Perspectives on
Identity, Migration, and Displacement

Edited by
Steven Tötösy de Zepetnek,
I-Chun Wang, and Hsiao-Yu Sun

U0153713

National Sun Yat-sen University
Humanities and Social Sciences Series and
the Sun Yat-sen Journal of Humanities Series

Published in 2010 by the Center for the Humanities and Social
Sciences and the College of Liberal Arts, National Sun Yat-sen
University, 70 Lien-Hai Road, Kaohsiung 80424, Taiwan

Published with financial assistance by
National Sun Yat-sen University

Printed and bound in Taiwan by okprint. Co., LTD., Kaohsiung

Perspectives on Identity, Migration, and Displacement
Edited by Steven Tötösy de Zepetnek, I-Chun Wang,
and Hsiao-Yu Sun
Editorial assistant: Yuanming Chang

ISBN: 978-986-02-3541-8
1. Identity 2. Migration 3. Culture
I. Tötösy de Zepetnek, Steven II. Wang, I-Chun III. Sun, Hsiao-Yu

書名(英文)：Perspectives on Identity,
　　　　　　Migration, and Displacement
編輯:陶鐸希、王儀君、孫小玉
出版者：國立中山大學人文社會科學研究中心、
　　　　文學院
國際書碼（ISBN）：978-986-02-3541-8
印刷廠:正合印刷有限公司
出版地:高雄
出版時間：民國九十九年六月
定價:新台幣 250 元

Contents

Introduction to *Perspectives on Identity, Migration, and Displacement*
I-Chun Wang and Steven Tötösy de Zepetnek

Culture and cultural expressions including literature and art contain many examples of life experiences related to migration and diaspora and in these texts we find elaborate descriptions — explicit and implicit — of matters and perspectives about and related to identity in all its formations and problematics. Migration and diaspora result in the problematics of assimilation and hybridity and in postcolonial scholarship, in particular, attention is paid to the concept of migration termed "Creolization" on the ground that cultural contact, cultural transmission, and cultural transformation result in the creation of new cultures. For example, Salikoko S. Mufwene suggests that Creolization is a social process and argues that in the process of Creolization language learning parallels the problematics of multiple identities because interactions and boundary crossings weave the patterns of identity ("Creolization is a Social, not a Structural Process," *Degrees of Restructuring in Creole Languages.* Ed. Ingrid Neumann-Holzschuh. Amsterdam: John Benjamins, 2000. 65-84). According to Douglas S. Massey, the four periods in the history of international migration include the mercantile period that lasted from 1500 to 1800, the period of European industrial migration after World War I, and the period of post-industrial migration since the 1960s (Worlds in Motion: Understanding International *Migration at the End of the Millennium*. Oxford: Oxford UP, 1998. 1-2). And Milton Sernett postulates that migration is a "theme of enduring historic significance" (*Bound for the Promised Land: African American Religion and the Great Migration.* Durham: Duke UP, 1997. 1).

Migration and diaspora are results of a multitude of social, political, and economic circumstances which, in turn, result in social, economic, and cultural marginalization. In Western history and culture, the expansion of the Roman empire caused migration as soldiers moved to conquered areas and movement of peoples such as the Germanic and Slavic tribes and clashes of cultures, as well as confrontations between ethnic tribes were common. In the Age of Exploration the Atlantic slave trade resulted in the movement of people within Africa and forced migration of large numbers of people. And the nineteenth century culminated in ethnic diasporas and the displacement of migrant workers throughout the Western world with the twenty-first century continuing global migration of peoples between continents resulting in much conflict cultural, social, political, etc., and this can be seen in a variety of cultural expressions.

The articles in the volume at hand are selected and peer-reviewed studies from National Sun Yat-sen University's Center for the Humanities and Social Sciences 2008 international conference *Perspectives on Migration, Nationhood, and Ethnicity*, as well as peer-reviewed articles following a general call for papers. The volume is divided in Part One: Identity and Migration with the articles "Distance, Culture, and Migration in Ancient China" by Chin-Chuan Cheng, "Sui and Tang Princess Brides and Life after Marriage at the Borderlands" by Jennifer W. Jay, "The Hybridities of Philip and Özdamar" by Sabine Milz, "The Ambivalent Americanness of J. Hector St. Jean de Crèvecoeur" by Susan Castillo, "Ethnicity and Nationhood in Achebe's *Arrow of God*" by Pao-I Hwang, "The Migration of Gender and the Labor Market" by Anders W. Johansson and Maria Udén, and "Migration, Diaspora, and Ethnic Minority Writing" by Steven Tötösy de Zepetnek, in Part Two: Identity and Displacement with the articles "Cosmopolitanism in Zhu's *Ancient Capital (Gudu)*" by Yu-chuan Shao, "British Muslims and Limits of Multiculturalism in Kureishi's *The Black Album*" by Shao-Ming Kung, "(Im)migration and Cultural Diasporization in Garcia's *Monkey Hunting*" by Jade Tsui-yu Lee, "Documentary Photography on the Internment of Japanese Americans" by Hsiu-chuan Lee, "Interculturalism and New Russians in Berlin" by Giacomo Bottà, and "From Diaspora to Nomadic Identity in the Work of Lispector and Felinto" by Paola Jordão, and in Part Three "Selected Bibliography of Work on Identity, Migration, and Displacement" by Li-wei Cheng, Steven Tötösy de Zepetnek, and I-Chun Wang.

Work published in the volume is intended for both scholars and a general readership interested in comparative aspects of migration in literary, historical, photographic, and filmic expressions of migration, displacement, and identity.

Author's profile: I-Chun Wang teaches English literature at National Sun Yat-sen University. Her interests in scholarship include comparative literature, Chinese and Taiwan drama, and English Renaissance drama. Among her recent publications are *Gendered Memories* (Studies in Comparative Literature 28), *Xing Bie yu Jiang Jieh* (Gender and Boundary), *East Asian Cultural and Historical Perspectives*, and *Identity Politics*: *Early Modern Culture*. She is currently working on Renaissance travel literature.

Author's profile: Steven Tötösy de Zepetnek works in comparative cultural studies and media and communication studies. For lists of his publications see <http://docs.lib.purdue.edu/clcweblibrary/totosycv>. He is editor of the Purdue UP humanities and social sciences quarterly *CLCWeb: Comparative Literature and Culture* <http://docs.lib.purdue.edu/clcweb>, the Purdue UP series of Books in Comparative Cultural Studies, and the Shaker Publisher series of Books in Comparative Culture, Media, and Communication Studies.

Part One
Identity and Migration

Distance, Culture, and Migration in Ancient China
Chin-Chuan Cheng

Abstract: In his paper "Distance, Culture, and Migration in Ancient China" Chin-Chuan Cheng explores the concept of distance, travel, and migration in ancient China. During the times of the Spring and Autumn and the Warring States (770-221 BC), most of the vassal states were in present-day Henan province and nearby regions of the Central Plains within a radius of some 700 kilometers of Luoyang. It is in this region where for example poems and songs were gathered and compiled in the *Book of Odes* and thus the culture of the Central Plains was formed. Places beyond the Central Plains were considered frontiers and were regarded as culturally primitive. In the ensuing years of Chinese dynasties including the Tang, Song, and Yuan, imperial courts often relegated high officials to towns and cities at least 700 kilometers away from the capital. However, this requirement with regard to distance was never mentioned in any decree or judgment of law. Cheng postulates that the said implicit rule of distance explains a number of factors with regard to geographic considerations in many activities and events in Chinese history and culture.

Formation of the Central Plains

The earliest record of the term "Middle Kingdom" occurred in the inscription on the bronze utensil He Jun unearthed at Jiacun, Baoji, Shaanxi in 1963 (see Wang). The utensil was made during the West Zhou Chengwang rein (1042-1020 BC). The inscription says that the king would rule from Chengzhou, the center of the country. Chengzhou was the city Luo, present-day Luoyang, Henan. During the Chengwang rein, the capital was Zongzhou also called Hao near present-day Xi'an, Shaanxi. Geographically speaking, Luo indeed was in the center of the states of China in the period. The maps I used to establish the relationships of distance and locations of oral transmission and exile I am discussing in my article was produced with the ArcView GIS 3.3 (2002) software by ESRI: Environmental Systems Research Institute, a geographic information system based on historical data taken from Qixiang Tan's *The Historical Atlas of China* and maps at the Academia Sinica. The geographic information system allowed me to measure the distance between any points and the result of my measurements was that the vassal states were all located within a radius of 700 kilometers from the center Luo.

In my article "Distance of Oral Transmission and Geographic Range of Human Interaction" I discuss a number of marriages between nobles of Zhou, the Spring and Autumn, and the Warring states on the basis of the inscriptions on bronze utensils. As gleaned from the inscriptions, many girls of the noble families in the Han and Huai river areas went north to marry nobles. The correlation of the location of the girls' families and the location of the families the girls married into shows that the longest distance of the two locations rarely exceed 700 kilometers, thus supporting my hypothesis of a built-in self-regulative pattern of migration which I postulate to be a phenomenon of early Chinese society and culture. The Spring and Autumn and the Warring states saw a flourishing of literature, philosophy, and culture in general. Many lasting thoughts and writings were formed during this period and the *Book of Odes*, for example, contains a wealth of songs and poems from the various states of the Central Plains and the book became one of the canons for the next two thousand years in China. On the map I generated as explained above, I drew a line between Chengzhou (Luo) and Qin and 650 kilometers indicated the distance between these two locations. Another line indicates 760 kilometers between Chengzhou and Qi. These distances show again that migration was within a radius of 700 kilometers from the center at Luo and thus I argue that these states with the phenomenon of geographical distance formation within which migration occurred resulted in social and cultural development. Further, based on the implied self-regulation of the distance of migration within the Central Plains, areas outside of 700 kilometers away from Luo were considered culturally less well developed frontiers. In consequence, I postulate that this implicit self-regulation of migratory distance permeates Chinese history and societal and cultural development. Following my postulate, I examine the concept of distance in oral transmission during the Han dynasty, the occurrences of exile as punishment and instances of law during the Tang, Song, and Yuan dynasties in order to test my postulate.

Distance of oral transmission

Written documents or printed books can be transported to distant places. Orally transmitted stories, however, have to rely on human interaction to traverse from one place to another. In ancient times when there were no technical devices of transmission, human contacts performed in orality were the major means of the circulation of information and knowledge. The said circulation of information and knowledge can be considered in terms of geographical distances as a major factor in human interaction.

The *Fengsu Tongyi* by Ying Shao (ca. 153-196 AD) of the Han dynasty recorded many stories heard from various places. Ying Shao, a native of present-day Henan, was an official in Luoyang for some time before he took up a position in Taishan, Shandong. We can assume that he heard many of the stories when he was in Luoyang and thus we can measure the distances of oral transmission between Luoyang and the places where the stories occurred. In the maps I generated I measured the straight-line distance between Yunzhong and Luoyang and found that the length was about 644 kilometers. This distance was one of the largest on the map. I thus concluded that the upper limit of the range of human interaction during that time was about 700 kilometers. Now we turn to the Tang, Song, and Yuan dynasties to show that the distance of 700 kilometers was an important consideration when sending government officials into exile.

Exile in the Tang, Song, and Yuan dynasties

The Tang dynasty produced much great literature and scholarship but many scholars and poets were exiled for one reason or another. Here is a list of exiled scholars and poets with the distance of their exile from their residence indicated: Han Yu (768-824) from Jingzhao Fu (Xi'an) to Chaozhou (Guangdong): 1,400 Km; Liu Zongyuan (773-819) from Jingzhao Fu (Xi'an) to Liuzhou (Guangxi): 1,090 Km; Liu Yuxi (772-842) from Jingzhao Fu (Xi'an) to Pozhou (Zunyi, Guizhou): 750 Km; Yuan Zhen (779-831) from Jingzhao Fu (Xi'an) toTongzhou (Daxian, Sichuan): 370 Km; Bai Juyi (772-846) from Jingzhao Fu (Xi'an) to Jiangzhou (Jiujiang, Jiangxi): 850 Km; Li Deyu (787-849)from Jingzhao Fu (Xi'an) to Yazhou (Haikou, Hainan): 1,600 Km. Their locations of exile indicate the radius of 700 kilometers around the capital Jingzhao Fu (Chang'an); however except Yuan Zhen the exiled scholars were sent into exile more than 700 kilometers away from the capital. This can be explained because the Tang Dynasty greatly extended its borders. During the rein of Tang Taizong (627-649) it was recorded in the Tang dynasty history that the territory covered 9,511 *li* (4,755 km) from East to West and 16,918 *li* (8,459 km) from North to South. Of note is that the banished scholars were not sent to border regions but to places in the culturally less developed areas within the country, that is, outside of the Central Plains.

Exile, culture, and migration

The states of the Central Plains — the areas around and those south of the Changjiang River — were rapidly developing in terms of economy after the armed rebellion led by An Lushan and Shi Siming in 755 and thus the southern prefectures had high percentage of increase in household numbers (see Wu, Yan, and Yang) and the various cities of the region show this: Ezhou (present-day Hubei) 100%; Xiangzhou (present-day Hubei) 194%;   Yingzhou (present-day Hubei) 93%; Suzhou (present-day Jiangsu) 48%; Hongzhou (present - day Jiangxi) 64%; Raozhou (present-day Jiangxi) 228%; Jizhou (present-day Jiangxi) 19%; Hengzhou (present-day Hunan) 33%; Guangzhou (present-day Guangdong) 15%. Further, silk has become an important commodity (delivered as tribute to the imperial court) and paper, tea, salt, and copper were also major products. Quanzhou of Fujian, Mingzhou of Zhejian and Guangzhou of Guangdong were bustling with trade business and night markets became favorite spots of commercial activities (see Wu, Yan, and Yang). This significant development in population meant of course also the development of culture in the states of the Central Plains and the above listed scholar Bai Juyi (772-846) who was sent into exile in Xunyang (present-day Jiujiang, Jiangxi) refers to the importance of culture in his poem "Song of a Pipa" ("Pipa Xing"). As said, what Bai Juyi missed was the refined culture of the capital Jingzhao Fu, a major center with 362,921 households while where he was sent in exile in the Xunyang prefecture had only 19,025 (see Xiu) and thus it was natural for Bai Juyi to think of himself in a remote frontier without culture. And the other exiled poet and scholar Han Yu wrote "I was banished to Chaoyang eight thousand *li*-s away." In the list given above the distance from Jingzhao Fu to Chaoyang was given as 1,400 kilometers, which is equivalent to 2,800 *li*. The number 8,000 was the poet's perception of remote frontiers.

Similar to the above situation of exiles with regard to distance, migration, and culture, the pattern of exile we have seen in the Tang Dynasty also occurred in the Song Dynasty. Here are selected poets and scholars who were exiled: Fan Zhongyan (989-1052) from Kaifeng to Raozhou (Boyang, Jiangxi): 660 Km; Su Shi (1036-1101) from Kaifeng to Qiongzhou (Haikou, Hainan): 1,700 Km; and Huang Tingjian (1045-1105) from Kaifeng to Yongzhou (Yongzhou, Hunan): 990 Km. In the case of Fan Zhongyan who was exiled from the capital of the state Henan during the period, the distance of his exile confirms the 700 km rule while the others were exiled to locations more than 700 kilometers away from the capital. However, this, too, confirms the rule of the minimum 700 kilometers of distance. During the Yuan Dynasty, again, the situation is similar: the penal code described in *Yuan History* (Song) had this stipulation: "For exile, Southerners are to be moved to the Northern part of Liaoyang and Northerners to Huguang." The question is why was it necessary to stipulate northern part of Liaoyang rather than just Liaoyang? The southwestern portion of Liaoyang was only a couple hundred kilometers from the capital Dadu (present-day Beijing) and thus the implicit rule of distance had to be 700 kilometers from the capital as the northern part of Liaoyang was outside the range of 700 kilometers and thus the penal code clearly reflected the idea of the said implicit rule of distance.

The implications of the implicit rule of 700 kilometers as illustrated above are that any distance greater than this distance would be hard to reach and this would create unnecessary administrative and bureaucratic issues. At the same time, also language can give us clues about the distance rule: in Chinese there are phrases for distance meaning "very far away" or "very hard to achieve." The crucial component of these phrases is "a thousand li" or "thousands of li." As a thousand li is equivalent to 500 kilometers, the point is that these phrases use "thousand" instead of the larger unit "ten thousand" as the measuring unit. We thus consider it to be roughly more than 700 kilometers. Here are further phrases of distance: *qianli tiaotiao, qianli zhiwai, qianli zhiyuan,* and *xiangqu qianli,* all using *qianli* "thousand li" to indicate very far away. The following phrases also use *qianli* to signal maximum size or distance: *qida qianli* "the size is as large as a thousand li", *qianli zhi xing shi yu zu xia* "a thousand-li journey begins with the first step", *shi zhi haoli miu yi Qianli* "an error of the breadth of a single hair can lead you a thousand li astray", *bu yuan qianli er lai* "make light of traveling a thousand li", *qianli ma* "a steed that can run a thousand li in a short time", and *qianli yan* "the eye that can see a thousand li away—farsighted person".

Another implication of the 700-kilometer rule relates to the size of administrative units. In order to govern people effectively, any unit of the size greater than 700 kilometers would be too large to manage. The vassal states of the Zhou Dynasty were as small as a town. After Qin Shi Huang united and ruled the entire country, the land was divided into three dozen smaller prefectures. The Han Dynasty also set up a system of local administration of prefectures and counties. The geographic ranges of these units were about 300 kilometers in diameter, much less than 700 kilometers. Such a size represented the range of accessible human connections. Even today China has administrative units of similar size.

Conclusion

Based on the measurement of distance in several historical periods on maps of ancient China, I argue that the upper limit of distance of communication and administrative communication was 700 kilometers. During the times of the Spring and Autumn and the Warring States (770-221 BC), most of the vassal states of ancient China were in present-day Henan province and nearby regions of the Central Plains within a radius of some 700 kilometers of Luoyang. It is in this region where for example poems and songs were gathered and compiled in the *Book of Odes* and thus the culture of the Central Plains was formed. Places beyond the Central Plains were considered frontiers and were regarded as culturally primitive. In the ensuing years of Chinese dynasties including the Tang, Song, and Yuan, imperial courts often relegated high officials to towns and cities at least 700 kilometers away from the capital. However, this requirement with regard to distance was never mentioned in any decree or judgment of law.

Works Cited

Cheng, Chin-Chuan. "Distance of Oral Transmission and Geographic Range of Human Interaction." *Journal of Chinese Language Teaching* 4.2 (2007): 1-11.
Ouyang, Xiu. *The New Tang Dynasty History.* Taipei: Zhonghua, 1965.
Academia Sinica. Chinese Civilization in Time and Space (2008): <http://ccts.ascc.net/>.
Song, Lian. *The Yuan Dynasty History.* Taipei: Zhonghua, 1965.
Tan, Qixiang. *The Historical Atlas of China.* Taipei: Xiaoyuan, 1992.
Wang, Hui. *Bronze Inscriptions of Shang and Zhou.* Beijing: Wenwu Publishing House, 2006.
Wu, Jinming, Wushan Yan, and Xiyan Yang. *Economic History of Shi, Tang, and Wudai in China.* Beijing: Renmin, 1994.
Ying, Shao. *The Fengsu Tongyi.* Beijing: Zhonghua, 1981.

Author's profile: Chin-chuan Cheng is academician of the Academia Sinica. He taught linguistics at the University of Illinois from 1970 to 2000 and since 2007 he teaches at National Taiwan Normal University. His research includes measurements of similarity and mutual intelligibility among Chinese dialects, Chinese phonology, lexical semantics, Chinese corpora, e-learning, and language geographic information systems, and he has published extensively books and articles in these areas of scholarship.

Sui and Tang Princess Brides and Life after Marriage at the Borderlands
Jennifer W. Jay

Abstract: In "Sui and Tang Princess Brides and Life After Marriage at the Borderlands" Jennifer W. Jay discusses the marriage outcomes of princess brides sent to the frontiers in sixth- to tenth-century China. Traditional China perceived the north and western frontiers as the zone demarcating agrarian, civilized China from the pastoral, uncivilized periphery. To deal with the military pressures frontier peoples exerted on the borders, the Sui and Tang states continued and extended the Han dynasty's policy of diplomatic alternative to war. This policy included the *heqin* practice of sending princess brides to the rulers at the frontiers, based on the assumption that the brides would play significant political roles and become civilizing agents in achieving the long-term objective of embracing the troublesome neighbors into the orbit of the Chinese imperial family and empire. The *heqin* brides found themselves permanently exiled from their homes and left to negotiate new identities and cultures to survive in the levirate states at the borderlands. Departing from the traditional scholarship of treating the women as victims and tools of foreign policy, Jay examines their exercise of agency, survival strategies, and response to opportunities to chart their fate.

The *heqin* marriage

In seventh century BC, Lady Li, from the border territory of Rong, wept profusely upon hearing that she and her sister were to depart from their homeland for a marriage alliance to Duke Xian in the state of Jin. After she received imperial favor, material comfort, and political power, she regretted ever shedding tears over her destiny and life after marriage in an unknown land. Member of an ethnic minority in the state of Jin, she changed from a weeping girl to an empowered concubine who got her son enthroned after exiling his rival half-brothers. Life after marriage turned out to be a much better outcome than the death sentence that she had earlier feared (see Zhuangzi 32). Lady Li's marriage can be seen as a precursor to the practice of *heqin* (harmonious kinship marriage), an instrument of foreign policy that preceded the Han (206 BC - 220 AD) and involved all dynasties except the Song (960-1276) and Ming (1368-1644) dynasties. The *heqin* policy of marriage was a practice where the Chinese state sent brides to the nomadic or semi-nomadic states for marriage in order to cease hostilities, cement friendship, and create divisive tensions among the neighboring states. The Chinese administration expected the brides to be designated as queens (*katun*s) so they could influence court politics in the nomadic states to the advantage of the Chinese state. The Sui (581-617) and Tang (618-906) dynasties were unique in contracting *heqin* marriages with a large number of nomadic peoples from extensive territories including the Tuyuhun, Xi, Khitan, Ferghana, Uighur, Gaochang, Tibetan, Eastern Turk, and Western Turk states.

In my study I analyse agency, national identity, and cultural negotiation in the lives of twenty-eight far-flung brides and one groom who completed the *heqin* marriage contract. I derived this list through a critical assessment of the sources on the discrepancies of the number of *heqin* marriages and brides in Sui and Tang China. Kuang Pingzhang lists twenty marriages, while Zhou Jiarong lists sixteen, and Yihong Pan includes sixty-seven marriages found in the dynastic histories. However, in reality there were more individuals involved, as each *heqin* marriage may have had an additional eight women sent to the nomadic states as concubines. Additionally, a number of lower-ranked women were married to the generals and ministers of these states. Similar to the experience of Lady Li, these individuals anticipated life after marriage to be dangerous and uncertain. They found themselves permanently exiled from their homes and left to negotiate new identities and cultures to survive in the levirate states at the borderlands.

Rather than focusing on the individuals as victims and tools of foreign policy, my primary objective is to observe their exercise of agency, survival strategies, and response to opportunities to chart their fate. I use the term "agency" as defined by Patricia Buckley: "women's agency means seeing women as actors. Women occupied positions of vastly different power, just as men did, and made choices that helped to recreate and subtly change the family and kinship system. Existing evidence can be read in ways that bring to the fore women responding to the opportunities open to them and accommodating or resting those around them" (xiv).

Sources on Sui and Tang *heqin* brides

Both the Chinese court and traditional historians considered the institution of *heqin* to be a matter of foreign policy and government concern, thus information on the *heqin* individuals appears in official sources and in standard histories. The primary sources were likely the reports written by the officials who accompanied the brides to the marriage and the reports were often updated by the envoys who visited them. There is inadequate and uneven coverage of the brides, but more information is generally available on the three biological daughters of emperors (i.e., Ningguo, Xian'an, Taihe) and those who stayed at the borderlands for more than ten years:

Qianjin/Dayi (14 years); Yicheng (33 years); Younger Ningguo (33 years); Wencheng (40 years; Jincheng (30 years); Xian'an (20 years), and Taihe (23 years). Below is the list of *heqin* brides with selected data about their times and marriages I am using in my analysis.

Sui and Tang *heqin* marriages (modified from Kuang 65-67)

dynasty	princess	surname	marriage	daughter of	marriages	after m.
N Zhou /Sui	Qianjin/ Dayi	Yuwen /Yang	580-593	kinsman	Turks: 3 Taspar	594, killed by husband
Sui	Guanghua	Yang	596	kinsman	Tuyuhun: 2	
Sui	Anyi	Yang	597	kinsman	E Turks: 1 Zamqan	d. 598
Sui	Yicheng	Yang	599	kinsman	E Turks: 4 Zamqan	630, killed by Tang soldiers
Sui	Huarong	Yuwen /Li	612	kinsman	Gaochang:2	
Sui	Xinyi	Yuwen	614	kinsman	W Turks	618, husb. killed
Tang	Honghua	Li	639	kinsman	Tuyuhun	
Tang	Wencheng	Li	641	kinsman	Tibet: 2	died in Tibet
Tang	Xiping	Li	641	kinsman	Tibet	
Tang	Jinchengxian	Li	652	kinsman	Tuyuhun	
Tang	Jinmingxian	Li	After 652	kinsman	Tuyuhun	
Tang	Jincheng	Li	710	kinsman	Tibet	died in Tibet
Tang	Nanhe	Li	711/13?	kinsman	E Turk	
Tang	Gu'an	Xin	717	kinswoman	Xi: 2	div./ return.
Tang	Yongle	Yang	717	kinswoman	Khitan: 2	719, return. Chang'

						an w/ new husb.
Tang	Yanjun	Murong	722	kinswoman	Khitan: 2	general killed her 2nd husb. & took her to Chang' an
Tang	Jiaohe	Ashina	722	granddau. of nomadic chief	Turgish king	
Tang	Donggua ng	Wei	722	kinswoman	Xi	
Tang	Donghua	Chen	725	kinswoman	Khitan	
Tang	Heyi	Li	744	kinsman	Ferghana	
Tang	Jingle	Dugu	745	kinswoman	Khitan chief Li Huaijie	killed by husb. who rebel.
Tang	Yifang	Yang	745	kinswoman	Xi chief Li Yanchong	killed by husb. who rebel.
Tang	Prince Dunhuan g	Li Chengca i	756	brother of Jincheng	Princess Bilga (Uighur daughter/sis ter in-law)	
Tang	Ningguo	Li	758	Suzong's daughter	Chinese: 2; Uighur:1, Moyancuo	return. Chang' an 759
Tang	Younger Ningguo	Li	758	kinsman	Uighur:3 Moyancuo	died 791
Tang		Pugu	758	high official	Uighur Bogu qaghan	
Tang	Chonghu	Pugu	769	high official	Uighur Bogu qaghan	
Tang	Xian'an	Li	788	Dezong's daughter	Uighur: 3 Bagha	died 808

					Tarqan qaghan	
Tang	Taihe	Li	821	Xianzong's daughter	Uighur: 4? Chongde qaghan	Return. Chang' an 843

In reporting on the brides and the marriages, the envoys and historians articulated sympathy for the brides being sent off to the distant lands, but there is a lack of interest in the lives of the brides before and after their marriage. Surprisingly, we know very little about the brides who returned to Chinese territory and who may have provided eyewitness accounts of life in the nomadic states. There is little written by the brides beyond several brief excerpts of letters and several short poems by Qianjin and Yifang. These poems, similar to those attributed to the *heqin* brides in the Han dynasty, were most likely not authentic and belong to the poetry of impersonation (see Frankel 133-56). Kuang also doubts the authenticity of Princess Yifang's poem because it is present only in the *Quan Tangshi*. These poems of impersonation were inspired by the actual poems that had been commissioned by the emperors for farewell ceremonies before the brides departed for the pastoral lands. For example, in 710 Zhongzong (ruled 705-711) ordered his officials to write poems to mark Princess Jincheng's departure for Tibet and in 808 Xianzong (ruled 805-820) commissioned the poet Bai Juyi to compose a poem to mourn Princess Xian'an, who had died in Uighur territory (see Sima 269.6639, 237.7648). Officials and poets often employed the powerful theme of involuntary exile in an alien culture, loneliness, and sacrifice to imagine the poignant sentiments of the brides. Almost all of these poems were penned by men and may be of limited use for recreating the gendered experience and mentality of the *heqin* brides. In sum, the scattered and incomplete nature of information in the dynastic histories and the limited use of literary sources explain the discrepancies in dates, marriages, and even the number of *heqin* brides.

Identity and the gendered experience

There is much variation in background, age, and ethnicity among the *heqin* brides. Because emperors were reluctant to send their biological daughters to the borderlands, most of the designated princess brides were selected from among the daughters of the imperial aristocracy such as kinsmen, imperial kinswomen, and high-ranking Chinese and non-Chinese officials. Thus the majority of the *heqin* women were not "true" princesses, but received the title of "princess" only when designated as *heqin* brides. Through the selection process we know the surnames of these women, which in most cases is the imperial surname of Li in marriage arrangements that create a fictive uncle/nephew or in-law relationship. In the cases of marriage with states such as Xi and Khitan — whose imperial families had been granted the Tang imperial surname of Li — Confucian taboo against patrilineal marriage required that the brides have a surname other than Li, and so daughters of kinswomen and high-ranking officials, whose surnames were not Li were selected as *heqin* brides.

Before setting out for marriage, some brides were adopted officially by the emperor and thus given a higher rank, and all were bestowed with the title of "princess" by which they became known in official correspondence and in historical documentation. Even the three biological daughters of emperors who became *heqin* brides had their birth titles replaced with newly acquired identities when they embarked on the journey to their new homes. Thus Princess Xiaoguo became Princess Ningguo, Princess Yan'guo became Princess Xian'an, and Princess Anding became Princess Taihe. These new titles, for examples, Princess Dayi (Princess of Great Righteousness) and Princess Yicheng (Righteousness Completed), express notions of harmony, trust, and integrity, indicating the collective objective of the marriages to rest upon securing peaceful relations between the Chinese and the nomadic states.

Being a *heqin* bride was a gendered position and the *heqin* marriage was the experience and lot of women. Empress Wu Zetian (ruled 690-705) questioned whether *heqin* had to be dictated by gender and in 697 sent her nephew Wu Yanxiu to marry the daughter of Bag Chor qaghan. But the qaghan rejected the marriage and sent him packing, and because the marriage did not materialize, Wu Yanxiu is not included in our list of twenty-nine *heqin* individuals. The only *heqin* alliance that involved a Chinese groom was the marriage of Prince Dunhuang (Li Chengcai), the younger brother of Princess Jincheng, herself a bride sent to Tibet. He had served as ambassador to the Uighurs and in 756 he married the Uighur Gele qaghan's sister-in-law. It is interesting to note that none of personal names of the *heqin* brides have been recorded, but we have the full names of the grooms, even the one whose marriage was canceled.

The *heqin* brides and the one groom came from various backgrounds and were treated accordingly. The size and membership of the entourage to accompany the brides depended on the status of the *heqin* bride. The Tang dynasty was unusual in marrying off biological daughters of the emperor (i.e., Ningguo, Xian'an, Taihe); however, the mothers of these daughters were lower-ranked concubines and not empresses or the emperor's favorites. Being daughters of emperors, these three *heqin* women were more privileged than the other women and were each given special household administrations of about a hundred people (see Twitchett 49-50). The other brides, daughters, and granddaughters of imperial princes, imperial kinswomen, and high-ranking officials were assigned smaller entourages. Marriage for some offered an opportunity for upward mobility (i.e., Princess Wencheng) and a chance to raise their social rank from obscure backgrounds or to escape from disgraced families (i.e., Princess Jincheng and her brother Prince Dunhuang).

The princess brides were supposed to represent the Chinese state and most of them identified themselves as Chinese in culture and language, but they were not of pure Chinese stock. Typical of the Sui and Tang imperial aristocracy that had a mixed blood ancestry in the early years of the dynasties, most *heqin* women were considered Chinese (Han), but had some Turkic/Mongol blood from several generations back. Princess Jiaohe, who went on the farthest journey to marry the Turkish qaghan in Sogdiana in 722, was the product of the intermarriage between a Western Turk qaghan who had submitted to Tang China, and a Chinese woman. When the Tang crushed the Turkish state in 739, Jiaohe declined to return to China and chose to live as a Buddhist recluse at a monastery in Kirgizya. Princess Chonghui, who married in 769, and her two older sisters who made the same journey in 756, were daughters of Tang's high-ranking Turkic official Pugu Huai'en, who later rebelled against the Tang. No matter what ethnicity, the *heqin* individuals found themselves minorities in their adoptive countries and had to adjust to new cultural and linguistic environments, all the while reminded by envoys that they had been sent out to represent the Chinese state and must remain loyal to it.

There was a wide range in the age of the *heqin* individuals. For example, Wencheng and Jincheng might have been as young as ten or twelve when they were sent to Tibet; Ningguo was older and had been twice married before she married the Uighur qaghan. The *heqin* women often found their designated husbands to be much older than they had expected. And when the husbands died, often soon after their arrival, they were subjected to the levirate and forced to remarry with the husband's relatives, who could be a brother-in-law, step-son, or even step-grandson.

Agency and living dangerously after marriage

The little information we have on *heqin* women before their marriages indicates that they were pawns of foreign policy and had little agency in being selected for marriage at the borderlands. The selection of the brides was the emperor's decision, as declared by Emperor Taizong (ruled 626-48): "We are the father and mother of the world; to benefit it, how could I begrudge [losing] one woman!" (see Liu 199b.5346). In their life after marriage the brides juggled to balance two processes at work: their assimilation into their husbands' nomadic culture and their duty to sinicize their adopted land, motivated as they were by survival strategies and loyalty to the Chinese state. The grasp of agency varied among the brides and was often contingent on forces beyond their control, such as the on-going foreign relations between the Chinese state and the nomadic state into which they married. Certainly there was little evidence of agency available to the two brides who were murdered by their husbands in 745, within six months of their arrival. Princess Yifang was killed by the Xi chief and Princess Jingle was murdered by the Khitan chief, who then rebelled against Tang China and joined the Turks. Other brides were luckier to encounter more opportunities to exercise agency and live longer. Survival strategies drove Qianjin/Dayi, Ningguo, Younger Ningguo, and Taihe to take bold action, and loyalty to the Chinese state guided Yicheng and Gu'an. Wencheng and Jincheng shouldered the burden of cultural transmission and diplomacy.

Princess Qianjin/Dayi followed her survival instincts to preserve her life through fourteen years of high political tensions in her new country, but she still died in 594 at the hand of her third husband (see Wei 51.1330). Born in the Yuwen clan in the Northern Zhou dynasty (557-581), Qianjin, a niece of the emperor, was traded as a hostage to the Eastern Turk qaghan in 579 in exchange for an enemy prince of Northern Zhou. Shortly after, the Sui founder crushed her native state of Northern Zhou and exterminated her entire family. As wife to the qaghan, Princess Qianjin had a certain degree of military influence and tried to turn him against the Sui, a strategy she continued to pursue with her second husband. In 584 she negotiated a peace treaty with the Sui and changed her surname to that of the Sui imperial house to assume a new identity (Princess Dayi) to represent the Sui in the Eastern Turk state. After her second husband died, she married his son (her stepson or step-grandson), all the time secretly nursing a hatred for the Sui imperial house that had wiped out her native dynasty and her family.

In 594, the Sui emperor bribed her third husband and he traded her for another princess bride (see Wei 51.1330).

While Princess Qianjin/Dayi ultimately failed to survive despite many attempts to change her fate, Princess Ningguo succeeded and returned to China after just one year of marriage. The Uighurs had been instrumental in saving Tang China from the devastating An Lushan rebellion and Tibetan invasion. To pay back the Uighurs, Tang negotiated two *heqin* marriages in 756: Princess Ningguo's marriage to the Uighur qaghan and Li Chengcai's marriage to the qaghan's sister-in-law. Ningguo was youngest daughter of Emperor Suzong (ruled 755-762) and had been married twice previously. A beautiful woman, Ningguo is reported to have bravely declared: "The affairs of the state are precarious; even if I die I will not regret this [*heqin* marriage]" (see Ouyang 83.3660). She arrived in the Uighur state in 758 and married Gele qaghan, an old man who died a few months after the marriage. The Uighurs pressured her to commit suicide and be buried live in a ritual of widow sacrifice. She protested and reminded them that they had demanded the marriage because they had admired Chinese culture and to now subject her to the widow sacrifice would be barbaric and repressive. She negotiated to mourn the qaghan for three years, as was traditional Chinese practice, and slashed and disfigured her face, as was customary in the nomadic societies. Her exercise of agency enabled her to avoid the death sentence and because she had no children she was allowed to return to China in 759 (see Ouyang 83.3660). After Princess Ningguo left, Princess Younger Ningguo, who had accompanied her and was married to the same qaghan, remained in Uighur territory for another thirty-two years, marrying three other qaghans in succession. We have few details about her survival strategies, but one would assume that she must have exercised agency to survive three decades of living dangerously in a world of shifting loyalties and complicated family relations in her multiple marriages. Her four sons and two daughters were killed in the internal strives, after which she still lived for another twelve years before dying in 791 (see Kuang 50-52).

Princess Taihe, the sister of Emperor Muzong (ruled 821-824), must have also employed strategies of note to survive twenty-two years of political upheavals as a *heqin* bride in the Uighur state (see Ouyang 83.3668.69; Kuang 53-55). Her intended husband had died while she was en route to be married, but she went on to marry four other husbands, including the one who held her hostage. When the Uighurs were defeated and she was captured and then returned to China in 843, many princesses, including her own sisters, did not come to greet her. Her return to China was controversial and she was blamed for the failure of the *heqin* policy to keep peace in the Uighur state.

The *heqin* marriage itself was an act of diplomacy, and *heqin* brides were expected to safeguard and promote the interests of their homeland. Princesses Yicheng and Gu'an were two *heqin* women whose strategies were motivated by loyalty to China. As in the case of Princess Qianjin/Dayi who remained loyal to her native state of Northern Zhou during dynastic change, Yicheng was loyal to the Sui after marriage in Turkic territory. She was subjected to the levirate and married four times in accordance with nomadic customs. Witnessing from afar the destruction of her dynasty and its replacement by the Tang, she plotted to restore the Sui, but hope faded when her adopted home, the Turkic state, disintegrated. Tang soldiers killed her in 630 and by then she had lived in the borderlands for thirty-one years (see Wei 84.1872). Similarly, Princess Gu'an remained loyal to the Tang dynasty after her marriage and life in the Xi state in 717-722. She arrived in Xi territory to marry the chief Li Dapu and when he died she married his younger brother Lusu, who treated her well. In a show of loyalty to the Tang, when a Xi official wanted to rebel against the Tang, she got him drunk and killed him. Emperor Xuanzong (ruled 712-755) rewarded her so lavishly that her stepmother in Chang'an became jealous of her good fortune and plotted to replace her with her own daughter. This she did by disclosing to the Xi state that Gu'an was not born from the principal wife of the emperor but from a concubine, and thus providing evidence that the Tang had deceived the Xi when contracting the marriage. In consequence Emperor Xuanzong had to order a divorce and give the Xi chief another bride, Princess Dongguang. Princess Gu'an had spent only five relatively happy years as a *heqin* bride in Xi territory and after the divorce it is not known whether she went back to Chang'an (see Ouyang 219.6174).

The experiences of Wencheng and Jincheng in Tibet suggest that life after marriage was a better alternative than had they stayed in Tang China. As *heqin* brides, Wencheng brought peace for several decades and Jincheng played a significant role in the negotiations between Tibet and Tang China. In 641 Wencheng traveled from Chang'an to Lhasa and married the Tibetan king, Sron-brsan sgam-po (ruled 626-650). Had Wencheng remained in China, she would have remained an obscure imperial relative, but in Tibet her marriage gave her the status of a Tibetan queen. Her large retinue included officials, scholars, craftsmen, and servants in charge of a huge inventory of Tang products, silk, porcelain, and literary and scholarly texts. Following her arrival, the Tibetan king told his people to stop the custom of face tattooing and painting which was offensive to Wencheng. However, this act of sinicization was at the most restricted to the Tibetan aristocracy and did not spread to commoners. As a result of the marriage alliance, Chinese scholars and texts were brought into Tibet and Tibetan aristocrats and students went to China for education. Wencheng herself, in communication with the Tang court, requested artisans and equipment to start wine making, sericulture, and printing. She lived in Tibet for forty years during which she facilitated exchange between the two cultures and brought peace to Tang China for about two decades (see Ouyang 81.3591; 216a.6073-78).

Between China and Tibet negotiations for another Chinese bride had begun in 703 and in 710 Princess Jincheng — who was then between ten to sixteen years old — was sent off as the adopted daughter of Emperor Zhongzong to marry the Tibetan king, Khri Ide gtsug brtsan (ruled 704-755). Jincheng's disgraced family status could have been the reason why several high-ranking officials refused to escort her on the difficult journey to Lhasa. But even as one of several queens, Jincheng had a much higher social status in Tibet than she would have had in a disgraced political family in Tang China. She often requested and obtained Chinese classics and products and thus acted as a cultural emissary (see Ouyang 216a.6081-86). Jincheng herself was literate and in 723, perhaps due to marriage difficulties, she wrote to the king of Kashmir, seeking asylum. But she was persuaded not to proceed and jeopardize relations with Tibet. Jincheng often communicated with the Tang Emperor Xuanzong (ruled 712-756), her father's first cousin. Several excerpts of her letters are extant, one each in 713, 716, 717, and two in 733. Yihong Pan places critical importance in Jincheng's role in negotiating peace and stabilizing relations between Tang China and Tibet (see 247-58). In 717 Jincheng requested that Tang's Xuanzong put down his personal signature on the peace treaty because it had critical significance of trust for the Tibetans, but she did not succeed. Still she persisted in her peace efforts and at the conclusion of a peace treaty in 733 she helped to erect a stone stele to mark the demarcation line between Tang China and Tibet.

Despite Jincheng's conspicuous role in the negotiations between Tibet and Tang China, hostilities continued during her three decades in Tibet. Although she was not successful in bringing permanent peace to the two countries, her support of Buddhism through financial contributions and patronage of Buddhist constructions made a longer, lasting impact. After her death, Jincheng's family continued to play a role in Tang history. In 756, in a successful case of marriage alliance, her younger brother, Li Chengcai, the only male groom in the *heqin* marriages, was designated Prince Dunhuang, and married to the Uighur qaghan's sister-in-law. In 763, the Tibetans invaded the capital of Tang China and installed another of her younger brothers as a puppet emperor of the Tang (see Liu Xu, 196a.5226-35).

Conclusion

In the popular tradition, *heqin* brides are given much credit for their civilizing and sinicizing roles in the borderlands, but this claim may be tenuous and much exaggerated. In the case of Princesses Wencheng and Jincheng, both left Tang China as teenagers (and perhaps even as pre-teenagers) and would not have been much schooled in Chinese culture and neither returned to China during their remaining life in Tibet, Wencheng for four decades and Jincheng for thirty years. It is likely that both became more Tibetan in the course of living two-thirds of their lives in Tibet. The assumption of the impact of sinicization is further diminished when we consider that the *heqin* brides were forced to violate Confucian kinship practice and patrilineal and generational taboos. The frequent occurrence of tribal regicide within the nomadic states made levirate remarriage a common experience for *heqin* brides. In levirate remarriage, the *heqin* brides must accept the levirate rules and marry, sometimes across generations, their deceased husband's brother, uncle, son, and even grandson. For example, Qianjin married her stepson and step-grandson; Anyi married her stepson; Yicheng married her stepson, step-grandson, and half brother-in-law; Gu'an married her brother-in-law; Younger Ningguo married her stepson; Xian'an married her stepson, step-grandson, and the minister who became the new qaghan; and Taihe married her stepson and went through another two or three marriages. The question then arises: if the *heqin* women were not even able to refuse remarriage and the levirate, how could they have drastically transformed the civilization of their adopted nomadic homes? Rather than simply attributing or denying a civilizing role to the *heqin* women, I argue that they adopted strategies and processes of mediation and negotiation. An example cited earlier was Ningguo's avoidance of widow sacrifice by disfiguring her face and mourning her husband for three years. The *heqin* women were much limited in their negotiation processes by virtue of the fact that they did not have male heirs who survived the frequent political upheavals. For instance, Younger Ningguo had four sons and two daughters and they were all killed during succession disputes. The *heqin* brides were not always treated well by the nomadic states, which complicated the situation when they contracted marriages with other neighbor states. Although a number of brides became queens, they had no sons or grandsons who ruled as qaghans — a situation that would have reinforced their power and influence in their life after marriage. Unfortunately there is little information about the children of the Sui and Tang *heqin* brides. One of Yicheng's husbands was Chuluo qaghan, who had a Chinese mother. Jincheng might have had a son, but it is not certain whether he was Kri de songtsen, who raided Tang China in 763. Similar to Lady Li in seventh century BC, life after marriage was not necessarily a death sentence; indeed, women such as Wencheng and Jincheng empowered themselves and they had a better life in their new country than were they to have remained in China. However, for most of the *heqin* women, their survival strategy was limited by forces beyond their control and they succumbed under the sheer power of the Chinese state that sent them out to the borderlands, as they struggled with the unfamiliar power relations and cultural practices of the new land where they had migrated.

Works Cited

Buckley, Patricia. *The Inner Quarters: Marriage and the Lives of Chinese Women in the Sung Period*. Berkeley: U of California P, 1993.
Frankel, Frankel H. "Cai Yan and the Poems Attributed to Her." *Chinese Literature: Essays, Articles, Reviews* 5.1-2 (1983): 133-56.
Kuang, Pingzhang. "Tangdai gongzhu heqin kao." *Shixue nianbao* 2.2 (1935): 23-68.
Liu, Xu. *Jiu Tangshu*. Beijing: Zhonghua shuju, 1975.
Ouyang, Xiu. *Xin Tangshu*. Beijing: Zhonghua shuju, 1975.
Pan, Yihong. "Marriage Alliances and Chinese Princesses in International Politics from Han through T'ang." *Asia Major* 10.1-2 (1997): 127-31.
Pan, Yihong. *Son of Heaven and Heavenly Kaghan: Sui-Tang China and Its Neighbors*. Bellingham: Center for East Asian Studies, Western Washington U, 1997.
Sima, Guang. *Zizhi tongjian*. Beijing: Zhonghua shuju, 1956.
Twitchett, Denis. "Tang Imperial Family." *Asia Major* 7.2 (1994): 49-50.
Wei Zheng. *Suishu*. Beijing: Zhonghua shuju, 1973.
Zhou Jiarong. "Tangdai heqin gongzhu di chushen wenti." *Xi'an lianhe daxue xuebao* 4.10 (2001): 59-62.
Zhuangzi. *Zhuangzi jizhu*. Qiwu lun. Neibian 2. Guiyang: Guizhou renmin chubanshe, 1987.

Author's profile: Jennifer W. Jay teaches Chinese history at the University of Alberta. Her main publishing activity has been in Chinese historiography — for example her 1991 book *A Change in Dynasties: Loyalism in Thirteenth Century China* — but she also works and publishes in literary study, philosophy, and politics, for example in her collected volume *East Asian Cultural and Historical Perspectives: Histories and Society, Culture and Literatures* (1997, with Steven Tötösy de Zepetnek). In recent years she has published articles in *the Harvard Journal of Asiatic Studies* and the *Journal of American Oriental Society*. Jay's current research projects include monographs on the institutional and social history of eunuchs in imperial China, marriage alliances and princess brides in imperial China, and Chinese-Canadian history and literature.

The Hybridities of Philip and Özdamar
Sabine Milz

Abstract: In her article "The Hybridities of Philip and Özdamar" Sabine Milz examines and compares strategies with which the Caribbean-Canadian woman writer Marlene Nourbese Philip and the Turkish-German woman writer Emine Sevgi Özdamar "de-colonize" ethnocentric Canadian and German discourse respectively and thus create their own spaces of hybridity. She argues that both Philip's and Özdamar's writings — by going beyond cultural-national categories and boundaries — display vital stimuli for multi-cultural and inter-national dialogue in a manner that facilitates cultural co-existence in spaces of hybridity. Responding to this stimulus, Milz's study in the mode of comparative cultural studies makes a critical contribution to the opening and broadening not only of the German and Canadian literary canons and contributes to the discourse of identity, migration, and displacement.

The 1980s and 1990s — the time when both the Caribbean-Canadian woman writer Marlene Nourbese Philip and the Turkish-German woman writer Emine Sevgi Özdamar came to prominence in Canada and Germany, respectively — have called for essential changes in the public and academic notions of what constitutes Canadian and German literature. With the displacement of the binary of "major" European and "minor" non-European literature, funding, publishing, and serious-critical reception of ethnic minority writers in both countries have improved considerably. Yet, critics from various academic disciplines in the humanities and the social sciences discern an "exclusion by inclusion" strategy underlying this change for the better. Michael A. Bucknor explains the paradox accordingly: On the one hand, ethnic minority writers are given much public and academic support, while, on the other hand, the very same institutions tend to reduce them to "ethnic ghettos" by racially and ethnically marking their works (13). As woman writers, Philip and Özdamar experience the "exclusion by inclusion" paradox not only through ethnic-cultural but also through gender labels. Their resistance against the marginalization and categorization of their art thus turns out to be a highly complex, multi-faceted undertaking. They resist the myths of universal art and fixed gender roles by means of re-contextualization and reconceptualization. Breaking genre boundaries and aesthetic norms they create an amalgamation or hybridization of literary traditions and subsequently their own hybrid spaces of multi-racial, multi-cultural interaction. They re-perform and complicate the invention of national narratives — of historical origins, linearity, and fixed national identities — by interspersing them with notions of diaspora, continuous displacement and cultural hybridity. Borrowing from Elisabeth Bronfen and Benjamin Marius, I assert the two texts as "changing narratives" (25-26), narratives that, for one thing, actively and radically change the traditional concepts of national literature in their specific contexts and, beyond it, show that narrative structures in general are not static but in a continuous process of transformation and hybridisation. The two writers' textual search for identity and belonging in the space of literary-cultural hybridity — which is composed of an Arabic-Turkish-German and African-Caribbean- Canadian cultural and literary mix, respectively — finds proficient expression in the two texts selected and compared here: Özdamar's prose-drama collection *Mutterzunge* and Philip's work of poetry *She Tries Her Tongue, Her Silence Softly Breaks*.

The theory of "cultural hybridity" — of the creation of new transcultural forms — has become widely employed and disputed not only in contemporary literary-academic discourse but also in scientific, philosophical, and sociological disciplines. The person who most decisively shaped the conception is the post-colonial critic Homi K. Bhabha. In his analysis of the interrelations between colonizer and colonized, he comes to the conclusion that any cultural identity in the "contact zone" of intercultural relations is constructed in a hybrid space, which he calls "the Third Space of enunciation ... [that] may open the way to conceptualising an *inter*national culture, based on ... the inscription and articulation of culture's *hybridity*" (*The Location of Culture* 37-38). He coins the term "in-between" to characterise the "Third Space [as] the inter — the cutting edge of translation and negotiation, the *in-between* ... that carries the burden of the meaning of culture" ("Cultural Diversity and Cultural Differences" 206). According to Bhabha's definition, living "in-between" cultures does not suggest a mere exchange between cultures; rather, it rather aims at the creation of new cultural forms (*The Location of Culture* 86-88; "Cultural Diversity" 206). Marie Louise Pratt emphasises the "third" space as an ambivalent contact zone that, on the one hand, offers perspectives of "copresence, interaction, interlocking understanding and practices" (7). On the other hand, these points are tense areas where "disparate cultures meet, clash, and grapple with each other" (Pratt 7).

In the ensuing discussion I analyze Philip and Özdamar within various contexts and thus explore the interconnections and hybridizations they originate with respect to the concepts of nationality, ethnicity, culture, and literature. Although Philip and Özdamar have very different ethnic-cultural and historical backgrounds and live in different cultural, national, and lingual environments, the experiences they undergo as non-White writers in a dominant White Western society show significant similarities on the social, political and academic-critical levels. With the comparative study of their writings, writerly positions, and reception, I endeavour to draw attention to the specific potential and forte comparative work and co-operation between the disciplines of Canadian and German literary-cultural studies — in this case contemporary postcolonial, cultural, comparative, and feminist studies — can effect. In support of Werner Sollors's criticism of the group-by-group or mosaic method and its conception of "pure pluralism" as an organising device of literary study and criticism (Sollors 151-54), my comparative method suggests a trans-ethnic, inter-national procedure that recognises cross-cultural interplays and literary-aesthetic connections between different ethnic-cultural groups and thus avoids a reduction of literature to ethnic typicalities. I agree with Aldo Nemesio's statement that "what happens within the boundaries of a culture [a language, a literature, an academic discipline as a heterogeneous construct] can be understood only if we relate it to what happens elsewhere" (see Nemesio <http://docs.lib.purdue.edu/clcweb/ vol1/iss1/1/>). Accordingly, the group-by-group method turns out to be too narrow and lacking for a study of literatures. Discussing the conditions and possibilities that develop from the coexistence and dialogue of different cultural notions and practices, Bronfen and Marius — who propose the theory of a postmodern, global, hybrid culture in *Hybride Kulturen* (25) — maintain post-colonial literature and theory/criticism as means of bringing "order" and "meaning" into the "hybrid, heterogeneous, and poly-contextual post-modern world" (29; my translation). I argue that *Mutterzunge* and *She Tries Her Tongue* — each text in its own individual way — put this idea into literary practice as they perform possibilities of identification and belonging in spaces of Arabic-Turkish-German and African-Caribbean-Canadian literary and cultural hybridity, respectively. My method then will be to choose as an organising device the comparison of Özdamar's and Philip's "cutting edges of translation and negotiation" (Bhabha, *The Location of Culture* 38) between the cultures and artistic expressions they are influenced by. With this approach, I take a distance from the traditional understanding of the discipline of comparative literature — the traditional centres being the United States and Europe, especially

France and Germany — as its limitation to national, Eurocentric perspectives stands in clear contrast to the positions of "ex-centricity" Philip and Özdamar take and proclaim in their writings. Connecting to their "ex-centric" positions on a theoretical-methodological level, I am instead corresponding to Steven Tötösy de Zepetnek's notion of "comparative cultural studies" that relates the "peripheral," which means non-Eurocentric comparatist procedures to European ones and especially to the impact of the field of cultural studies (see Tötösy de Zepetnek, *Comparative Literature*, "From Comparative Literature"). Tötösy de Zepetnek's theoretical and methodological postulate is "to move and to dialogue between cultures, languages, literatures, and disciplines ... The claim of ... institutional power of national cultures [being] untenable in this perspective" ("From Comparative Literature" <http://docs.lib.purdue.edu/clcweb/vol1/ iss3/2/>). His postulate and conception of the discipline of comparative cultural studies is significative of a more general shift of focus taking place in the discipline of comparative literature: A shift from poststructuralist (textualist, formalist) criticism to a cultural studies (contextualist) emphasis (see also Pivato; Hutcheon; Zima and Strutz; Zelle; Bernheimer; Kadir).

In keeping with this development, I analyze Philip and Özdamar from and within (re)contextualized perspectives that reflect present multicultural realities in Canada and Germany. In the 1995 issue of *World Literature Today*, Nathalie Melas suggests a mode of comparison along the lines of "conceiv[ing] of equivalences that do not unify ... that might not synthesize similarities into a norm" set up by traditional comparative standards (275). I fully agree with Melas's claim which I try to follow here; but yet I am also aware of the fact that my comparative method, in turn, is influenced by my academic and ethnic-cultural context that again shapes a "common ground" on which I build the ensuing comparison. Aware of this bias, namely that it provokes the question whether there could ever be a procedure that would not be restrictive, assumptive, and normative — I deem it indispensable to apply a comparative cultural studies perspective in its given multi-cultural, inter-national, and multi-lingual context.

Critical, public, and academic reception

Özdamar and Philip both belong to the first waves of Turkish and Caribbean immigrants to Germany and Canada, respectively, and they have chosen their new countries as their permanent residence consciously. In this context, their works and in turn the reception of their works have to be viewed within the framework of immigration: they deal with the political, social-cultural, and economic conditions they were and are confronted with in the host countries. The question of how Germany and Canada define their notions of the nation-state and especially of its different members living therein is of essential significance to an understanding of Özdamar's and Philip's writings discussed in my study. From the legal-political viewpoint, the two writers seem to be confronted with completely different circumstances. While the Canadian nation-state is defined by the *jus soli* — the law of citizenship according to soil and parentage, which adjudges its immigrants the right of Canadian citizenship (a right Philip chose to assert for herself) — Germany base its national self-understanding on the *jus sanguinis* — the law of citizenship according to blood that delimits the non-German immigrant from most civil and political co-determination (Özdamar is not a German citizen but a so-called "resident alien"; this law has been repealed recently but in the period I am writing about it was exercized). Yet, in spite of these notably different conceptions of the nation-state and the place of its residents, the definitions and implementations of the countries' immigration policies — termed politics of multiculturalism in Canada and integration politics in Germany — show a striking similarity of "exclusion by inclusion." Multicultural policy in both countries reveals the paradoxical ideal of the multi-cultural and at the same time homogeneous nation-state, of cross-cultural understanding and at the same time cultural retention (see, for example, O'Brien 451-52; Brinkler-Gabler and Smith 6-7; Harney; Hutcheon and Richmond, "Introduction"). It is a paradox that decisively influences the concept of national literature and — as exemplified in the following — of public and critical literary reception.

In 1994, the English translation of Özdamar's prose-drama collection *Mutterzunge* (*Mothertongue*) was enthusiastically reviewed in *The New York Times Book Review* as one of the best works of fiction published in that year (Horrocks and Kolinsky 419). It is only recently that academic and public interest in non-mainstream "ethnic" writing — even on an international range — has increased discernibly. In the course of multicultural politics initiated in Canada and Germany in the late 1960s and the subsequent protest of ethnic minority writers against being ignored by dominant literary discourse, non-White writers in the two countries have progressively received more serious public and critical attention (see Khalil 115; Bucknor 13). In 1991, Özdamar's novel *Das Leben ist eine Karawanserei* was the first "non-originary" German text — the first text written by a writer who is not an "originary" German according to the law of *jus sanguinis* but a German of Turkish origin — to win the prestigious Ingeborg-Bachmann Prize, organized annually by the German-speaking countries of Austria, Switzerland, and Germany in order to give authors and critics who work in the German language the chance to publicly discuss literary texts and "consider what constitutes good literature" (Jankowsky 261). Philip has received several literary prizes as well (Bucknor 139). She was the first Anglophone woman and the second Canadian to win the illustrious Casa de las Americas Prize for the manuscript version of *She Tries Her Tongue* in 1988 (back cover of the poetry collection). Clearly, the pluralization of the conceptions of Canadian and German literature, a process instigated by multicultural policy, has given publication support and visibility to ethnic minority authors, in this case to Caribbean-Canadian and Turkish-German writers. The considerable success of writers such as Philip, Dionne Brand, Claire Harris, and Austin Clarke in the late 1980s and 1990s would not have been possible without the funding of the Canada Council, the Multiculturalism Directorate of the Secretary of State, or the Ontario Arts Council. Likewise, Özdamar's artistic prestige in Germany has — among other factors — depended on and profited from political-literary financial support given, for instance, through the Deutsche Literaturfonds e.V. (The German Literary Fund) or Arbeitsstipendien der Länder (specific scholarships funded by the German federal states).

However, the improved reception of non-mainstream, non-White writing within the German and Canadian fields of literary studies and public-political spheres cannot be acknowledged without reservation (for a selected bibliography of criticism in Canadian ethnic minority writing, see Tötösy de Zepetnek, Sayed, and Salzani, <http://docs.lib.purdue.edu/clcweblibrary/canadianethnicbibliograp hy>). Its development and current practice has a paradoxical nature, which — in my opinion — is hard to evaluate since it remains rather vague whether its workings result from a purposeful, subtle strategy or, instead, from engrained taken-for-granted assumptions. In spite of the increased interest by German literary scholars since the 1980s, for instance, the circulation of reviews on non-originary German literature is still relatively limited and exclusionary, this especially with respect to ethnic minority writers who are still conventionally reduced to an interesting but minor addition or enrichment of the normative German canon (see Suhr 75; Khalil 115, 120-21). The widely held, stereotypical reception of Turkish society and culture — as that of the non-intellectual, exotic "Other," of, in Sargut Sölcün's words, "rückständigen Bauern, gastfreundlichen Hirten, [Geschichtenerzählern], fanatischen Moslems und einer Minderheit nicht weniger fanatischen Stalinisten" / "backward farmers, hospitable shepherds, [storytellers], fanatic Muslims, and a minority of not less fanatic Stalinists" (144; my translation) not only leads to national but also to literary categorisations (Sölcün 145-46). In the Canadian context, Bucknor also observes that the gesture of literary and political consideration "often reduces Caribbean-Canadian writers to an 'ethnic ghetto'" (11); the majority are marginalised because they do not fit the conventions of the established literary institutions. Philip describes her own problematic positioning of "exclusion by inclusion" in the introduction to *She Tries Her Tongue* when she emphasises that "as a female and a black presently living in a society that is, in many respects, still colonial ... and a society which is politely but vehemently racist, while I may have gained some control of my word and its image-making capacities, control of information and production is still problematic" (25).

The taxonomies of national narratives and of the nation-state

The term "ethnic" has carried a sense of marginalisation or marginality ever since its earliest English use which pertained to culturally different "heathen" or "pagan" nations (*Oxford English Dictionary*). In contemporary usage, it suggests cultural groups that are not traditionally identified with the dominant national mythology of a country or other social grouping (Ashcroft 82). The ethnic marker serves mainstream/dominant literature to justify the denial of non-mainstream writers' potential to constitute Canadianness and Germanness, respectively. The subsequent binarisation not only fosters the preservation of the myth of a normative Canadian and German literature but consequently that of the ethnically and culturally homogeneous nation-state (Bucknor 12-13; Suhr 72-73). The cultural-artistic scene becomes a projection of the political-national sphere insofar as it constantly (re)invents the collective identity of the — in Benedict Anderson's words — "imagined community" of the multicultural and yet homogeneous nation-state. In accordance with Anderson's line of argumentation — "Kulturelle Wurzeln" (31, 44-48) — I locate the Canadian and German nation-states in the landscape of the mind. The ideal of the multicultural nation-state on equal ethnic-cultural terms is far from being practice let alone fact; rather, it is a collective invention and idealisation proclaimed by dominant discourse in order to preserve its superiority.

Interestingly, the exclusionary notion of "major" German national narrative and identity finds extensive reflection in public and literary-academic terminology. One major reason why it has taken non-originary German writers so long to be recognised and taken seriously is the persistent usage of the terms *Gastarbeiterliteratur* (the literature of the so-called *Gastarbeiter* meaning "guest workers" who, in the 1960s, were recruited from southern European countries and especially from Turkey to compensate for shortages in the German labour force) and *Ausländerliteratur* (literature of foreigners/aliens) for all kinds of non-originary German writing. The ethnic-cultural categorisations inherent in these literary terms ignore the fact that more and more contemporary German writers of a non-German background have never been guest workers and have never lived in their countries of ancestry (see Khalil 115, 120; Suhr 74, 78-83; Müller 133-34). Whereas the halt to immigration — caused by the economic crisis in the 1970s and the need for trained labour — allowed foreign workers to permanently settle in Germany with their families, the image of the *Gastarbeiter* as well as the term itself are still prevailing and dominant in social as well academic/scholarly discourse. In his essay "Social and Economic Integration of Foreigners in Germany," Wolfgang Seifert notes that "the guest-worker system was abandoned; however, the ideology of temporary migration survived" (84). Even in the most recent contexts of mass migration and internationalisation (burning examples being the construction of a United Europe and the massive emergence of war diasporas), political, social, public, media, and academic German discourse largely refuses to recognise Germany as the country of immigration it is. Writing about German participation in international postcolonial discourse Paul M. Lützeler, for instance, exemplifies how German writers such as Bodo Kirchhoff, Peter Schneider, Günter Grass, or Franz Xaver Kroetz "participate in postcolonial discourse through their travel reports [with which] they wish to raise their readers' as well as their own awareness of the dilemma facing the Third World" (540). Yet, at the same time, he also acknowledges that "the theory of postcolonialism was worked out by Third World intellectuals who are currently teaching at leading universities in Europe or the U.S. ... that it is above all the so-called hyphenated intellectuals who are involved" (539). The paradoxical nature of these two statements —

a) the necessity of "German" writers to travel to so-called Third World countries in order to partake in postcolonial discourse and b) the recognition that postcolonialism as an academic-political-social movement is most active in Western countries; that it thus cannot be limited to the geographical space of the "Third World" — in my opinion clearly shows the (subconscious or conscious) non-recognition of the multicultural, and also postcolonial, reality prevalent in German society and culture, including literature. This misconception subsequently pervades all levels of discourse: non-originary Germans and immigrants continue to be represented as *Gastarbeiter*, *Ausländer*, and/or *Zuwanderer* (meaning newcomers/migrants; the term *Zuwanderer* results from the latest change in official terminology and is hardly known and used in public discourse). While the immigrant would be perceived as "a person who migrates into a country as a [permanent] settler" and subsequently a citizen (*Oxford English Dictionary*), the *Ausländer* unmistakably remains "a subject of another country than that in which [she]/he resides" (*Oxford English Dictionary*). She/he is a "resident foreign in origin [and] excluded from (the citizenship and privileges) of the nation" (*Oxford English Dictionary*), which makes her/him "a stranger, outsider; a person other than oneself" (*Oxford English Dictionary*). Through this process of "Othering," the originary German imposes a label of identification that depersonalises and homogenises the immigrant at the same time that it stresses the distinctness or distinctiveness of the foreign "Other" from the familiar "Self" (Itwaru 12-14; Kristeva 19-20). However, more recent terms employed in German such as *Migrantenliteratur* (literature of migrants), *Minoritätenliteratur* (ethnic minority literature) or *Schreiben in der Diaspora* (diaspora literature) are no less problematic (Fischer 63; Wierschke 203-204) as they are still conceptual categorizations established from a dominant Eurocentric viewpoint that classifies the culturally unfamiliar or unknown as strange or "Other." Commenting on the ambiguous nature underlying her winning the Ingeborg-Bachmann Prize, Özdamar remarks ironically that "I was accepted, but merely as a 'guest writer'" (afterword to the *Mothertongue* collection). The Austrian, Swiss, and German critics evaluating *Das Leben ist eine Karawanserei* did not address her as a German but as a foreign writer who had chosen the German language to express herself. Even though the critical discussion of her work reckoned the multicultural diversity of writers in German, the very acknowledgement re-enforced the division of migrant and originary German literature by ethnically marking Özdamar and her work

(Jankowsky 262-63, 267).

A comparable process of ethnic-cultural labelling of foreignness can be observed in Canadian literary studies. In the introduction to *Other Solitudes*, Linda Hutcheon argues that already the label "ethnic" for non-Anglophone and non-Francophone Canadian writings is exclusionary and thus enhances the clear-cut ethnic-racial boundary underlying the binary assumption of normative, "non-ethnic" White literature and peripheral, "ethnic" non-White literature. Non-White writers are "Othered" by White writers' ignorance (whether subconsciously or consciously is a widely disputed issue) of their privilege of Whiteness, which reduces the concept of the "writer" to an ethnocentric White category. Although unlike in Germany, immigration and multiculturalism are legal matters of Canadian national self-definition -- the conception of the Canadian nation-state is constructed politically, based on the aforementioned concept of *jus soli* and accompanied by a governmental policy of multiculturalism (Cook 5-12; Harney) — the traditional understanding of national identity and canonical literature shows distinct signs of Anglo-Canadian and Franco-Canadian ethnocentrism. According to Bucknor, the political promotion of the ideal of multicultural difference/pluralism in the unified Canadian nation-state gives decisive impetus to the ghettoisation and misrecognition of non-White writers in the field of literary studies, especially in literary theory and criticism (14-15). On the one hand, the Multicultural Act of 1988 makes a call to "(c) encourage and promote exchanges and cooperation among diverse communities of Canada," whereas, on the other hand, it endeavours to "(e) encourage the preservation, enhancement, sharing, and evolving expression of the multicultural heritage of Canada." In spite of the fact that the pluralist conception of multicultural politics has improved the situation of ethnic minority writers, its paradoxical and asymmetrical composition leads to compartmentalisation and "exclusion by inclusion" that keeps alive the myth of a genuine Anglo/French literary canon. The political claim to uphold one's ethnic identity and at the same time to participate to the full in national life turns out to be rather spurious in reality: "Canada ... is located in the landscape of the mind" (Itwaru 20); the ideal of the multicultural nation-state on equal ethnic-cultural terms is not a fact but a collective invention and idealisation — in Anderson's words "an imagined community" — proclaimed by dominant White discourse in order to preserve its superiority (31, 44-48). Under these conditions, the ideal of mosaic-like cultural and literary pluralism turns out to be a mere metaphor for a pedagogy that leads to the proliferation of labels, to compartmentalisation, and to further entrenchment of ethnic boundaries, a dilemma Philip depicts in her collection of critical essays *Frontiers*: "I carry a Canadian passport: I, therefore, am Canadian. How am I Canadian, though, above and beyond the narrow legalistic definition of being the bearer of a Canadian passport; and does the racism of Canadian society present an absolute barrier to those of us who are differently coloured ever belonging? Because that is in fact, what we are speaking about — how to belong — not only in the legal and civic sense ... but also in another sense of feeling at "home" and at ease" (16-17). In the following, her reaction to this dilemma is outspokenly resistant, a resistance that she endeavours to conduct through her writerly activities: "But more importantly than that, Canada *needs* to m/other us. Her very salvation depends on m/othering all her peoples. ... In the words of my only mother tongue, the Caribbean demotic: 'We ent going nowhere. We here and is right here we staying." In Canada. In this world so new. To criticize, needle and demand; to work hard for; to give to; to love; to hate — for better or for worse — till death do we part. And even after — in the African tradition of our ancestral role after death of advising and guiding our offspring — our descendants. African Canadians — Canadians'" (*Frontiers* 20-23).

Writerly resistance in spaces of hybridity

"True" belonging in the German or Canadian nation-state is envisioned through the re-performance of German or Canadian national community away from the traditional conception of the organically grown, homogeneous nation towards an imagined community that — as a heterogeneous, culturally hybrid amalgamation — builds on the productivity of internal differences: Philip: "she / swung / a skilled trapezist -- / no net / below / no one / to catch / her / ... /one breast / white / the other black / headless / in a womb-black night / a choosing -- /one breast /neither black nor white/ (*She Tries Her Tongue* 40, 33). And Özdamar: "A guest worker, standing there, said: 'Sonra interpreter geldi. Formanle konustu. Bu income tax kaybetmis dedi. Tax office cok fena dedi. Income tax Yok. Residence da yok. Immigration police vermiyor. Housing office da yok diyor. Employment office da permit vermedi" (*Mothertongue* 96) ("Ein gestandener Gastarbeiter sprach: 'Sonra Dolmetscher geldi. Meisterle konustu. Bu Lohn steuer kaybetmis dedi. Finanzamt cok fena dedi. Lohnsteuer Yok. Aufenthalt da yok, Fremdpolizei vermiyor. Wohnungsamt da yok diyor. Arbeitsamt da

Erlaubnis vermedi" [*Mutterzunge* 77]).

In the latter quotation, German words are interspersed in the mother tongue in order to name concepts and institutions that are specifically German and thus cannot be named in the Turkish language. The heteroglossia that emerges from this blend poses a problem for both originary speakers of German and of Turkish. It is created by and tailored to the context of those living in-between languages and cultures, those who "sew their Turkish clothes out of German materials" (*Mothertongue* 115) ("aus deutschen Stoffen ihre türkischen Kleider nähen" [*Mutterzunge* 92]). It is the space of personal and national-cultural instability (of the "skilled trapezist — not net below"), displacement ("one breast white, the other black"), and in-betweenness/hybridity ("one breast neither black nor white") that opens possibilities of mutual ethnic-cultural competence and interaction in the two women's writings. The polyvalence of Philip's and Özdamar's art, especially their imaginative mobility, skilfully displays the cracks and gaps in cultural-literary Canadian and, similarly, German discourse. Both writers are well aware of the fact that they cannot write outside of the traditional conventions of German and Canadian literature; yet, what they can do and actually do in their writings is enter into a critical, challenging dialogue with the mainstream. They take — what Hutcheon calls — "ex-centric" or "frontier" positions at the margins of dominant culture and literature (*The Canadian Postmodern* 3). It is with and in their "ex-centric" narratives that they problematise and re-envision the notions of a "pure" literary canon and national identity.

In "Discourse on the Logic of Language," Philip breaks with Eurocentric poetic structural-formal norms by decentring the poem on the page and surrounding it with a mythical short story, historical edicts, and a physiological-scientific description of how speech takes place that is underlined by multiple choice questions. With the conjunction of these different texts she disrupts the modernist poetic convention of humanism, which she refers to as "Eliot's objective correlative" that dehistoricises and depersonalises poetry by averring its autonomous and universal nature (Hutcheon, *The Canadian Postmodern* 1-2, 10). Interspersing the elements of mythic vision, colonial history, and scientific, racist, sexist masculine discourse, Philip deliberately "put[s] the poem, that particular poem, back in its historical context, which is what poetry is not supposed to do" (Philip qtd. in Williamson 228). She thus alludes to a subtle process Arun P. Mukherjee overtly denounces in her essay "Canadian Nationalism, Canadian Literature and Racial Minority Women" when she points out that "what seems universalist and apolitical on the surface often turns out to be a Euro-Canadian conceptualization" (429). Unveiling the seemingly universal Canadian values as culture-specific, Eurocentric constructs, Philip attributes a significant role to the mythical Afro-Caribbean short story, which is not only thematically distinguished from the other textual parts of the poem but also through its particular positioning. It is the only text for which the reader needs to turn the page in order to read it. By this accentuation of the ancestral African story, Philip seems to interrogate the relevance and hence to challenge the dominance of the western texts juxtaposed with it. I argue that she thus indicates to her readers how important the aspects of perspective and context are in the production of meaning(s), how important it is to read the different texts of the poem in their relational co-existence that forms a new, trans-cultural/textual "whole."

Challenging the traditional Western notion of the universality and the generic categorisation of art, Özdamar who herself is an actress, director of plays, and writer creates the narrative space in-between theatre and prose. Her *Mutterzunge* stories can be characterised as prose drama or — depending on the perspective — dramatic prose. In a conversation with Annette Wierschke, Özdamar claims that the theatre, her first active encounter with art, has always been part of her writing ("Das Theater ist immer" 252). The Karagöz story, for instance, was first written as a play before she transformed it into a prose text that still expresses her experiences of staging it. In both play and prose text, Özdamar reviews her artistic relationship with the Turkish and Western European theatre (for more details see Milz, "Introduction"). Doing so, she creates an inseparable blend of the tradition of the Turkish Karagöz shadow-play with that of Bertolt Brecht's epic theatre and Heiner Müller's avant-garde theatre. What her prose-drama shares with all three pretexts is an actor-recipient relationship that is not based on the western classical aesthetics of realistic representation and sympathetic identification but on a critical understanding of social processes, of how we act our roles in society. Özdamar's conjunction of the Brechtian drama and the Turkish shadow-play in the Karagöz story is not coincidental. A precursor of the absurd and epic, the Karagöz play can be described as a socially critical comedy or caricature of society and its morals (Wierschke 198; van Heyst 115-16). Like the shadow-play, Özdamar's story is named after the main character Karagöz (*Schwarzauge* in German and *Black Eye* in English) who — in both the original and re-contextualised version — is performed as a rough, uneducated Turk or Arab. Together with his intellectual friend Hacivad (represented by the donkey in Özdamar's text), he gets into numerous tragic-comic situations and arguments, which reveal and challenge social, political, and economic inequality. The prologue to the original Karagöz shadow-play clearly anticipates what Özdamar only insinuates in her version: the performance is not meant to be a piece of universal fiction but rather a critical mirror, a parody or caricature of real life (Kühn 5). As exemplified in the Karagöz tradition, Özdamar complicates her stock characters (the guest worker, the financially dependent and constantly pregnant wife, the simple-minded villagers, the Marxist intellectual, the fascist, the bourgeois German and numerous other character types) and thus demonstrates the inconsistency and senselessness of stereotypes. In *Mutterzunge*, the construction of identity is performed as a multi-dimensional, dynamic process. It is ambivalent and indeterminable insofar as it rejects both an assimilation into German culture and a return to Turkish cultural practice.

Özdamar's hybrid prose-dramas oppose thematic, linguistic, and stylistic norms as they inseparably combine the oral with the written, the traditional with the modern, European-German culture with the Turkish-Arabic. If compared to western literary norm, her narrative style is bumpy and unsmooth; it abounds with abrupt changes of narrative perspective. Özdamar lines up grotesque, ambivalent, and fractured scenes that do not seem to make much sense when one first reads them. Another means of confusing her German (European) readership is that of constantly interspersing conventional themes and structures with unfamiliar Turkish-Arabic elements. The *Mutterzunge* stories abound with Turkish and Arabic words, phrases, proverbs (worldly wisdoms), folklore, songs, and fragments of Islamic religious texts. With the help of these insertions, Özdamar creates her own polyvalent space of textual and cultural hybridity. Blurring the strange or foreign with the common or familiar, Özdamar's writing calls upon her German as well as upon her non-German readers to re-think their often one-dimensional and tenacious national-cultural expectations of each other.

As my discussion indicates, Özdamar and Philip re-perform German and Canadian national narratives in *Mutterzunge* and *She Tries Her Tongue* as they choose not to belong exclusively to any national community or literary model (Wierschke 266; Philip, *Frontiers* 22). In the interview with Wierschke, Özdamar declares that for her home and belonging is wherever her friends are (258-60). Giving an account of the circumstances and experiences as stage-director of her play "Karagöz in Alamania," she brings ethnic-national identification ad absurdum with a seemingly farcical anecdote: "On one occasion the donkey bit the Turkish star in the back of his neck ... One of the Turkish stars said: 'A Turkish donkey would never do a thing like that.' (The donkey was from Frankfurt.) A German star replied: 'I get on very well with the donkey. He'd never do anything like that to me.' But then the donkey kicked him too" (Horrocks and Krause 61-62]). In this scene, the mutually prejudiced, multi-ethnic cast goes so far as to attribute ethnic-national characteristics to the donkey incapable of this kind of discrimination. The persistent myths of ethnic-national identification and belonging are brought ad absurdum and thus demythologised (Horrocks and Krause 67). Özdamar's assertion that she simultaneously feels related to many places (Wierschke 265) shows affinities to Philip's self-understanding as an exiled subject, for whom "be/longing *anywhere* is problematic" (*Frontiers* 22): "From one exile to another, island hopping, first to Trinidad 'for an education' ... next to Jamaica for a continuation at the tertiary level, and then to a more permanent exile in North America. Only to understand, finally, that exile had begun a long time before I left Tobago for Trinidad" (*Frontiers* 9-10). In *She Tries Her Tongue*, Philip describes her people as a diaspora, which Western colonialism has deprived of its belonging and identification: the African cultural space. On the endless search for belonging and being they have become "wanderers/ in the centuries of curses / the lost I's / the lost equation:/ you plus I equals we / I and I and I equals I / minus you ("African Majesty" 48).

Employing the trope of the "Black Atlantic" in his discussion of the Black diaspora, Paul Gilroy manifests place as a continually shifting passage; the metaphor suggests that all places are places of repeated displacement. The diasporic condition thus unsettles the static cartographical markers of the nation-state. In her latest collection of critical essays, *A Genealogy of Resistance*, Philip also perceives the identification of displacements as the precursor to the identification of place (58). She thus attributes a positive force to the state of being displaced, which also shows in *She Tries Her Tongue*. Re-appropriating Ovid's Ceres and Proserpine story in the poem sequence "And Over Land and Sea," she makes use of the quest narrative to describe her people's search for the lost place, language, memory and identity. In the interview with Barbara Carey, she pronounces that "'finding out' ... is the quest itself, and not its result" (Carey 20).

Belonging and home are provisional, fluid and dynamic

processes for Özdamar as well. As the long title of her *Karawanserai* novel indicates, life — like a caravanserai — is a place where one stays for a short while and then leaves again: "life is a caravanserai: has two doors, I entered through one of them, I exited through the other" ("Das Leben ist eine Karawanserei: hat zwei Türen, aus einer kam ich rein, aus der anderen ging ich raus." In the *Mutterzunge* collection, traveling by train is used as a common image to express the fluidity of belonging: "Train station. Trains leave, trains arrive" (*Mothertongue* 95) ("Bahnhof. Die Züge fahren ab, die Züge kommen an" [*Mutterzunge* 76]). In the Karagöz story, the guest worker and especially his wife continually travel back and forth between Turkey and Germany, between "where they're from" and "where they're at": Remembering the wisdom of her grandmother, the farmer's wife describes her problematic positioning in-between the two cultures: "My grandmother used to say: 'Humans are like birds. Open eyes and you are here. Close eyes and you are there.' Goodbye, Alamania!" (*Mothertongue* 93) ("Meine Großmutter sagte: 'Der Mensch ist ein Vogel. Machst du Augen auf, bist du da. Machst du Augen zu, bist du dort.' Wiedersehen Alamania!" [*Mutterzunge* 75]).

"Where" is the space in-between?

The performative, ex-centric positions presented in *Mutterzunge* and *She Tries Her Tongue* draw attention to a highly complex problem, namely that of finding creative spaces in-between cultures. Ien Ang's claim of a politics of diaspora that neither privileges the (real or imaginary) country of immigration nor the (real or imaginary) homeland but that instead keeps a "creative tension" between the two (16) proves to be a very complicated, if not impossible, undertaking in both texts (and I would presume in any text) as each one, in its specific socio-cultural, literary context, reveals biases and positions that can become rather delicate (for a detailed discussion see Milz, Chapter Two and Conclusion). In the light of this complication the question if Philip's and Özdamar's third spaces of hybridity can really offer a viable alternative to the binaries investigated and challenged in their writings evokes itself. To affirm this provocative question, I want to expose a significant parallel in the two women's artistic endeavours: Notwithstanding the problematic issues their writerly politics and thus their works raise, they display vital possibilities and stimulus for multi-cultural, inter-national dialogue and competence. With their writing, Philip and Özdamar go "beyond" cultural-national categorisations and boundaries, which means that they re-perform cultural coexistence from spaces of hybridity. In *Frontiers*, which is dedicated to "Canada in the effort of becoming a space of true be/longing," Philip voices the conciliatory call to find out "what we [all Canadians] can offer to and accept from each other. It is the only way we will transform this place from a stranger place to one of true be/longing" (25). Likewise, Özdamar envisions German society as a multicultural community of relational difference where "you see people without judging them, set out to find the tragic and the comic in their lives, and proceed on the assumption that every person is a novel and that the life of every person is a novel. And that one never loses the interest in this novel. And that one sets out to search for all the great feelings in the life of this person" (Özdamar qtd. in Wierschke 266; my translation). Constantly pointing out the importance of relational differences, *Mutterzunge* and *She Tries Her Tongue* suggest a multicultural Canadian and German nation-state respectively, in which diasporas and ethnic minorities are highly problematical but nonetheless constitutive, integral parts. Yet, as actualities show multicultural German and Canadian societies on equal terms are still visions; but I want to stress here that they are visions that are widely shared and enforced by a polyphony of artists and critics in both countries. Critical texts on ethnic minority writers such as Philip and Özdamar or on cultural-literary hybridity are numerous, especially in the areas of minority discourse, post-colonialism and feminism. However, linkages between the areas of a) German and Canadian literary research on writings of ethnicity/nationality and of b) cross-disciplinary comparative studies are, in spite of the rich comparative potential unfolding between the two countries' ethnic-cultural and receptive situations demonstrated here, still rare. The line of argumentation chosen in this comparative study implies that critical-academic contributions to the opening and broadening of the (German and Canadian) literary canons have to be multi-perspectival, cross-cultural, inter-national, and inter-disciplinary approaches that acknowledge and constitute identity and belonging as fluid processes in-between cultures, ethnicities, literatures, histories, and languages correlating in invented collective spaces such as the imagined geographical community of the nation or that of national literature.

Literary-academic discourse revised

As Özdamar playfully yet satirically shows in the Karagöz story of the *Mutterzunge* collection, the alternative proposed above turns out to be a highly complex and problematic undertaking in dominant literary-academic discourse. She discloses intellectual patronizing and stereotyping by depicting a German intellectual who — reminiscent of Peter Weiss's challenging *mise en scène* of the life of the French revolutionary Jean-Paul Marat in the drama *Verfolgung und Ermordung Jean-Paul Marats* — sits in a bathtub in front of the "Door to Germany" (*Mutterzunge* 90-92; *Mothertongue* 112-16). Employing the devices of irony and exaggeration, she exposes the intellectual's unwitting complicity with dominant discourse. The intellectual "Others", who wait for their admittance in front of the "Door," in a "benevolently" racist-totalizing manner: "The intellectual took off his trousers — passionately, dropped to his knees, said: 'Understand how important it is to do something for these people. Are you feeling that? Believe me, the culture shock of the Gastarbeiter puts everything into question. Economical — cultural — political. Do you understand how important that is?'" (*Mothertongue* 114) ("Der Erleuchtete zog seine Hose aus — aus Leidenschaft, ging auf Knien, sprach: 'Versteht ihr, wie wichtig es ist, für diese Leute etwas zu tun. Are you feeling that? Was meint ihr, der Kulturschock der Gastarbeiter stellt alles in Frage. Economical — cultural — political. Versteht ihr, wie wichtig das ist?'" [*Mutterzunge* 91-92]).

Instead of entering into a serious dialogue with the donkey -- which represents the perspective of the intellectual immigrant -- the German intellectual is much too fixated on his own, one-perspectival vision of the interstitial cultural, economic, and historical space in-between backward-Ottomanic Turkey and progressive-Western Germany: "'I believe … that my imagination gets the better of me again, that is perhaps ottomanic'" (*Mothertongue* 116) ("'Ich glaube … meine Phantasie reitet mich wieder, das ist vielleicht otomanisch'" [*Mutterzunge* 92]. The donkey's ironic-sarcastic reply to this racist, condescending utterance is "manic" / "manisch" (*Mothertongue* 116; *Mutterzunge* 93). With the provocative "Ottomanic — manic" / "otomanisch — manisch" wordplay, he overtly mocks the intellectual's stereotyping image or invention of the Ottomanic-Oriental immigrant. Yet, the evident sarcasm in his remark remains unrecognised by the addressed person, the self-important intellectual.

Being a "White woman intellectual" who approaches the field of ethnic minority and non-White women's literature in the contexts of Philip's *She Tries Her Tongue* and Özdamar's *Mutterzunge*, I am fully aware that the donkey's thought-provoking criticism of Western intellectualism includes the field of academic literary study which I am part of. By means of the donkey-intellectual scene, Özdamar asks me — the White academic reader and critic of her text — to self-reflexively and self-critically re-think my position within dominant Western discourse. And I realise that my very position "within" — especially if lacking awareness and self-reflexion — might turn this study, against its intentions, into an accomplice of dominant literary discourse. Once alert to this danger, the question arises whether it is still justifiable or wise of me to write on the given issues? My answer is affirmative since I believe that the critical recognition and questioning of my "complicit" status is constituent to the challenge and unlearning of traditional White discursive patterns and privileges. I argue that multi-ethnic/cultural co-operation and cultural-literary equality in the imagined communities of the German and Canadian nation-states are only possible if White academics are willed to unlearn the ethnocentric perspective offered to them through their status and to instead choose alternative, multi-ethnic and comparative perspectives. The texts of Philip and Özdamar take on new significance in light of the comparative context that — as Diana Brydon and Helen Tiffin point out in the introduction to their work *Decolonising Fictions* (15-20) — cuts across the ethnocentric Canadian and German nexus to focus instead on the polyphony of transethnic encounters. Philip's *She Tries Her Tongue* and Özdamar's *Mutterzunge* reveal an impressive artistic potency in "decolonising" ethnocentric Canadian and German discourse respectively, which means in writing back against imperial, universalised fictions and subsequently in incorporating alternative, re-contextualized ways of seeing, living, and speaking in the Canadian/German societies (11). Both writings accentuate that to "decolonise is not simply to rid oneself of the trappings of imperial power [but] also to seek non-repressive alternatives to imperialist discourse" (Brydon and Tiffin 12). The de-universalized alternatives Philip and Özdamar offer are contextualized in the hybrid spaces of African-Caribbean-Canadian and Arabic-Turkish-German cultures and literatures respectively. *Mutterzunge* and *She Tries Her Tongue* seek to enter into a vital dialogue with their non-White *and* White audiences by opening possibilities of multi-racial, multi-cultural discussion on the issues of racism, nationalism, (hetero)sexism and gendering. A comparative dialogue with the texts opens the possibility of an effectual immersion in the specific contexts they are imbedded in.

Note: The above article is a revised version of Milz, Sabine. "Comparative Cultural Studies and Ethnic Minority Writing Today: The Hybridities of

Marlene Nourbese Philip and Emine Sevgi Özdamar," *CLCWeb: Comparative Literature and Culture* 2.2 (2000): <http://docs.lib.purdue. edu/clcweb/vol2 /iss2/4/>. Copyright release by Purdue University Press.

Works Cited

Anderson, Benedict. "Kulturelle Wurzeln." *Hybride Kulturen: Beiträge zur anglo-amerikanischen Multikulturalismusdebatte*. Ed. Elisabeth Bronfen, Benjamin Marius, and Therese Steffen. Tübingen: Stauffenburg, 1997. 31-58.
Ang, Ien. "On Not Speaking Chinese: Postmodern Ethnicity and the Politics of Diaspora." *New Formations* 24 (1994): 1-18.
Ashcroft, Bill, Gareth Griffiths, and Helen Tiffin. *Key Concepts in Post-Colonial Studies*. London: Routledge, 1998.
Bernheimer, Charles, ed. *Comparative Literature in the Age of Multiculturalism*. Baltimore: The Johns Hopkins UP, 1995.
Bhabha, Homi K. "On the Irremovable Strangeness of Being Different." *PMLA: Publications of the Modern Language Association of America* 113 (1998): 34-39.
Bhabha, Homi K. *The Location of Culture*. New York: Routledge, 1994.
Bhabha, Homi K. "Verortungen der Kultur." *Hybride Kulturen. Beiträge zur anglo-amerikanischen Multikulturalismusdebatte*. Trans. Anne Emmert, and Joseph Raab. Ed. Elisabeth Bronfen, Benjamin Marius, and Therese Steffen. Tübingen: Stauffenburg, 1997. 123-48.
Brinker-Gabler, Gisela, and Sidonie Smith, eds. *Writing New Identities: Gender, Nation, and Immigration in Contemporary Europe*. Minneapolis: U of Minnesota P, 1997.
Bronfen, Elisabeth, Benjamin Marius, and Therese Steffen. *Hybride Kulturen. Beiträge zur anglo-amerikanischen Multikulturalismusdebatte*. Trans. Anne Emmert, and Joseph Raab. Tübingen: Stauffenburg, 1997.
Brydon, Diana, and Helen Tiffin. *Decolonising Fictions*. Sydney: Dangaroo P, 1993.
Bucknor, Michael A. *Postcolonial Crosses: Body-Memory and Inter-nationalism in Caribbean / Canadian Writing*. PhD Diss. London: The U of Western Ontario, 1998.
Carey, Barbara. "Secrecy and Silence." *Books in Canada* 20 (1991): 17-21.
Cook, Ramsay. "Nation, Identity, Rights: Reflections on W.L. Morton's Canadian Identity." *Journal of Canadian Studies* 29 (1994): 5-18.
Fischer, Monika. *Intercultural Alterity or Borderland Experience: Minor Literatures of Germany and the United States*. Oregon: U of Oregon P, 1997.
Gilroy, Paul. *The Black Atlantic: Modernity and Double Consiousness*. Cambridge: Harvard UP, 1993.
Harney, Robert F. "'So Great a Heritage as Ours': Immigration and the Survival of the Canadian Polity." *Daedalus* 117.4 (1988): 51-97.
Heyst, Ilse van. *Alles für Karagöz*. Stuttgart: Klett, 1982.
Horrocks David, and Eva Kolinsky, eds. *Turkish Culture in German Society Today*. Providence: Berghahn Books, 1996.
Horrocks David, and Frank Krause. "Emine Sevgi Özdamar: 'Black Eye and his Donkey:' A Multi-Cultural Experience." *Turkish Culture in German Society Today*. Ed. David Horrocks, and Eva Kolinsky. Providence:

Berghahn Books, 1996. 55-69.

Hutcheon, Linda. "Productive Comparative *Angst*: Comparative Literature in the Age of Multiculturalism." *World Literature Today* 69 (1995): 299-303.

Hutcheon, Linda. *The Canadian Postmodern: A Study of Contemporary English-Canadian Fiction*. Toronto: Oxford UP, 1988.

Hutcheon Linda, and Marion Richmond, eds. *"Other Solitudes": Canadian Multicultural Fictions*. Toronto: Oxford UP, 1990.

Itwaru, Arnold H. *The Invention of Canada: Literary Text and the Immigrant Imaginary*. Toronto: TSAR, 1990.

Jankowski, Karen. "'German? Literature Contested: The 1991 Ingeborg-Bachmann-Prize Debate, 'Cultural Diversity,' and Emine Sevgi Özdamar." *The German Quarterly* 70.3 (1997): 261-74.

Kadir, Djelal, ed. *World Literature Today: Comparative Literature: States of the Art* 69 (1995).

Khalil, Iman O. "Zur Rezeption arabischer Autoren in Deutschland." *Denn du tanzt auf einem Seil. Positionen deutschsprachiger MigrantInnenliteratur*. Ed. Sabine Fischer and Moray McGowan. Tübingen: Stauffenburg, 1997. 115-31.

Kristeva, Julia. *Strangers to Ourselves*. Trans. Leon Roudiez. New York: Columbia UP, 1991.

Kühn, Monika. *Karagöz und Rumpelstilzchen. Türkisches und deutsches Schattentheater*. Donauwörth: Ludwig Auer, 1994.

Lützeler, Paul M. "The Postcolonial View: Writers from the German-Speaking Countries Report from the Third World." *World Literature Today* 69 (1995): 539-46.

Melas, Nathalie. "Versions of Incommensurability." *World Literature Today* 69 (1995): 275-80.

Milz, Sabine. *Hybridity in Culture, Literature and Language: A Comparative Study of Contemporary Caribbean Canadian and Turkish German Women Writing Exemplified by the Writers M.N. Philip and E.S. Özdamar*. M.A. Thesis. Hamilton: McMaster U, 1999.

Mukherjee, Arun P. "Canadian Nationalism, Canadian Literature and Racial Minority Women." *The Other Woman: Women of Colour in Contemporary Canadian Literature*. Ed. Makeda Silvera. Toronto: Sister Vision P, 1995. 421-44.

Müller, Regula. "'Ich war Mädchen, war ich Sultanin.' Weitgeöffnete Augen betrachten türkische Frauengeschichte(n). Zum Karawanserei-Roman von Emine Sevgi Özdamar." *Denn du tanzt auf einem Seil: Positionen deutschsprachiger MigrantInnenliteratur*. Ed. Sabine Fischer and Moray McGowan. Tübingen: Stauffenburg, 1997. 133-49.

Nemesio, Aldo. "The Comparative Method and the Study of Literature." *CLCWeb: Comparative Literature and Culture* 1.1 (1999): <http://docs.lib.purdue.edu/clcweb/vol1/iss1/1/>.

O'Brien, Peter. "Germany's Newest Aliens: The East Germans." *East European Quarterly* 30.4 (1997): 449-70.

Özdamar, Emine S. *Das Leben ist eine Karawanserei hat zwei Türen aus einer kam ich Rein aus der anderen ging ich raus*. Köln: Kiepenheuer & Witsch, 1994.

Özdamar, Emine S. *Mother Tongue*. Trans. Thomas Craig. Toronto: Coach House P, 1994.

Özdamar, Emine S. *Mutterzunge*. Köln: Kiepenheuer & Witsch, 1998.
Özdamar, Emine S. "Schwarzauge und sein Esel." *Die Zeit* (25 February 1992): 90.
Philip, Marlene N. *A Genealogy of Resistance and Other Essays*. Toronto: The Mercury P, 1997.
Philip, Marlene N. *Frontiers: Selected Essays and Writings on Racism and Culture 1984-1992*. Stratford: Mercury, 1992.
Philip, Marlene N. *She Tries Her Tongue: Her Silence Softly Breaks*. Toronto: U of Toronto P, 1989.
Pivato, Joseph. *Echo: Essays on Other Literatures*. Toronto: Guernica, 1994.
Pratt, Mary L. *Imperial Eyes: Travel Writing and Transculturation*. London: Routledge, 1992.
Schwenk, Katrin. "Introduction: Thinking about "Pure Pluralism." *Cultural Difference & The Literary Text: Pluralism & the Limits of Authenticity in North American Literatures*. Ed. Winfried Siemerling, and Katrin Schwenk. Iowa City: U of Iowa P, 1996. 1-9.
Seifert, Wolfgang. "Social and Economic Integration of Foreigners in Germany." *Paths of Inclusion: The Integration of Migrants in the United States and Germany*. Ed. Peter H. Schuck, and Rainer Münz. New York: Berghahn Books, 1998. 83-113.
Sölcün, Sargut. *Sein und Nichtsein. Zur Literatur in der multikulturallen Gesellschaft*. Bielefeld: Aisthesis, 1992.
Sollors, Werner. "Comments." *Cultural Difference & the Literary Text: Pluralism & the Limits of Authenticity in North American Literatures*. Ed. Winfried Siemerling, and Katrin Schwenk. Iowa City: U of Iowa P, 1996. 151-61.
Suhr, Heidrun. "Ausländerliteratur: Minority Literature in the Federal Republic of Germany." *New German Critique* 46 (1989): 71-103.
Tötösy de Zepetnek, Steven. *Comparative Literature: Theory, Method, Application*. Amsterdam: Rodopi, 1998.
Tötösy de Zepetnek, Steven. "From Comparative Literature Toward Comparative Cultural Studies" *CLCWeb: Comparative Literature and Culture* 1.3 (1999): <http://docs.lib.purdue.edu/clcweb/ vol1/iss3/2/>.
Tötösy de Zepetnek, Steven, Asma Sayed, and Domenic A. Beneventi. "Selected Bibliography of Work in Canadian Ethnic Minority Writing." *CLCWeb: Comparative Literature and Culture* (*Library*): <http://docs. lib.purdue.edu/clcweblibrary/canadianethnicbibliography>
Wierschke, Annette. *Schreiben als Selbstbehauptung. Kulturkonflikt und Identität in den Werken von Aysel Özakin, Alev Tekinay und Emine Sevgi Özdamar. Mit Interviews*. Frankfurt: Verlag für Interkulturelle Kommunikation, 1996.
Williamson, Janice. *Sounding Differences: Conversations With Seventeen Canadian Woman Writers*. Toronto: U of Toronto P, 1993.

Zelle, Carsten, ed. *Allgemeine Literaturwissenschaft. Konturen und Profile im Pluralismus*. Opladen: Westdeutscher, 1999.
Zima, Peter V., and Johann Strutz *Komparatistik. Einführung in die Vergleichende Literaturwissenschaft*. Tübingen: Francke, 1992.

Author's profile: Sabine Milz teaches literature at Fanshaw College. Her interests in research include culture policy, contemporary ethnic minority writing and culture in Canada and Germany, and publishing. Milz's recent publications include "Canadian Cultural Policy-making at a Time of Neoliberal Globalization," *English Studies in Canada* (2009) and "Inside and Outside the Hyena's Belly: Nega Mezlekia and the Politics of Time and Authorship," *Journal of Canadian Studies* (2008).

The Ambivalent Americanness of J. Hector St. Jean de Crèvecoeur
Susan Castillo

Abstract: In her article "The Ambivalent Americanness of J. Hector St. Jean de Crèvecoeur" Susan Castillo analyzes Crèvecoeur's concept of the melting pot and its relation to his own personal history as expatriate Frenchman and pre-revolutionary inhabitant of New York. Crèvecoeur's vision has had a profound impact, not only on European definitions of what it means to be a citizen of the United States, but also in discussions of which texts are deemed worth of literary canonical status. Castillo discusses Crèvecoeur's life as an Anglophile farmer in colonial New York and his notion of "Americanization" as a process available to all white male Northern European settlers who are willing to toil industriously. Castillo analyzes Crèvecoeur's dismay when he is forced to choose between his European identity and his adopted home on the North American continent and concludes by linking Crèvecoeur's ideas on American pre-revolutionary identity to multiculturalism and to current debates on the literary canon in United States literature.

As we are all aware, the concept of the melting pot is one which has strongly shaped perceptions of the United States since it was first articulated in the texts of Hector St. John de Crèvecoeur (on Crèvecoeur, see, e.g., Bishop; Castillo; Iannini; Schell; White). What most people are not aware of, however, is that Crèvecoeur himself is a truly transnational figure, a shape-shifter and man of many masks, whose career illustrates in graphic fashion some of the dilemmas of identity in the Early Republic. Born in Caën to an affluent family of Norman gentry, he spent some time in England visiting distant relatives in Salisbury and would remain an Anglophile for the rest of his life. It is said that there he fell in love with a young Englishwoman, a merchant's daughter who died before they were able to marry. In 1755 he embarked for New France as a soldier. France's position in North America at the time was strong; in the previous century, *voyageurs* such as La Salle and Hennepin had laid claim to extensive territories in the Great Lakes area and in the upper Mississippi Valley. In the decade prior to Crèvecoeur's arrival in New France, tensions along the frontier between France and England's American possessions had steadily increased; both groups wished to expand their territories in order to increase trade of all sorts, particularly in furs and in 1754 what would come to be known in North America (i.e., Canada, the U.S.A., and Mexico) as the French and Indian War broke out. Crèvecoeur was wounded in the battle in which the French general Montcalm lost Canada for France and after the war ended he headed south to the British colonies. There, as a cartographer and surveyor, he quickly found employment, and became a resident of New York and a naturalized subject of King George III. Later, he took part in 1767 in a party which explored the Appalachians, parts of the Ohio River Valley, and the upper Mississippi. In connection with his work, he traveled widely up and down the Atlantic coast from Nova Scotia to Virginia. In 1769 Crèvecoeur married a well-to-do young woman called Mehetable Tippet, bought a farm in New York (not Pennsylvania, as his narrative would later suggest) and settled down to the live of a gentleman farmer and man of letters. The ensuing years were clearly the happiest in his life. By dint of hard work, Crèvecoeur, his farm and his family prospered, and three children were born. At the same time, he was able to devote himself to intellectual pursuits and writing. Crèvecoeur's epistolary meditations on what it means to be an American, and the conflicts and dilemmas of American identity, would later be one of the texts that has most directly constructed perceptions of America throughout the world. It should be kept in mind, however, that Crèvecoeur's own lived experience and those of his many narrators (such as the Anglophile Farmer James and Andrew the Hebridean) are not necessarily the same, although the author clearly has drawn heavily on events of his own life.

Crèvecoeur's *Letter III* is titled "What is an American?" and he begins by speculating about the thoughts and feelings of an "enlightened Englishman" upon his arrival on the continent. This putative Englishman, he argues, would feel pride at the accomplishments of his countrymen, who had taken refuge in America "when convulsed by factions, afflicted by a variety of miseries and wants, restless and impatient" (66). There, says Crèvecoeur, they have carried their national genius which can flourish unimpeded. He contrasts life in America with the extremes of wealth and poverty existing in Europe, and declares that even the most basic log cabin is a "dry and comfortable habitation" (67). He characterizes American society as secular and American religion as undemanding and tolerant. He is fascinated by the diversity of national origins to be found among American's inhabitants: "What, then, is the American, this new man? He is either an European or the descendent of an European; hence that strange mixture of blood which you will find in no other country...He is an American, who, leaving behind him his ancient prejudices and manners, receives new ones from the new mode of life he has embraced, the new government he obeys, and the new rank he holds. Here individuals of all nations are melted into a new race of men, whose labours and posterity are the western pilgrims who are carrying along with industry which began long since in the East; they will finish the great circle" (70). It is important to note here that Crèvecoeur is writing about his years in New York (1769-1776) when it was still a British colony and not part of the United States.

This discourse about America (and later, the US) as a vast melting pot into which all (Northern European) ethnicities are blended into an amorphous and uniform mass, shedding their old languages and identities in order to be reborn as people of the New World, has proved remarkably powerful and resilient. It is also problematic on many levels. Crèvecoeur's definition of [US]Americanness excludes large swathes of North America's population: women, African slaves, and Native Americans. For him, the ideal American is a European transplanted into an environment where he can grow and prosper unhindered by rigid European political, economic, and social structures. He adds that the colonies on the Eastern seaboard (those that are closest geographically to Europe) are the most "civilized" and advanced; those nearest the sea are bold and enterprising, those dwelling in the middle colonies are living in an Arcadian, egalitarian idyll; and those furthest from Europe, on the frontier, are "no better than carnivorous animals of a superior rank" (72). Thus, in a marvellous example of Eurocentric Catch-22 reasoning, the more European one is, the more US-American. Crèvecoeur speaks of an archetypal immigrant, who on getting off the boat is hired and immediately put to work and accepted as "a member of the family" (82). This person spends two or three years acquiring practical knowledge about agriculture, and once he has done so buys land; allegedly his good name will procure him the necessary credit to purchase two hundred acres of land. By dint of hard work, "From nothing to start into being; from a servant to the rank of a master; from being the slave of some despotic prince, to become a free man, invested with lands to which every municipal blessing is annexed! What a change indeed! It is in consequence of that change that he becomes an American" (83).

Obviously, reality was not quite so rose-tinted for all immigrants, particularly those taken to America against their will as slaves. On a visit to Charleston Crèvecoeur was confronted in all too graphic form with the horrors of plantation slavery. His *Letter IX* begins with a description of the opulence of Charles Town or Charleston, South Carolina, and the carefree existence of the planter caste. He then describes the contrast of this state of affairs with the economic exploitation of the toil of slaves and the destruction of slave families, with whom he finds a common humanity. As the essay draws to a close, we learn that Crèvecoeur's melancholy reflections were prompted by an incident when he was walking through the woods to a dinner engagement with a planter. In the woods, he comes upon swarms of birds hovering above a slave who is confined in a cage hanging from a tree: "horrid to think, and painful to repeat, I perceived a Negro, suspended in the cage and left there to expire! I shudder when I recollect that the birds had already picked out his eyes; his cheek-bones were bare; his arms covered with a multitude of wounds. From the edges of the hollow sockets and from the lacerations with which he was disfigured, the blood slowly dropped and tinged the ground beneath" (178). Crèvecoeur gives the dying man water, and laments that he has no bullets in his gun to put an end to the slave's agony. Later, he learns from his hosts that the man's crime was to have killed the overseer on the plantation. The agony of the dying slave embodies all too graphically the limitations of Crèvecoeur's thought: his vision of America as the land of opportunity, where those who work hard will prosper is directly refuted by the caged slave, who symbolizes a large group of non-European human beings who, despite working from sunup to sundown, were unable to better their lot.

Crèvecoeur lived at a time when tensions between England and its American colonies were growing steadily more acute, and his Arcadian idyll would soon be torn apart by the whirlwinds of history. His Anglophile sympathies were well-known and created bad feeling with his neighbours; and on the other hand, there was the threat of Indian raids. Crèvecoeur tried for as long as he could to avoid taking sides, but eventually was forced by circumstances to make plans to return to France, and in 1778 left his family and farm in the care of friends. On arriving in New York, however, he fell under suspicion from the English as the result of an anonymous letter and was put in prison; his papers were confiscated. As a consequence, and although he was released shortly thereafter, his health was as a result permanently impaired.

Crèvecoeur's *Letter XII*, "Distresses of a Frontier Man," is a poignant testimony from a man who is torn apart by his conflicting allegiances. The title itself foregrounds the author's identity as a "frontier man," a man not only had lived on the American frontier but whose entire life had flowed across so many borders. He begins by stating that the time has come for him to flee and abandon his beloved farm, and describes his mental anguish: "I can never leave behind me the remembrance of the dreadful scenes to which I have been witness; therefore, never can I be happy! Happy — why would I mention that sweet, that enchanting word? Once happiness was our portion; now it is gone from us, and I am afraid not to be enjoyed again by the present generation! Whichever way I look, nothing but the most frightful precipices present themselves to my view, in which hundreds of my friends and acquaintances have already perished; of all animals that live on the surface of this planet, what is man when no longer connected with society, or when he finds himself surrounded by a convulsed and half-dissolved one?" (200-201). Crèvecoeur is grieving not only for his lost agrarian idyll, but also for his lost community. The image of "frightful precipices" is reinforced by images of his family's living in constant fear, plagued by nightmares, starting at any unexpected noise. He describes his moral paralysis, one moment experiencing "spontaneous courage," later falling into "the deepest despondency" (202). One of the most revelatory passages, however, describes in graphic terms the dilemma of Crèvecoeur's paradoxical emotions as post-colonial subject trapped in the tumult of historical change: "If I attach myself to the mother country, which is 3,000 miles from me, I become what is called an enemy to my own region; if I follow the rest of my countrymen, I become opposed to our ancient masters: both extremes appear equally dangerous to a person of so little weight and consequence as I am, whose energy and example are of no avail. As to the argument on which the dispute is founded, I know little about it. Much has been said and written on both sides, but who has a judgement capacious and clear enough to decide?" (204). In the first sentence of this excerpt, Crèvecoeur sets forth the conflicting loyalties that he feels at the invidious choice he is being forced to make between his European roots and his presence in what would later become the U.S. However, his protestation that his lack of "weight and consequence" are not important, and that he knows little about the arguments underlying the current conflict, are at best disingenuous: clearly he is hoping to safeguard his and his family's interests by sitting on the fence and avoiding commitment to either side.

Similar to many texts of the period emerging from a colonial context, Crèvecoeur's "Distresses of a Frontier Man" (and indeed his *Letters from an American Farmer* in general) are woven thick with familial metaphors. From the notion of Britain as benevolent faraway parent as seen in his rose-colored *Letter III* ("What is an American?"), he moves to the image of Britain as neglectful, abusive parent: "Must I, then, bid farewell to Britain, to that renowned country? Must I renounce a name so ancient and so venerable? Alas, she herself, that once indulgent parent, forces me to take up arms against her. She herself first inspired the most unhappy citizens of our remote districts with the thoughts of shedding the blood of those whom they used to call by the name of friends and brethren. That great nation which now convulses the world, which hardly knows the extent of her Indian kingdoms, which looks toward the universal monarchy of trade of industry, of riches, of power: why must she strew our poor frontiers with the carcasses of her friends, with the wrecks of our insignificant villages, in which there is no gold?" (209). The tone here is that of an abandoned child bemoaning its betrayal at the hands of an abusive parent. The accusations veer, however, between that of rebellious anger and of accusations of neglect. The curious last sentence seems to imply that if gold had actually existed in these territories, Britain would have been justified in shedding American blood. This reflects the thought of many intellectuals in the fledgling Republic, who sought to distance themselves from the abuses of Spanish and Portuguese imperial policy while characterizing the British as somehow kindler, gentler colonizers. The implication is that Britain has adopted the worst facets of imperial policy without the consequent payoff that might justify them.

The solution finally found by Crèvecoeur's putative US-American Farmer James is to Go Indian and to remove himself as far as possible from Europe and European conflicts, in order to live as man in a state of nature in an Indian settlement:

It is that which leads to the tenants of the great — village of — where, far removed from the accursed neighbourhood of Europeans, its inhabitants live with more ease, decency, and peace than you imagine; who, though governed by no laws, yet find in uncontaminated simple manners all that laws can afford. Their system is sufficiently complete to answer all the primary wants of man and to constitute him a social being such as he ought to be in the great forest of Nature. There it is that I have resolved at any rate to transport myself and family: an eccentric thought, you may say, thus to cut asunder all former connexions and to form new ones with a people whom Nature has stamped with such different characteristics! (211)

The notion of Native Americans as living in an idyllic state of nature would resonate with philosophers such as, for instance, Jean-Jacques Rousseau. An escape to this Arcadian, ahistorical paradise, however implausible in reality, would go down well with European audiences. In Crèvecoeur's own life, however, and as opposed to his fictional alter ego, such an initiative was simply not viable for a Frenchman with Tory sympathies, down on his financial luck, and with family in the U.S. and estates in France. He finally managed to return to England on a ship that had managed to evade the French naval blockade, and in May 1781 sold the manuscript of

Letters from an American Farmer to the English firm of Davies and Davis for thirty guineas.

When the book was published in London the following year, Crèvecoeur had escaped to France. There he became part of Parisian intellectual circles, and in 1787 he published an expended version of the *Letters* in French. He also wrote for the Ministry of the Marine an exhaustive report on England's American colonies, now the United State of America. This placed him in prime position to become France's first consul in New York, a post which he took up in September 1783. He returned to a scene of devastation: his wife had died, his beloved Pine Hill Farm had been burned to the ground and his children were scattered, although he later managed to track them down. Although he longed for his lost paradise, and although a tone of melancholy pervades his writings, Crèvecoeur was by any standard an efficient and effective diplomat, establishing shipping connections between the two countries and encouraging the importation of French commodities such as wine, brandy, pianos, gloves, and human hair (Albert E. Stone, "Introduction" to Crèvecoeur's *Letters from an American Farmer*). As well, under the literary pseudonym "Agricola," he wrote essays on practical agriculture and founded botanical gardens in New Haven and in New Jersey. In 1790, owing to his declining health — and the gathering clouds of the French Revolution — he returned to his estates, where he lived quietly until his death in 1813.

Although Crèvecoeur 's *Letters from an American Farmer* was not a huge success in the U.S., its reception in Europe was a different story. In the following five decades, the book went though editions in London, Dublin, Belfast, Leipzig, Leyden, Paris, and Maastricht, and was translated into French, Dutch and German. Its influence on European perceptions of the new nation was extraordinary. Its descriptions of an Arcadian utopia resonated powerfully with writers such as Coleridge and the followers of Rousseau, and its optimistic portrayal of the self-made man who is able to shed European linguistic and cultural constraints to go from rags to riches has become a powerful and seductive myth of United States identity.

In our own times, the limitations of the theory of the melting pot, however, with its notion that Americanization implies the loss of ethnic and cultural identity and the adoption of an amorphous, undifferentiated, Anglophone US-Americanness, have become ever more evident. Crèvecoeur was writing at a time when the violence of the American Revolution was tearing apart his Arcadian view of the British colonies as idyllic Anglophile havens. Some of the issues discussed in his Letters, however, are particularly relevant to present-day debates about which texts are worthy of inclusion in anthologies of United States literature and in university syllabi. In the last twenty years, with the rise of multiculturalism and the diversification of the ethnic, racial and gender composition of university populations in the United States, there has been a very considerable backlash against the notion of US-America as a melting pot, as signalled by the publication of a major new anthology, the Heath. Later, however, there was a reaction against multiculturalism. On the website of the revised version of the *Heath Anthology*, its editors state:

Today's *Heath* maintains its emphasis on the multiple origins and histories of the cultures of the United States and on the need to see literary works in relation to the particular historical circumstances in which they appeared, were circulated, and read. But we are increasingly interested in the ongoing conversations among these cultures; how they engage with and influence one another; whether (as Bartolomeo Vanzetti put it) some voices "must speak loudly to be heard" while others "have only to whisper and even be silent to be understood"; and just how these conversations have come to define America as plural, complex, heterogeneous — a chorus, perhaps, rather than a melting pot. We have emphasized works that illustrate how the borders between these cultures were, and have remained, places of political and cultural tension but also permeable, open to interaction and change. We have striven not only to clarify regional and cultural differences but to offer more of a hemispheric view, while maintaining the focus necessary to most courses on the literatures of what is now the United States. (qtd. in Castillo, "Shifting Canons" 13)

The original *Heath Anthology* emerged in response to demands of students, professors, and critics to open cultural conversations beyond the limitations of the traditional literary canon. The paragraph quoted above, however, reveals that its editors have taken on board the notion that multiculturalism can be atomistic and divisive, and here they emphasize the notion that the different cultures which exist in the United States interact in dynamic fashion with one another. The mention of the turn toward a more hemispheric perspective reflects what probably is the most dramatic development in US-American Studies in recent years: the acknowledgement that, in an era of cultural and economic globalization, it is no longer viable to view the nation/state as primary interpretative lens through which literary texts can be analyzed.

What, then, can we learn as scholars from the career of de

Crèvecoeur? The notion of a literary canon restricted to white male Northern European authors, just as Crèvecoeur's definition of US-Americanness is restricted to white male Europeans, is clearly no longer viable. His notion of the typical immigrant trajectory as the monolingual, acculturated journey of an immigrant who comes to the U.S., goes from rags to riches, and lives there forever after, is equally unsatisfactory, given the diasporic movements of large sectors of the population; Crèvecoeur himself left his own country, emigrated, acquired cultural and material capital, and returned to his country of origin, very much in the mode of the *sojourner* described in Asian-American literary scholarship. What is important, it seems to me, is to ensure that the "chorus" described by the Heath editors be open to different, often clashing and disharmonious voices; that it not embrace Anglophone perspectives uncritically but at the same time be capable of lucid analysis of the commonalities in US culture as well as of its diversities. In short, that United States Studies manage to avoid the pitfalls of Crèvecoeur's ambivalent Americanness while welcoming his multilingual, border-crossing, cosmopolitan contradictions.

Works Cited

Bishop, James E. "A Feeling Farmer: Masculinity, Nationalism, and Nature in Crèvecoeur's *Letters*." *Early American Literature* 43.2 (2008): 361-77.

Castillo, Susan. *Colonial Encounters in New World Writing, 1500–1786: Performing America*. London: Routledge, 2006.

Castillo, Susan. "Shifting Canons." *Letterature d'America* 27.1221-22 (2007-2008): 5-18.

Crèvecoeur, J. Hector St. John de. *Letters from an American Farmer*. Ed. Albert E. Stone. New York: Penguin, 1986.

Crèvecoeur, J. Hector St. John de. *Lettres d'un cultivateur américain addressées á Wm Seton, Esq*. Paris: Cuchet, 1787.

Iannini, Christopher. "'The Itinerant Man': Crevecoeur's Caribbean, Raynal's Revolution, and the Fate of Atlantic Cosmopolitanism. *The William and Mary Quarterly* 61.2 (2004): <http://www.historycooperative.org/cgibin/justtop.cgi?act=justtop&url=http://www.historycooperative.org/journals/wm/61.2/iannini.html>.

Schell, Jennifer. "Figurative Surveying: National Space and the Nantucket Chapters of J. Hector St. John de Crèvecoeur's *Letters from an American Farmer*." *Early American Literature* 43.3 (2008): 581-604.

White, Ed. "Crèvecoeur in Wyoming." *Early American Literature* 43.2 (2008): 379-407.

Author's profile: Susan Castillo teaches American literatures at King's College London. Castillo's book publications include *Colonial Encounters in New World Writing: Performing America* (2005), *The Literatures of Colonial America* (edited with Ivy Schweitzer) (2001), *Notes from the Periphery* (1994), and *American Literature to 1865 in Context* (2010). Castillo is editor of *Journal of American Studies*. She is also a published poet and literary translator.

Ethnicity and Nationhood in Achebe's *Arrow of God*
Pao-I Hwang

Abstract: In her article "Ethnicity and Nationhood in Achebe's *Arrow of God*"
Pao-I Hwang postulates that although Nigeria is a globally recognized nation,
it is frequently seen as the creation of a colonial regime and not understood
as a geographical site consisting of many ancient states that had strong
pre-colonial identities. Chinua Achebe's *Arrow of God* is a study of an African
man struggling to come to terms with his identity when a nationalizing
colonial force undermines the structures of his community and destroys his
sense of security. The novel shows that two issues central to the
protagonist's identity crisis remain a problem to Nigerians today: If Nigeria is
a nation, are the Ibo or Yoruba just tribes? African writers have warned that
until the people of Africa understand their pre-colonial foundations and
re-structure their society accordingly, they cannot hope to build nations with
harmonious ethnic co-existence. Hwang focuses on the social disruption and
personal trauma that nation-building causes and questions whether ethnic
reclamation should be taken more seriously.

African writers are divided over the use of colonial languages as
national languages. While Chinua Achebe has shown that English, if
carefully and purposefully used, can be an effective tool for
promoting and even developing Nigerian culture and thought, Ngugi
wa Thiong'o has reverted to Kikuyu and shown that a writer using
his/her own native language can be equally productive and valuable
to his/her society. Although language is crucial to the development
of a country, particularly a country that has to struggle with the
shadows of a colonial past, the question of identity is far more
problematic and deep-rooted. It is the messy nature of identity
formation that both allows political leaders to make loud, patriotic
claims and yet also deters them from analyzing earnestly their
nation's past. If political leaders, who want to guide their people
toward a better future, are afraid to look too deeply into themselves,
the work of writers like Achebe and Ngugi have been doing the
opposite. *Arrow of God* is a good example of a narrative that probes
the postcolonial identity by seeking to identify the moment of
transition of a society with a pre-colonial identity to one with a
national identity.

In a series of lectures published as *Home and Exile*, Achebe
ruminates over the choice of describing his people as a "tribe" or a
"nation." According to his sources, a tribe is a "group of (esp.
primitive) families or communities linked by social, religious or
blood ties and usually having a common culture and dialect and a
recognized leader" and a nation is "a community of people of mainly
common descent, history or language, etc., forming a state or
inhabiting a territory" (5). Despite his preference for the latter

definition, it is clear that Achebe does not feel completely at ease with the term: to call the Igbo people "a nation as I now prefer to do is not without problems of its own" and it "may not be a perfect fit for the Igbo, but it is close" (5). Having taken the effort to define the two terms, we may wonder why his conclusion is so hasty and even dismissive. On the one hand, it could be that he did not want to dwell on a complicated issue that would be too long for a lecture; on the other hand, it could be because he had already gone over this ground at length in the novel that he had written thirty-six years earlier.

Although *Arrow of God* is set around the start of Britain's colonization of Nigeria in 1894, the identity crisis that it treats is in fact the early birth throes of the Nigerian nation in 1960. Nigeria, like many other African countries, has often been considered the creation of a colonial regime and rarely portrayed as a state, never mind a state with a preconceived identity. That is, until Achebe rectified this misconception in his novels by showing that modern concepts of Nigeria actually emerged from the destruction of a pre-colonial identity. Although Nigeria is now a globally recognized nation, there are still very few literary works that depict as clearly as Achebe's *Arrow of God* the country's pre-colonial origins and the thorny progress of nationhood.

If the nation is a Western construct, as Anthony D. Smith claims, it may explain precisely why Britain had so many problems trying to graft its civic concepts onto the ethnic Igbo stock in order to finally create "Nigeria." Ideally, nations are meant to emphasize both their political and cultural bonds. Nations define a definite social space within which members live and work, they also demarcate a historic territory that locates a community in time and space. Nations provide individuals with "sacred centers," with objects of spiritual and historical pilgrimage which reveal the uniqueness of their nation's "moral geography" (Smith 16). However, according to Smith, the modern nation has its origin in two distinct types: "ethnic" nations that are non-Western and based on sharing the same history, culture and territory and "territorial" nations that are Western and focus more on politics, the economy, and legal systems. The distinguishing feature of the ethnic nation is its "emphasis on a community of birth and native culture," whereas the components of the more Western model are, "Historic territory, legal-political community, legal-political equality of members, and common civic culture and ideology" (Smith 11). Thus, "the Western concept laid down that an individual had to belong to some nation but could choose to which he/she belonged, the non-Western or ethnic concept allowed no such latitude" (Smith 11). Although neither type excluded completely elements of the other, but actually combined both to various degrees and forms, the diametrical focus of each type may help to explain the pre-national identity crisis described in Achebe's *Arrow of God* where a very territorially minded "political master" attempted to govern very ethnically minded "nominal subjects."

The traumatic consequences of colonial administration on native life are neatly summed up in a government memorandum in the novel:

To many colonial nations native administration means government by white men. In place of the alternative of governing directly through Administrative Officers there is the other method of trying while we endeavor to purge the native system of its abuses to build a higher civilization upon the soundly rooted native stock that had its foundation in the hearts and minds and thoughts of the people and therefore on which we can more easily build, moulding it and establishing it into lines consonant with modern ideas and higher standards, and yet all the time enlisting the real force of the spirit of the people, instead of killing that out and trying to start afresh. We must not destroy the African atmosphere, the African mind, the whole foundation of his race. (*Arrow of God* 56-57)

Although it is not explicitly stated, the memorandum calls attention to an issue that is central to the novel — the question of installing a more Westernized identity over the more African ethnic identity. It is not difficult to deduce that the "higher civilization" is the Western concept of nationhood and the "soundly rooted native stock" refers to the ethnic roots of the Igbo people. Although such a letter may not have been written in reality, it portrays accurately the contradictions in the Indirect Rule that Britain was trying to apply at the time. On the one hand, the colonial administration wanted to include non-white men, but on the other hand it distrusted them because they belonged to a system that was seen as uncivilized and needed purging. The policy to borrow "native stock" that is "soundly rooted" for the opposite reason of "moulding" and more "easily" building something else is a recipe for chaos. It speaks of nurturing the spirit through cooperative advancement that is in fact a subversive destruction of everything African, including the atmosphere, the mind, and the foundation. The grand political agenda, which is to unite the disparate communities under British rule, is paradoxically a disruption of the original and culturally rooted harmony to create an unnatural entity that is superficially progressive and orderly but belies a spirit that is fraught with contradictions and discontent. Ultimately, the disintegration of the villages and the mental breakdown of the protagonist in *Arrow of God* can be seen as the slow torture of a society forced to undergo an alien project of nationalization.

Indirect Rule played a very large part in Britain's administration of its colonies, but very little is said of its destructiveness, especially from the perspective of the colonized. As Colin Newbury expounds, the policy was actually transferred from India, where it fostered corruption and internecine feuds, to Africa, where it failed to take root. The British government adopted Indirect rule because it was easier to centralize and consolidate political power by fostering a "lop-sided friendship" with the original rulers – Britain endorsed corruption and granted favors on the sole condition that the nominal subjects recognized Britain as the political master (see Newbury). This system was more disruptive when applied to Nigeria than India, for example, for two major reasons. Firstly, the hierarchy of rulers in Nigeria was much more democratic and fragmented, political power was not only divided amongst a number of chiefs but also did not extend beyond a spoken community. Secondly, and this was likely owing to the first reason, native rulers were often overlooked for appointments to new British posts. So, instead of working with the original rulers and their system of rule, the British government chose to appoint new people who, as upstarts but Christians, would theoretically be more compliant.

Britain's centralizing of political power in Nigeria overruled the native chiefs because it questioned their democratic leadership, their resistance and therefore their usefulness. The first person in *Arrow of God* to be appointed Warrant/Paramount Chief, a previously non-existent rank, is James Ikedi and not the native Chief Priest because Ikedi was "an intelligent fellow who had been among the very first people to receive missionary education" (57). When Winterbottom, the District Officer who appointed Ikedi, comes round to asking Ezeulu it is more because the Chief Priest sided with him in a court case than because he was the head of six villages. At no point in the story does Winterbottom, who prides himself on decision making based on in-depth research and thought, show his understanding of why Ezeulu cuts an impressive figure. Even at the very end, he still refers to Ezeulu as a "fetish priest" instead of the chief of all the priests, a recognition that would have shown some respect for Ezeulu's high status and an understanding of the importance of religion in Igbo chieftainships.

The history of the Igbo people is at least 5000 years old. Igboland, as Achebe prefers to call his home, was composed of a large number of independent states made up of villages sharing a common language and similar customs but not unified by an overarching government. A typical Igbo state was a small, democratic community of independently governed villages. In *Arrow of God*, Umuaro is such a community:

The six villages — Umuachala, Umunneora, Umuagu, Umuezeani, Umuogwugwu and Umuisiuzo — lived as different peoples, and each worshipped its own deity. Then the hired soldiers of Abam used to strike in the dead of night, set fire to the houses and carry men, women and children into slavery. Things were so bad for the six villages that their leaders came together to save themselves. They hired a strong team of medicine-men to install a common deity for them. This deity which the fathers of the six villages made was called Ulu ... The six villages took the name of Umuaro, and the priest of Ulu became their Chief-Priest. (14-15)

The reality of Achebe's portrayal can be confirmed by a brief comparison to Raisa Simola's more historical rendition:

A village group is a political structure which consists of a number of villages. At the village-group level, a representative system has been adopted. At the village level of government, the accepted practice has been a direct democracy ... Each village is autonomous and sovereign in most matters affecting it. The village is then further segmented into a number of lineages and each lineage into major and minor sublineages. At the lineage level the most important ritualistic figure is the *okpara*. He holds the lineage *ofo* (a staff and symbol of power) which is very important in Igbo political processes. The compound then consists of a number of economically independent households, each with a man or a woman as the householder. (64)

Despite being fictional, Achebe's portrayal is not far from historical truth. From his own accounts, from historical records, and from the praise of his critics such as Simola, Charles Nnolim, and Robert Wren, Achebe's treatment of the colonial experiences of the Igbo people has been noted for being realistic. Achebe's description reveals that village life is largely centered on religious beliefs and traditional practices. Thus the political union between villages, a practical move necessitated by external threats, is only completed with the installment of a deity. Furthermore, Simola's description points to the ancestral dynamics at play in the political organization of the Igbo community. A town can be divided into villages that can be divided into families. The direct lines of descent both allow people to relate to each other and facilitate the transference of power, some of which are inheritable and others only acquirable through personal merit. In these ways, Umuaro can be said to display more qualities of an ethnic nation than a territorial one, because its cohesion shows stronger cultural and historical bonds than political and economical ones.

Like their religious beliefs, the Igbo social and political structures are also very accommodating and democratic. While Okonkwo in *Things Fall Apart* becomes a powerful figure through his own achievements, Ezeulu in *Arrow of God* inherits his priesthood from his father. In any case, as Victor Uchendu states, a young man may earn a title and acquire great wealth, but to maintain his power over his peers and elders, his position "must not only be achieved, but constantly validated" (20-21). Therefore, both Okonkwo and Ezeulu achieve a high status and wield great power, but throughout their lives they are constantly challenged and inevitably displaced. Politically, villages are organized and represented by men of title, chiefs who often also represent a deity, for example, Ezeulu for Ulu and Ezidemili for Idemili. Although each village holds celebrations and rituals for its own deity, the villages also share some festivities and mutually respect all the deities, because they believe in them equally for the power that each carry. Despite the title of Chief Priest, Ezeulu is not a "king" with absolute power over the six villages. In fact, at the first meeting in the novel, it is suggested that the priesthood of Ulu was offered "to the weakest among them to ensure that none in the alliance became too powerful" (15). Ezeulu's role involves observing the agricultural calendar, naming significant festivals such as the New Yam Feast and cleansing the villages of their sins. When meetings are called, Ezeulu gets to speak, but so do all the men of title and even those in the audience. Thus no one has sole power regarding the welfare of the villages, and decisions rely on majority rule.

If we follow Smith's definitions, it is possible to argue that ethnic nations tend to focus on promoting a more fluid cohesion through the sharing of a common ancestral identity, while territorial nations tend to superimpose identities on people within a given territory by drawing on legal and economical structures to demarcate "them" and "us." Consequently, when the British arrived with their more territorial blueprint for nation-building, the ethnically structured Igbo community was thrown into disarray. In *Arrow of God*, this message is conveyed by three significant incidents: the unexpected territorial dispute that spirals out of control, the unprecedented clash between a representative of wealth and a representative of tradition and the prophetic destruction of the native social-political structure.

From all accounts, the dispute over a piece of land between Umuaro and Okperi only begins as a result of British interference. It is clear that Umuaro and Okperi have never had any problems sharing their land, so why does it become a problem under British rule, especially when the British government was supposedly trying to unite all the communities as one nation? Although no concrete reasons are given in the novel, the frequent allusion to the white man's presence calls attention to two very different concepts of land. For the Igbo people, their ethnic identity may be more important to them, which means they are able to achieve cohesion through historical and cultural sharing. On the other hand, the British, who not only have a more territorial system of identification but as a colonial power certainly cannot rely on tradition and culture to rally unity, have to use geographical demarcation to force disparate ethnic groups together. When Ezeulu appeals to his people for a peaceful negotiation with Okperi he reminds them of their history: "my father said this to me that when our village first came here to live the land belonged to Okperi. It was Okperi who gave us a piece of their land to live in. They also gave us their deities – their Udo and their Ogwugwu" (15). Nwaka, an advocate for war, counters Ezeulu by similarly referring to the past:

If Ezeulu had spoken about the great deity of Umuaro which he carries and which his fathers carried before him I would have paid attention to his voice. But he speaks about events which are older than Umuaro itself … My father … told me that Okperi people were wanderers. He told me three or four different places where they sojourned for a while and moved on again … Would they go today and claim all those sites? Would they have laid claim on our farmland in the days before the white man turned us upside down? (16)

Both Ezeulu and Nwaka use their fathers to verify and strengthen their claims, although what they claim is contradictory. Ezeulu appeals to his people's beliefs and traditions as another reason for maintaining peace with their neighbor. Nwaka strikes back by arguing that even if accounts differ, that is not the point: the point is that their history with the land goes back to time immemorial and the only reason they are having this dispute is because of the white man. And this argument is also reflected in the thoughts of the younger generation. When Nwaka wins the vote to send a messenger to settle the dispute with Okperi, his political acumen directs him to the belligerent Akukalia, whose mother happened to be from Okperi, for two reasons. Firstly, because Akukalia's hot-tempered behavior under the circumstances when was even more likely to take things personally and feel obliged to prove his impartiality by advocating war and secondly because Akukalia's actions strengthened Nwaka's claim that the white man's presence was destroying the bonds of kinship. Yet, no matter how convincing Nwaka is or how primed Akukalia is for war, it does not stop anyone from sensing that something is wrong and that they are symbolically, if not literally, attacking themselves. Akukalia and his companions reflect on this as they travel to Okperi:

"I remember coming with my father to this very place to cut grass for our thatches," said Akukalia. "It is a thing of surprise to me that my mother's people are claiming it today." "It is all due to the white man who says, like an elder to two fighting children: You will not fight while I am around. And so the younger and weaker of the two begins to swell himself up and to boast." "You have spoken the truth," said Akukalia. "Things like this would never have happened when I was a young man, to say nothing of the days of my father." ... "What you should ask them," said the other companion who had spoken very little since they set out, "what they should tell us is why, if the land was indeed theirs, why they let us farm it and cut thatch from it for generation after generation, until the white man came and reminded them." (19-20)

Here, Akukalia and his friends refer to their fathers and their father's times as sources of validity and stability. They use familial imagery to understand their situation, stressing that the piece of land belonged to the family either through the father or the mother, thus any dispute occurring is and ought to be between siblings. In addition, they turn their frustrations on the white man because not only does he not understand the dispute that he has caused, but as the presiding authority has even chosen to side with one party without taking the trouble to truly understand the causes of the dispute from the other side. As the last speaker in the conversation clarifies, there had never been quarrels over the land, at least not until something in the colonizer's administration triggered a sense of inequality and altered the concept of the ownership of land. Even the young men can remember sharing the land peacefully with their neighbors; there were no territorial demarcations and each farmed or took from it what they needed. Thus the confused tone in their questioning and their need to find an explanation for their disgruntlement.

Since the British were forceful in their possession of the land, they tampered with the people's sense of belonging because inevitably they did not understand the history. By their self-invested power to confer or take away land, they interfered with the tradition and established practice of sharing between villages and encouraged a desire for selfish possession, thus necessitating a previously unheard-of legal reinforcement. Winterbottom represents this disruptive force in a biased foreign administration. Winterbottom's account of the land dispute varies greatly from that of Nwaka's or Akukalia's:

The people of Okperi and their neighbors, Umuaro, are great enemies. Or they were before I came into the story. A big savage war had broken out between them over a piece of land. This feud was made worse by the fact that Okperi welcomed missionaries and government while Umuaro, on the other hand, has remained backward ... this war started because a man from Umuaro went to visit a friend in Okperi one fine morning and after he'd had one or two gallons of palm wine — it's quite incredible how much of that dreadful stuff they can tuck away – anyhow, this man from Umuaro having drunk his friend's palm wine reached for his *ikenga* and split it in two. (37)

This inaccurate account of the war between Umuaro and Okperi is, if nothing else, demeaning. Firstly, Umuaro and Okperi were not "great enemies" who had been fighting for a long time over a piece of land. Akukalia's reminiscences tell otherwise. Secondly, it certainly did not start because two friends got drunk and the ungrateful visitor pointlessly split his host's *ikenga*, or personal idol, in two. In fact, Akukalia was sent to Okperi with a grave message — the choice of peace or war. Understandably, when he arrived he refused the hospitality of his hosts, but when his hosts refused to summon the leaders for a hearing and insult was returned with insult, Akukalia lost his temper. He wounds one of the people, who runs home for a gun, and seeing his life in danger, Akukalia reacts by symbolically splitting his opponent's *ikenga* and effectively "killing" him. When Akukalia performs this abominable act, everybody condones his death. Hence, the war that ensued was not a simple act of revenge resulting from frivolous circumstances.

Winterbottom's satisfaction at having solved the dispute single-handedly, and even forcefully, illuminates the imbalance of power and the careless reasoning that sometimes accompanies it. Ultimately, Winterbottom's decision to grant the land to Okperi is not an objective act based on evidence. His judgment is weighed in favor of Okperi because of its early conversion and easy governance as compared to Umuaro's "backwardness." When he claims that the land belonged to Okperi "without a shade of doubt" he does not have any evidence to prove it except for Ezeulu's words. And he complains that all the witnesses were liars since African people have a tendency to lie like children. Both Winterbottom's distortion and careless interpretations are necessary for legitimizing his presence and interference; it is not an unusual or unrealistic example either of the colonizer's inability to understand or appreciate the importance of the native people's customs and actions.

Although what occurred between Umuaro and Okperi was a war, it was not so "savage" as to solicit intervention. Elizabeth Isichei has noted that in reality, skirmishes that occurred between villages were rarely serious and death was usually minimal (75-78). Arguably, Winterbottom's armed interference was more a display of power than anything else. And this confirms Simola's explanation that there were three stages of British colonial invasion: "the first pattern could be called 'letting the guns talk,' the second pattern combined diplomacy and war, and the third combined diplomacy and magic" (75). As a matter of fact, Simola's suggested pattern of colonial occupation maps the collapse of Igbo society in *Arrow of God*. Military force compelled political negotiations that would finally lead to religious and educational indoctrination. The wider repercussions of colonial interference forms the central issue in *Arrow of God*, and indeed as a sequel to *Things Fall Apart*, it attempts to show exactly how the Igbo community fell apart.

In the narrator's account of the land dispute, also remembered as the Breaking of the Guns, it is clear that the first and second stages of the invasion have already taken place. In a way, the narrator's voice serves to verify this fact and act as a more objective third party: "The white man, Wintabota, brought soldiers to Umuaro and stopped it. The story of what these soldiers did in Abame was still told with fear, and so Umuaro made no effort to resist but laid down their arms ... The white man, not satisfied that he had stopped the war, had gathered all the guns in Umuaro and asked the soldiers to break them in the face of all, except three or four which he carried away. Afterwards he sat in judgment over Umuaro and Okperi and gave the disputed land to Okperi" (27-28). The fighting stops as soon as the soldiers appear because the people were reminded of Okonkwo's generation, when the murder of a white man brought destruction on a whole village. As Simola observed, any form of resistance or petty crimes could sometimes lead to "collective punishments," where individuals or culprits were not singled out but whole communities had to pay the price. From an administrative point of view, it was regarded as a good opportunity to instill fear in people (see Simola 81). Therefore, despite the people's compliance and there being no evidence that they were fighting with their guns, all the guns were destroyed or confiscated (ending up as an antique display in Winterbottom's living room).

The breaking of the guns was a symbolic act and a good excuse to disarm the people; it was unnecessary but allowed Winterbottom to remind the people of his power and the British authorities endorsing his actions. Military power ensured cooperation in legal matters. Thus, as Winterbottom intones, "they're no longer very troublesome — not to us anyhow; the punitive expedition taught them a pretty unforgettable lesson" (108), and the administrative work can begin. All that is required for the British to do is to set up a Native Court, with nothing more than a single District Officer to preside and rule as he pleases.

James Ikedi provides a good example for the analysis of British political interference and its consequences. Ikedi is an unmistakable echo of Joyce Cary's Mister Johnson. Both are "intelligent" Christians who have been given British administrative positions, and both abuse their power over local people who regard them as "foreigners." Both profit from British road building and attempt to set up their own private empires. What Winterbottom — and, incidentally, Cary — find difficult to comprehend is the black man's "ingratitude" and "arrogance." What they see is that the black man is a corrupt, money-grabbing upstart prone to self-aggrandizement. What they do not see is how the white man is exactly the same. If Ikedi and Johnson are not exactly of "soundly rooted native stock," at least they are malleable and make great progress in copying and building British-styled courts, prisons, and a tax-collecting system, albeit all considered "illegal" by the British. Undoubtedly, for the British government the main problem with such successful imitators was that they would eventually refuse to take orders from anyone and this forced the "legitimate" colonizers to share the resources.

Winterbottom cannot see the similarities in his and Ikedi's position when they are equally usurpers. Winterbottom interprets Ikedi's behavior as that of an African prone to "cruelty of a kind which Africa alone produced. It was this elemental cruelty in the psychological make-up of the native that the starry-eyed European found so difficult to understand" (58). Instead of acknowledging the fact that placing nominal chiefs over rightful ones was the authorization of disruption, he preferred to view the concomitant corruption as resulting purely from incompetence and greed. Winterbottom's presence and his installation of Warrant Chiefs are both acts of unwarranted interference that politically destabilize the established Igbo system. They represent the second stage of colonial invasion, that of diplomacy and political intervention.

In the society we have been looking at in this story, one does not do things in the name of the son but in the name of the father.

And this is exemplified in the story of Ezeulu. The legitimacy is with the elders, the ancestors, with tradition and age. With the new rulers there is a new dispensation of power in which youth and inexperience earn a new legitimacy. This almost amounts to turning the world upside down. It is significant and poignant that Ezeulu's madness is portended by his best friend at a moment of great domestic turmoil. When Akuebue brings up the problem of the community's dissatisfaction, he admits later that he was unaware that Ezeulu's family was wracked with internal strife, his wives arguing with each other and his children physically attacking each other. Ezeulu's manic laughter frightens his friend but at the same time served to reveal something about the future. This is a significant scene and the narrator is indirectly making a comment on the pervasive influence of colonialism, how the disruption of the community filters down to the family and finally the individual. Ezeulu's laughter indicates two things. First, he may have laughed to hide his disappointment and sense of helplessness because the villagers did not listen to him when they went to war with Okperi, then after putting so much effort into negotiating with the white man for their sake, even sending his son to church against his wife's wishes, they turn on him and still accuse him of betrayal. Second, he may have laughed because he has finally realized that as a leader he is truly alone, and in order to carry out the will of his god he has little choice but to sacrifice himself completely — physically, emotionally, mentally.

Apart from Akuebue, Ezeulu's son Obika is probably the only other person to understand Ezeulu completely. And both of these people remind us that Ezeulu is well-intentioned, if a little hard-headed and misguided sometimes. Obika knows his father well and even resembles him in appearance. Despite being hot-tempered and addicted to alcohol, he keeps his words and is loyal to his friends. When hostility is penetrating Ezeulu's compound from every direction and Matefi, Obika's mother, asks him to persuade Ezeulu to defy his god Ulu, Obika asks, "How can I listen to you when you join outsiders in urging your husband to put his head in a cooking pot?" (212). Obika's respect for his father is so great that when he is whipped and his father does not take his side, he storms off in a rage and gets drunk. If Obika loves and respects his father, Ezeulu loves his son equally and has high hopes for him despite his flaws. It is telling that Obika then dies from performing a strenuous funeral ritual for a friend while suffering from an illness. The breaking of this last thread of love finally breaks Ezeulu's heart and sends him spiraling into madness. Unable to serve his god and his people anymore, he surrenders his sanity and joins his son in oblivion. According to the narrator, this was not a punishment but a merciful act for it spared Ezeulu from seeing the "final outcome" of his beloved community and their ways.

Achebe gave Ezeulu a vision and made him a representative of the Igbo people. Ezeulu is an upright man and a good leader, who dies trying to do right by his people. He makes true democratic efforts to accommodate the foreign presence in his community, but when it threatens to swallow them he tries to fight back. He sends his son to church in the hopes of understanding the new religion but also with a premonition of the white man's pervasive invasion. However, as colonization is spreading too rapidly through the land, he is forced to take radical steps to hold his society together. Since the democratically organized Igbo society is not accustomed to or ready to accept a paramount leader, Ezeulu's early efforts at rallying for unity is considered inappropriate and dictatorial, thus making him an easy target for ruthless political rivals. When Ezeulu refuses to name the New Yam festival, the decision seems to confirm Nwaka's early admonitions that Ezeulu is an autocrat seeking absolute power for personal gain. However, Nwaka is wrong. Ezeulu's final act was not one of selfishness. If it was, the gesture of punishing his people would not have come after he had refused to become a British-warranted overlord. Until the very end, Ezeulu believed that he served Ulu and his tradition. It was very clear to Akuebue, and it is the obvious reason why Ezeulu succumbed to Obika's death as Ulu's final command. Ezeulu's breakdown was highly symbolic for not only did it reflect the disintegration of his community and signify the dying of a long tradition, but it called attention to the Igbo social-political structure.

The Igbo social-political structure cracked under the colonial onslaught, but it managed to convey two important messages. The first is that colonialism is such a sly and pervasive adversary, the chaos it brings is lethal and may remain with the people indefinitely. The second is that if the past is to survive in any shape or form under these circumstances, it calls for a concerted and dedicated effort at preservation from the people. Regarding the first, Abdul JanMohamed's analysis of the colonial strategy of polarization serves as a succinct summary:

The limited choice of either petrification or catalepsy is imposed on the African by the colonial situation; his subjugation and lack of political power prevent him from constructively combining the [European and African] cultures and leave him more vulnerable to further subjugation. If he chooses to be faithful to the indigenous values, he remains, from the colonialist's view point a "savage" and the need to "civilize" him perpetuates colonialism. If, however, he attempts to espouse Western values, then he is seen as a vacant imitator without a culture of his own. Thus colonialist ideology is designed to confine the native in a confused and subservient position. (5)

As for the second, Achebe has this to say, the "autonomous Igbo villages and towns, so deeply suspicious of political amalgamation ... should ever face an enemy able to wield the resources of a centralized military power, acting directly or through local surrogates. They would need every fortification to maintain their delicate solidarity" (*Home and Exile* 17). The protagonist echoes the author when he urges his people again and again to wake up to the real source of danger. Ezeulu reminds his people: "We went to war against Okperi who are our blood brothers over a piece of land that did not belong to us and you blame the white man for stepping in. Have you not heard that when two brothers fight a stranger reaps the harvest?" (131). Whether Ezeulu succeeded as a politician was not important — Nwaka was a good reader of human nature and a powerful orator but he used his skills to very little personal gain and great public tragedy — but whether his madness taught his people a lesson was more important. *Arrow of God* is not a novel recommending nation-building; it is a novel exploring the merits of solidarity. By examining a critical moment in history, when traditional values and identities were being replaced by foreign ones, Achebe encourages his people to embrace solidarity and take pride in their ethnic roots. If colonialism succeeds in destroying the African's simple social harmony and basic human dignity then all will be lost and everything will fall apart. This fear is conceived in *Things Fall Apart* and carried to term in *Arrow of God*. It is not an overstatement to say that the world has persistently measured Africa by European standards, and today Africa's development looks dismally retarded when measured by economic output, technological improvement and, especially, political stability (see, e.g., Brown; Herbst). Achebe's works offer insight into the alternative cultural and political structure of a non-European "nation," reminding us that ultimately Africa must not be measured by any yardstick but those specifically created for Africa. Otherwise, African countries will always be haunted by their colonial pasts, and if African communities do not conform to European notions of nationhood, it does not follow that Africans learnt the concept of democracy from the West. Rather, lessons on democratic rule and even multiculturalism may be learnt from what may have been pre-colonial African socio-political structures. The communal governance, and the ethnically strong identity it fostered, emphasized greater tolerance of others and focused less on territorial demarcation. When Achebe published *Arrow of God* and suggested that his ancestors were living more civilized lives than they were given credit for in European history books, he did not know exactly how much. Today, instead of questioning where multiculturalism is taking us or whether post-nationalism is possible, it is probably equally important to question the process of ethnic reclamation.

Works Cited

Achebe, Chinua. *Arrow of God*. New York: Doubleday, 1989.
Achebe, Chinua. *Things Fall Apart*. London: Doubleday, 1994.
Achebe, Chinua. *Home and Exile*. New York: Anchor Books, 2001.
Brown, Michael E. "The Causes of Internal Conflict." *Nationalism and Ethnic Conflict*. Ed. Michael E. Brown, Owen R. Coté, Jr., Sean M. Lynn-Jones, and Steven E. Miller. Cambridge: MIT P, 1996. 3-25.
Gates, Henry Louis Jr. *Loose Canons: Notes on the Culture Wars*. New York: Oxford UP, 1992.
Herbst, Jeffrey. "Responding to State Failure in Africa." *Nationalism and Ethnic Conflict*. Ed. Michael E. Brown, Owen R. Coté, Jr., Sean M. Lynn-Jones, and Steven E. Miller. Cambridge: MIT P, 1996-67. 374-98.
Isichei, Elizabeth. *A History of the Igbo People*. London: Macmillan, 1976.
JanMohamed, Abdul R. *Manichean Aesthetics: The Politics of Literature in Colonial Africa*. Amherst: U of Massachusetts P, 1983.
Lindfors, Bernth. *Conversations with Chinua Achebe*. Jackson: UP of Mississippi, 1997.
Mathuray, Mark. "Realizing the Sacred: Power and Meaning in Chinua Achebe's *Arrow of God*" *Research in African Literatures* 34.3 (2003): 46-65.
Newbury, Colin. "Patrons, Clients, and Empire: The Subordination of Indigenous Hierarchies in Asia and Africa." *Journal of World History* 2.2 (2000): 230-52.
Okechukwu, Chinwe Christiana. "Oratory and Social Responsibility: Chinua Achebe's *Arrow of God*." *Callaloo* 25.2 (2002): 567-83.
Simola, Raisa. *World Views in Chinua Achebe's Works*. Frankfurt: Peter Lang, 1995.
Smith, Anthony D. *National Identity*. Harmondsworth: Penguin, 1991.
Uchendu, Victor C. *The Igbo of South-East Nigeria*. New York: Holt, Rinehart and Winston, 1966.

Author's profile: Pao-I Hwang teaches literature at National Taiwan University. His recent publications include "The Postmodern Writer and His Alter Ego: Julian Barnes versus Dan Kavanagh," *Wenshan Review* (2009) and "Mental Nations: The Identity of Meaning in Iain Sinclair's *Lights Out for the Territory*," *Hwa Kang Journal of English Language & Literature* (2008).

The Migrationof Gender and the Labor Market
Anders W. Johansson and Maria Udén

Abstract: In their article "The Migration of Gender and the Labor Market"
Anders W. Johansson and Maria Udén postulate that public interventions to
promote innovation have been motivated by the existence of market failures.
Information asymmetries have been recognized as one major cause of these
failures. In the article, theories of Michael Spence concerning signalling costs
are used to analyze three cases. The three cases illustrate how women
entrepreneurs and sectors dominated by women can be expected to face
higher signalling costs compared to male-dominated industries. Johansson's
and Udén's conclusion is that public interventions are likely to strengthen
existing structures instead of compensate market failures and thus the
upward mobility of women — their migration into male-dominated spheres
of business activity — can be affected although still remaining compromised.

Introduction

The Lisbon strategy proposes to make Europe the most competitive
economy in the world, as well as the most sustainable and socially
inclusive society. To achieve these goals the stimulation of
innovation has been formulated as one of the keys. The reason
formulated for state intervention is the existence of market failures.
These can be of different kinds such as knowledge spillovers,
imperfect and asymmetric information, and coordination failures.
State aid is a measure to increase research and development in and
of the economy as the market alone cannot guarantee an "optimal
outcome." The argument is macroeconomic in nature focusing the
potential of the SMEs (Small and Medium Enterprizes) job creation.
However social objectives are added thereby justifying government
intervention for reasons of equity and sustainability (see Harvie and
Lee).

A recent report from the Swedish Agency for Economic and
Regional Growth (see Nutek, *Utfall och styrning*) shows that in
average less than 20% of the public financial business venture
funding has been allocated to women entrepreneurs. As a
comparison, 21% of the total of all small businesses are led by
women and twice as many men than women are starting new
business ventures (see Nutek, *Kvinnor och mäns*). If we assume
that women and men are equally innovative in their capacity to
produce optimal economic outcome, women and men should be
equally represented among SMEs. The current unequal distribution
we thus regard as a market failure. Further, if business venture
funding by the state is to compensate for market failures, the

majority of the support for new ventures should reasonably be allocated to women entrepreneurs in order to increase their share of the total number of companies. Instead, public money is used in a way that this market failure could be expected to be even larger when compared to a situation where no intervention by funding is made. Our assumption about the relationship between state aid and its distribution with the purpose of compensating for market failure is built upon postulates in Michael A. Spence's 1973 article "Job Market Signaling."

Asymmetric information and signaling costs

The article "Job Market Signaling" was one of the early works that later came to render Spence the 2001 Nobel Prize in Economics with George Akerlof and Joseph Stiglitz. Currently well-known concepts of signaling and asymmetric information were introduced with this article and it were these economists who made the call for government intervention to correct market failures (see, e.g., Stiglitz). It should be noted, however, that also sociologists such as J.E. Rosenbaum have illustrated similar unequal patterns although not using the concept of market failures.

Spence discussed in his article the labour market with special attention to women and we apply his argumentation with regard to state funding for the promotion of innovation. Spence himself claimed his theory to be of general applicability and he defined the application of a decision under uncertainty and the employment procedure a matter of interpreting signals comparable to lottery: the employer deduces the productivity of a potential employee and sets the wage in accordance with this supposition, that is, "the employer pays the certain monetary equivalent of the lottery to the individual as wage. If he is risk-neutral, the wage is taken to be the individual's marginal contribution to the hiring organization" (357). This particular level as such is not of importance, it can be set as chosen, but here Spence introduced a model for how to calculate the interaction between employers and potential employees:

Primary interest attaches to how the employer perceives the lottery, for it is these perceptions that determine the wages he offers to pay. We have stipulated that the employer cannot directly observe the marginal product prior to hiring. What he does observe is a plethora of personal data in the form of observable characteristics and attributes of the individual, and it is these that must ultimately determine his assessment of the lottery he is buying ... With respect to the basis for employers' judgement and thereto connected decision making Spence identified a distinction, which played a major role in his outline of a theory of market signaling. It is the distinction between *signals* and *indices*: Of those observable, personal attributes that collectively constitute the image the job applicant presents, some are immutably fixed, while others are alterable. For example, education is something that the individual can invest in at some cost in terms of time and money. On the other hand, race and sex are not generally thought to be alterable. I shall refer to observable, unalterable attributes as indices, reserving the term signals for those observable characteristics attached to the individual that are subject to manipulation by him. (357)

However, it is meaningless to analyze hiring as an event that happens once and isolated. The employer gains experience, which is why "signals and indices are to be regarded as parameters in shifting conditional probability distributions that define an employer's beliefs" and "New market data are received and conditional probabilities are revised or updated. Hiring in the market is to be regarded as sampling, and revising conditional probabilities as passing from prior to posterior. The whole process is a learning one" (358). The feedback loop in the market need not lead to changes over time. A system can be in a continual state of flux but, "the system will be stationary if the employer starts out with conditional probabilistic beliefs that after one round are not disconfirmed by the incoming data they generated" (358). Such beliefs Spence defines as self-confirming. For the job market education is the typical signal of productivity signal. To acquire education entails costs for the individual: "We refer to these costs as *signaling costs.* Notice that the individual, in acquiring an education, need not think of himself as signaling. He will invest in education if there is sufficient return as defined by the offered wage schedule. Individuals, then, are assumed to select signals … so as to maximize the difference between offered wages and signaling costs" (358). In the manner of traditional economics Spence maintained that "people with the same preferences and opportunity sets will make similar decisions and end up in similar situations" (370). Even so, he found the conclusion wrong that indices as gender therefore can have no informational impact: "If employers' distributions are conditional on sex as well as education, then the external impacts of a man's signaling decision are felt only by other men. The same holds for women. If at some point in time men and women are not investing in education in the same ways, then the returns to education for men and women will be different in the next round. In short, their opportunity sets differ" (370).

We consider the state providing subsidy — at times in

cooperation with other actors — as the "employer" of innovation and entrepreneurial activities and liaisons. In the case of sectors being the "applicants," the decision makers corresponding to "employers" would be governments assisted by ministries and regional authorities as for instance the European Commission. Asymmetric equilibrium can settle so that an industry or sector perceived initially as less productive never gets the chance to contradict this assumption. If government policy reinforces the resources for innovative activity for a sector, this sector will become integrated in the review process for public spending and thus has the chance to prove it self. A sector that is not favored in terms of public spending on innovation and entrepreneurial undertakings will have difficulties to contradict an image as "unproductive" in these respects, both because it will not have access to the reinforcing resources from public funding and because it does not get included in consistent information flows which the judgement of decision makers.

The same reasoning as for sectors applies to women and men. Man and women can settle at different equilibriums, where the two genders face different signaling costs. In fact much more so as certain sectors are dominated by men and other sectors are dominated by women. If we have a case where women are thought of initially as low productive in terms of innovation, asymmetric equilibrium will imply that returns for investment differs so that women have to invest more than men to reach the level where they acquire signaling criteria for high productivity. Such criteria can for instance be technical education and/or inclusion in high-tech environments. Investment may occur at a level unreasonably high or even unreachable to most women. In that case, it will be wiser for the majority of women to settle for low productivity signaling capacity. This fact will "feed" women into the (perceived) low productivity sector and an information loop is created where the scarce presence of women in high productivity sectors results contradictory information that never reaches the decision makers who continue to act so that the investment cost for women to enter high-tech sectors remain unrealistic.

We conclude that in general men are likely to have different signaling cost with respect to the production of innovation than women. We present three cases as illustrations where all three concern innovation, but they differ with respect to how they are recognized as such. To compare with the job market we could say that there are different question marks attached to the three cases whether "education" at hand is qualified, or, in other words, if innovation is regarded as productive or not.

Case 1 traditional technological innovation

The first case represents technological innovation, a type of innovation that can be expected to face comparatively low signaling cost as being "safe" objects for "hiring" by decision makers allocating public funds for promoting innovation. Navid Ghannad provides an in-depth analysis of three entrepreneurs and their firms:

Liko is a medium sized firm with 180 employees worldwide. It was founded in 1979 by Gunnar Liljedahl. The company is specialized in developing, manufacturing, and marketing lift and transfer equipment to people whose mobility in impaired. This is a niche market with about 20 major players. Ghannad reports that it was no easy task for Gunnar to establish and develop Liko in 1979 as a rather substantial amount of money was needed in order to invest in development costs as well as in industrial buildings. The firm was situated in the north of Sweden, a region where such investments were regarded as more risky compared to central Sweden. Therefore Gunnar was forced to lodge not only his own but also his parents house. (Ghannad 184)

Index is a small company which manufactures and sells high quality and technically advanced Braille printers. The company is a world leader within the segment of selling single and double-sided Braille embossers with high print speed. The company was founded in 1982 by Björn Löfstedt. In 2009 the company has ten employees and 97% of the firm's total sales are exported to around eighty countries. Already in 1980, two years before the company was founded, Löfstedt managed to persuade Nutek (the Swedish government's agency for economic development) as well as the university, where he was working at the time, to borrow some money for his project to develop the printer. As Ghannad reports, he was not alone with this idea, but the product idea was interesting for most people and organizations at that time.

Our second example is Polaris founded in 1979, a privately owned mid-size niche company that manufactures and sells rimless eyewear. At present the company has eighty employees worldwide. The company designs, manufactures, and sells a wide range of rimless eyewear with almost 93% of total sales generated in foreign markets. The company was founded by Staffan Preutz, who was trained by his father who operated a watchmaker's and optician's shop. At an early age Staffan started to design and manufacture eyewear, from the beginning as a response to wealthier women customers in his home town, Boden. In 1979 Polaris moved to a high-end location in Boden. The new production facility was financed by loans from Nutek, local development agencies, and commercial banks.

What the above entrepreneurs have in common is that they at some time in their early development phase have received loans from Nutek. They were considered worthy to be picked out in the lottery (to use Spence's concept) of the innovation market to represent qualified innovators. Apparently they all signaled productivity. We argue that this kind of firm and the appearances of this kind of male entrepreneurs fit perfectly with the image of the innovative entrepreneur and thus they were placed in a favourable loop and therefore had relatively low signaling costs. The decisions to provide public funding for these entrepreneurs were taken almost thirty years ago. Still, given the figures presented above about the current allocation of financial aid, a male entrepreneur associated with traditional technological innovation seems still to be the typical receiver of funding, while the following two cases represent situations where the productivity of innovation is questioned by the decision makers.

Case 2 technological innovation on the margin

The context in this case is the Sámi territory in northern Sweden, associated traditionally with nomadic reindeer herding. The funding is centerd on a project named "The Sami Network Connectivity" which aims at creating internet solutions for a territory beyond the outreach of regular internet connectivity.

In Sweden the average of business entrepreneurship in reindeer herding is one woman business leader out of eight reindeer herding companies (see Amft; Kråik) and this suggests an unequal relationship between genders. The first steps towards supporting SNC were taken in 2001 with 500 members in Sirges, the largest Sámi village in Sweden. The aims were to stimulate the economic growth of Sirges, build business capacity among the village's women especially in reindeer herding, and achieving larger influence for Sirges's women in management and other communal matters. Already at the stage of planning, researchers specialized in gender and technology studies at Luleå University of Technology (LTU) were contacted so as to integrate scientific assistance. Social and technical conditions for work and business development were in focus and an affiliated but separately funded university project was formed.

A center that hosted coalition projects between LTU and the information and communication technologies (ICT) industry, Center for Distance Spanning Technology (CDT), in Swedish Center för distansöverbryggande teknologi, was chosen for a first attempt to create contact with an ICT environment. The response was immediately positive. A guest researcher from the U.S. presented a tailor-made proposition for creating connectivity in the reindeer grazing lands. This was unexpected for everyone involved. Not least the amazement lay in the fact that a senior internet specialist with international reputation took interest in the request for co-operating with the Sámi women. The proposition was embraced as it offered the possibility to develop sought after business applications for use in reindeer herding and because of the general benefits access to the internet can offer. The women in the project also saw that their position in the herding community would be considerably strengthened by having a role in high-tech development and hoped this could serve as model for how women's capacity and role in the Sámi villages was to be judged in the future.

From May 2002, a group of four women — two reindeer herders, one gender studies researcher, and one internet specialist — came to work jointly for establishing and carrying SNC through. An important backup at local level was the Sámi Educational Center (Samernas utbildningscentrum) in Jokkmokk. Fundamental to the strategies developed by the group has been that all parts from the start agreed that the impact of SNC on the local community depended on more than providing a technological solution and thus the objective was agreed on to create and maintain a local project ownership and to locate as much as possible of the technical and other development activities in the area of Jokkmokk. The SNC project came through because individuals took unconventional initiatives within existing resources. The project gave space for women reindeer herders to elaborate some of their ideas. Further, the project gave a university based platform for identifying potentials and initiating contacts, and the 2002 guest research position at LTU was the SNC originator's platform for launching the proposition. After it became clear that the LTU environment would not be able offer full assistance to the project, it became an urgent matter to establish new unions with key organizations involved with high tech ICT research and development. But, when possible partners and funding sources were approached, it was a recurring answer to refer to the LTU computer science environment as the appropriate organ for channeling resources.

As the decision makers at LTU were the very same that had

advised the regional funding authorities, the situation became desperate. Likewise, the locally based project strategy faced the same type of problem. Individuals and establishments that became interested in the project when approached by the members of the project judged it as "not (sufficiently) within their jurisdiction" and passed on to offices and individuals in the "right" positions, in this case civil servants and politicians dealing with Sámi topics and reindeer herding but who were not in the ICT industry. Unfortunately, these persons and institutions showed explicitly negative attitude or simply did not answer back when approached by the project members or leaders. However, a PhD student in computer science — Anders Lindgren — became interested in one of the key problems that the SNC proposition presented. His research reinforced the credibility of the project and was thus valuable not only for bringing the connectivity problem addressed by SNC closer to its solution but also to strengthen the whole SNC team's possibilities to find allies. Also, an LTU professor, Anders Östman, of a needed complimentary science subject (Geographical Information Technology) joined SNC. This supported the project with scientific expertise and also a base within a "legitimate" subject for ICT development at the regional university (LTU).

In comparison with Case 1, instead of a single entrepreneur a whole community of Sámi women, as well as the whole Sami territory, is involved. And instead of a few Nutek officials a collective of researchers and practitioners are involved in the process. It would be naive not to expect dissenting voices in such a coalition of people and interests. Still, we think the story presented contains enough to illustrate that when technological innovation takes place in a context led by women from a minority group, the signaling costs are much higher. The innovation as such is much more complex compared to Case 1 as it involves both technological and social innovation and a structural re-formation of society. It is not the technical aspects of the feasibility of the innovation project that comes to the surface; rather, it is the question whether SNC signals high innovation productivity or not in the eyes of resources controlling stakeholders/"employers." Speaking with Spence, the endeavour seems to have jumped from a fairly stable equilibrium — some of which read signals and indices in favourable ways, some of which excluded the very idea of including SNC, or rather the team behind it — to the sector of high productivity of "innovation" sector. Thus, Spence's metaphor of the lottery is clearly applicable.

Case 3 social innovation

The third case is situated in a high school context in Köping, a city in the middle of Sweden. Even if information technology is involved the innovation that will be illustrated here has the character of social innovation. We propose that social innovation (see, e.g., Sundin and Tillmar) in general have higher signaling costs compared to technological innovation in manufacturing industries (Case 1). Social innovation can more easily be questioned as to whether it is productive or is to be recognized as innovation at all. Our argument is that the quality of innovation is as much present in this case as in the two previous cases.

This case is a sub-project of Dropin <http://web.vkl.se/dropin/> funded by the European Union. The sub-project was with focus on the development of the practice of health dialogues with students guided by a school nurse at the high school in Köping. Health dialogue in Sweden is an established method within the school health service. The way it is carried out does, however, vary between schools and is dependent on the individual school nurse, the school management, and other administrative staff. In project Dropin the school nurse was as a front figure. Before becoming a school nurse she worked at a district health care center. She then attended a university course in preventive health care. The idea was that the district health care center would develop the preventive part of their service. When she had finished her education, the center was no longer ready to do so. However, she developed a concern for preventive care and thus she started a company of her own and that she operated for eleven years. As self-employed she traveled around the country and provided workplace profiles including individual health profiles. She remembers many happy people jumping out of her car after she had presented their profiles to them. The reason for this joy was that the employees received an overall picture of their health and life style and were able to see on paper what was good and bad and thus most of them were in a general sense encouraged about their lives. Some years ago she came to discuss how to make the outcome of the health dialogues visible outside the high school. Because of the severe policy of secrecy, the dialogues were not forwarded to any other person at the school and so the two nurses at the school decided to write up summaries of the outcome to some of the questions they used in their dialogues and presented the information at the homepage of the school nurse care center. This was meant also as a response to signals that the students became tired of steadily recurring surveys without receiving any feedback. Within the broader Dropin project this preventive health care work was acknowledged. As a part of the project it was decided to further develop this way of a tool for health dialogue (the above information is based on interviews with the staff of the nurse center).

After different attempts to organize the process, the said school nurse took the lead. As well, one of the ICT teachers became interested and was engaged to create a data based tool, a tool that after a while became a web-based tool. This way the two developed together VISAMT (Vi samtalar: We talk together) <http://www.visamt.com/indexeng.html>. During the school year 2006-2007 this tool was used for the first time by three school nurses. The website contains a set of questions used in connection with health dialogue students complete and whose results are presented in the form of diagrams. A long bar indicates that the student within a certain area scores positively and a short bar indicates an area where his/her health is less good. It is optional to take part in the dialogue, but almost every one of the students chose to take part and most of them enjoy it according to the nurses (this information is based on their interaction with the students). The students think the exercise is helpful and that it is good to see the outcome (Interviews on 16 March 2007). The nurses want the students to "own" the outcome of their dialogue so that they can bring it with them in conversations with teachers, the school's welfare officer, the vocational guidance officers, the headmaster, etc., so that the student in these conversations can provide a documentation of their own health profile. In addition it is possible to use the data of the website as an aggregate outcome of the situation of health of each class and the whole of the school. Further, the website as a tool is well suited for other coaching dialogues, something a number of the teachers at the school have recognized all from the beginning and implemented. The website triggered interest beyond the school and in the Dropin project members from other countries expressed interest in having the website and its data translated.

The development and implementation of VISAMT is an example of social and health care innovation. It is not a radical innovation in the sense that something has been discovered which cannot be found anywhere else. However, the same could be said of the innovations presented in Case 1 where they do neither represent radically new procedures or new technology. At the same time, VISAMT is unique because it has been developed within a specific context and with a specific pedagogical way of thinking adjusted well to the specific context it used in. While the same kind of creativity emanating from solving practical everyday problems characterize the innovations taking place in both Case 1 and Case 3, we argue that the signaling cost is much higher in Case 3. First of all there is no regular market for innovations of the kind described. Of course the website could be marketed and sold, but the tool in itself is only one part of the innovation. The pedagogical use of the tool is, we believe, more context dependent and thus innovative. The way it should be brought out in another context probably involves some additional loops of innovation in a new context in order to have it work as well in the new context. Because of these intangible aspects of the content of innovation, these kinds of innovations are usually not recognized as innovations. With regard to Spence's concept, this innovation faces unfavourable loops and equilibrium.

Conclusion

Economists have argued successfully that the existence of market failures calls for governments to take action and subsidize specially SMEs as they are disadvantaged compared to large firms. Special interest in recent years has involved the stimulation of innovation as this is thought to be a key for not only economic progress but also for a better world in general. There is little scholarship where the outcome of this policy has been examined in relation to the expressed motive to compensate for market failures. We argue that the outcome of public intervention suggests to compensate for market failures may instead contribute to make these even greater. C. Harvie and B.C. Lee in their review of policy arguments conclude that the subsidizing of public assistance of SME activities in various areas are not economically justified and propose a wider use of networks between SMEs as more effective. We take takes as point of departure the concept of information asymmetries while focusing on how Spence ideas can be applied to the allocation of public funding. Further, we propose by illustrating with case studies that it is likely that public funds are allocated in a way the existing structures are strengthened instead of changed to the worse. The results of our investigation suggest that women's migration into higher echelons of economic competence can be impacted by well-structured public funding regardless of entrenched male patriarchal practices and processes of business, although at the same time still compromised.

Works Cited

Amft, Andrea. *Sápmi i förändringens tid*. PhD Dissertation. Umeå: Umeå U, 2000.

Ghannad, Navid. *The Entrepreneur and the Born Global Firm*. PhD Diss. Växjö: Växjö U, 2009.

Harvie, C., and B.C. Lee. *Public Policy and SME Development*. Wollongong: Wollongong U, 2003.

Kråik, Maria. "Sámi Women Equal Rights: Yesterday and Tomorrow." *Taking Wing*. Helsinki: Ministry of Social Affairs and Health Finland, 2002. 151-61.

Nutek. *Kvinnor och mäns företagande. En statistisk beskrivning*. Stockholm: Nutek, 2006.

Nutek. *Utfall och styrning av statliga insatser för kapitalförsörjning ur ett könsperspektiv*. Stockholm: Nutek, 2007.

Rosenbaum, J.E. "Tournament Mobility: Career Patterns in a Corporation." *Administrative Science Quarterly* 24.2 (1979): 220-41.

Spence, Michael A. "Job Market Signaling." *Quarterly Journal of Economics* 87 (1973): 355-74.

Stiglitz, Joseph. "The Theory of 'Screening': Education and the Distribution of Income." *The American Economic Review* 65.3 (1975): 283-300.

Sundin, E., and M. Tillmar. "A Nurse and a Civil Servant Changing Institutions: Entrepreneurial Processes in Different Public Sector Organizations." *Scandinavian Journal of Management* 24.2 (2008): 113-24.

Author's profile: Anders W. Johansson teaches business administration specializing in entrepreneurship at Växjö University and at Mälardalen University. His recent publications include "Entrepreneurship, Discourses and Conscientization in Processes of Regional Development," *Entrepreneurship and Regional Development* (with Karin Berglund, 2007) and he has published the article "Emancipation or workability? Critical versus Pragmatic Scientific Orientation in Action Research," *Action Research* (with Erik Lindhult, 2008).

Author's profile: Maria Udén teaches gender studies and technology at Luleå University of Technology. Udén's areas of interest include engineering, innovation systems and gender, and women's conditions in the Arctic economy. Her recent publications include "A Located Realism: Recent Development within Feminist Science Studies and the Present Options for Feminist Engineering," *Women's Studies International Forum* (2009) and "Indigenous women as entrepreneurs in global front line innovations systems," *Journal of Enterprising Communities* (2008).

Migration, Diaspora, and Ethnic Minority Writing
Steven Tötösy de Zepetnek

Abstract: In his article "Migration, Diaspora, and Ethnic Minority Writing"
Steven Tötösy de Zepetnek proposes — based on the theoretical and
methodological framework of "comparative cultural studies" — a framework
for the study of migration and life writing. In an application of the proposed
framework, Tötösy de Zepetnek analyses selected texts of life writing by
women in Canada and the U.S. whose background is Central European
Jewish. Among others, Tötösy de Zepetnek's analysis is based on his notion
of "in-between peripherality" and the problematics of displacements,
historical, cultural, geographical, and personal.

Narratives — fictional or other — of migration and displacement
abound in literature and occur to a large measure in life writing (for
a recent discussion of the genre, see, e.g., Vasvári). In the following,
I propose a theoretical and methodological framework for the study
of such texts. The proposed framework is itself located in the
"comparative cultural studies" (Tötösy de Zepetnek, *Comparative
Literature*, "From Comparative," "From Comparative <http://docs.
lib.purdue.edu/clcweb/vol1/iss3/2>; for the theoretical and
methodological background of comparative cultural studies see
Siegfried J. Schmidt's work in the Empirical Study of Literature, e.g.,
<http://docs.lib.purdue.edu/clcweb/vol12/iss1/1>).   In   most
instances national literatures and/or large-language literatures
possessing a decisive number of elements such as a historical locus
and established parameters of tradition, thus with their power bases
of politics and economics determine visibility and importance.
However, there is a significant "other" corpus of literature, namely
that of diaspora, migration, and ethnic writing. This type of writing
is by no means small and depending from the point of view of its
readership, critics, and scholarship, it is either with focus on the
original literature wherefrom the text is created — either in
thematics, or language, or in any further or other parameters and in
this case it is designated as "diaspora writing" — or with focus on its
new location in which case it is designated as "ethnic writing." In
other words, Chinese or Hungarian literature written in Canada is
designated as diaspora writing in Chinese or Hungarian literary
scholarship and it is designated as ethnic writing in Canadian
literary scholarship. And such literatures are, in recognition and in
function within the system of culture, peripheral in all cases.
  Diaspora, migration, and ethnic literature is difficult to account
for, difficult to canonize, difficult to recognize. As recognition and
canon formation of literature occurs in a complicated and
fragmented way based on various factors and in areas such as
critical and academic attention, readership, production and
distribution parameters, sales figures, literary historical attention,

etc., diaspora, migration, and ethnic writing is and remains hard to assess and, and consequently, to accept as a significant corpus of literature in the scholarship of literature and culture. However, in recent years there has been increasing interest in all aspects of diaspora and ethnic writing in all major Western literatures. In the North American English-speaking theoretical and critical landscape, Charles Bernheimer's (ed.) *Comparative Literature in the Age of Multiculturalism*, Ella Shohat and Robert Stam's *Unthinking Eurocentrism: Multiculturalism and the Media*, Gurbhagat Singh's (ed.) *Differential Multilogue: Comparative Literature and National Literatures*, Susan P. Castillo's *Notes from the Periphery: Marginality in North American Literature and Culture*, Winfried Siemerling's and Katrin Schwenk's (eds.) *Cultural Difference and the Literary Text: Pluralism and the Limits of Authenticity in North American Literatures*, David Palumbo-Liu's (ed.) *The Ethnic Canon: Histories, Institutions and Interventions*, Sneja Gunew's *Framing Marginality: Multicultural Literary Studies*, or Satya P. Mohanty's *Literary Theory and the Claims of History* are good examples.

Based on tenets of comparative cultural studies, I developed the notion of "in-between peripherality," a notion that can be applied in several ways for the study of migration, diaspora, and ethnic minority literature (see, e.g., "Configurations"). In the said framework developed for the study of Central and East European literature and culture, I propose that the cultures and literatures of the region exist traditionally on the periphery of the major European literatures, following their historical, economical, and political marginalization, including the field of literary scholarship. However, because of their cultural self-referentiality, they are not only "peripheral" but also "in-between," that is, in-between their own national cultural self-referentiality and the cultural influence and primacy of the major Western cultures they are influenced by. While my notion may be understood as a macro theory because it deals with "national" literatures, the notion of in-between peripherality can be also applied to diaspora, migration, and ethnic writing as a parallel macro theory based on the large corpus of writing in existence. The parameters are similar: the diaspora author and text is "in-between" the original culture and literature the author and his/her text emanate from and both are "peripheral" with regard to the original culture and literature and their location. My notion is not new, in principle. For example, Homi K. Bhabha writes in his *The Location of Culture* that multicultural writing is the "the cutting edge of translation and negotiation, the *inbetween* space that carries the burden of the meaning of culture" (38). And in English-language scholarship in general, there are many further examples and attempts to define diaspora, migration, and ethnic minority writing In US-American scholarship the notion of "border writing" (see, for example, Jay), or Amin Malak's "ambivalent affiliations" and "in-betweenness," François Paré's "exiguity" and the "margins of literature" may serve as excellent examples.

It appears to me that — following tenets of comparative cultural studies — in particular the contextual (systemic and empirical approach) and its framework's ability to avoid the mistake of downgrading the literary, indeed, polyvalence and consequently canonical value of some, if not all, diaspora, migration, and ethnic literature is most advantageous. In other words, the contextual approach allows us to take into account extra-literary factors which often mark, indeed, designate, the perception of diaspora, migration, and ethnic minority literature. As mentioned previously, in general terms diaspora, migration, and ethnic minority literature appears to be more often than not having difficulties in the overall canonization process in the sense of primary or even secondary recognition. The reasons for this are manifold and here are some examples of the why of this marginalization. For example, Robert S. Newman writes that "it is safe to say that we normally expect exile or refugee literature to be transparent. That is, we assume that those who encounter it will accept it at face value and perhaps even understand its subtextual implications. But the varying reception of exiles and refugees over the years should make us wonder about this model of transparency" (87). An alternative is proposed, for example, by Francesco Loriggio, who suggests that "One of the more interesting aspects of ethnic literature as a field of study is the obligations it entails. The critic is forced to work on many levels simultaneously. S/he must name the texts, disseminate them, and, at the same time, at this particular stage of the game, define them, situate them within the agenda of the century and the debate it has fostered" (575). This *a priori* positioning of the study of diaspora, migration, and ethnic minority literature is among other reasons why I designate the approach and its object of study as contextual, that is, systemic. More to the point, once the "systemic" positioning of the diaspora/migration/ethnic text is performed, it already obtains a higher order of perception with regards to its more sophisticated analysis, and hence, possible recognition toward canonization. Because in a contextual/systemic context the text is located within the framework of the interrelation between its function as a peripheral text that is related to both the "home" literature and the literary origins based in its location of production. Following Loriggio's argumentation that the positioning of an ethnic text involves historical strategies, in which "ethnicity is active disemia, disemia congenital to one's biography and behaviour, historically and institutionally over-determined" (585), the contextual/systemic positioning of diaspora, migration, and ethnic minority writing with reference to what appears to be the criticized historical and autobiographical element, becomes, evidently, multi-layeredness and creative sophistication. In other words, the tenets of the contextual and systemic approach to literature and culture which proposes to observe and to describe the extra-textual factors of a literary text in a specific manner are appropriate as well as advantageous for the study and legitimization of diaspora, migration, and ethnic minoritywriting.

Following the above briefly outlined theoretical and methodological presuppositions — which, in turn I propose is applicable for the study of diaspora, migration, and ethnic minority writing — I apply here the framework to a particular aspect of Central and East European literature and culture. Ever since the collapse of the Soviet empire in 1989-90, Central and East Europe gained new currency in general social discourse, in politics, economics, as well as in literature and culture. In general social and political discourse, the designation of "Central Europe" and the discussion around it has been at times fierce; nevertheless, the discussion itself raised many questions about identity and culture. Milan Kundera, Timothy Garton Ash, Czeslaw Miosz, György Konrád, Péter Esterházy, Claudio Magris, Adam Michnik, Danilo Kis, and scores of other prominent intellectuals and writers discussed and discuss the notion of Central Europe and whether it exists in various shapes and forms or not. More often than not, the debate ends, in an affirmation of the notion of Central Europe. Perhaps the most astute and informed as well as impartial piece of writing being Garton Ash's 1986 article, "Does Central Europe Exist?" The current interest in the idea of a Central Europe — as well as its tandem notions of East Central Europe, South Eastern Europe, the debate on *Mitteleuropa* in Austria and in Germany, the historical relevance of *Zwischeneuropa*, etc. — relates to the economics and the political aspects of Europe and the European Union and the larger problematics of globalization and markets. With regard to the history of the notion of Central Europe, we must pay attention to Milan Kundera, who argues that "the geographic boundaries of Central Europe are vague, changeable, and debatable … Central Europe is polycentral and looks different from different vantage points: Warsaw or Vienna, Budapest or Ljubljana … Central Europe never was an intentional, desired unit. With the exception of the Hapsburg emperor, his court, and few isolated intellectuals, no Central European desired a Central Europe. The cultures of the individual peoples had centrifugal, separatist tendencies; they far preferred to look to England, France, or Russia than one another; and if in spite of that (or perhaps because of that) they resembled each other, it was without their will or against their will" (12).

If the history and genesis of a Central Europe or a Central European culture is questionable as Kundera suggests, the notion, as he states, "that they resemble each other" is a more accepted idea. Virgil Nemoianu, for instance, argues in his article "Learning over Class: The Case of the Central European Ethos" that there is a structure of Central Europeanness which he calls an "ethos" and which explains as being a specific configuration of education and the Roman Catholic religious imagination, resulting in a specific cultural and behavioral value system. Another recent example is Louis Rose's *The Freudian Calling: Early Viennese Psychoanalysis and the Pursuit of Cultural Science* where he argues in many aspects similarly to Nemoianu that humanist education (*Bildung*) in a context of traditional aesthetic culture and the leadership by a Roman Catholic aristocracy created a specific characteristic and cultural space of and in the region (28-29). In my book, *Comparative Literature: Theory, Method, Application*, I too argue for the existence of a Central European cultural space and I propose the said theoretical designation of "in-between peripherality" — a framework that takes into account the forty-year impact of Soviet colonial and communist rule over all previous Habsburg lands except Austria and where I argue for cultural specificities and a common cultural character of Central Europe. The framework is then applied to contemporary Hungarian and Romanian literary texts: the result of the application makes it clear that the argument for the existence of a contemporary Central European literature as representing certain characteristics specific to the region may be valid. Further, in recent years, the theme of Central European philosophy, connected with but independent of literature, has been given more thorough attention. The Polish logical school, logical neo-positivism, phenomenology, the Prague school of linguistics, and analytic philosophy, Gestalt psychology, the Vienna economics school — as well as individual thinkers — are all movements and groups specifically Central European and continuing to make a strong impact on thinking and artistic expression today.

In general social discourse about culture, the existence and location of a specific Central European space (a cultural *noyau*) is generally accepted, it appears, despite Kundera's and many others' more cautious and differentiated view. The difficulty arises when it has to be explained in detail and exemplified. What is needed, therefore, is a comparative and synthesizing approach and method which take into account several areas of cultural expression from a good number of cultural regions of Central Europe. In addition, it may also be of some importance from which location the observation is performed (i.e., second-order observation as per radical constructivism). For instance, while Kundera is right in his assessment of the history of the notion and idea of Central Europe, what his argument lacks is the perspective from the outside. True, the Hungarian in Hungary or the Slovak in Slovakia is foremost Hungarian and Slovak, respectively (that is, "still" but perhaps not as homogeneously as before). And he/she would certainly pay more attention to Germany or the USA than to a notion of Central Europe when he/she is in Hungary or Slovakia. And the same observation can be made in scholarly discourse. The perspective changes, however, once the individual is outside of his/her original location, cultural or other. In other words, when Milan Kundera lives in Paris, or Josef Škvorecký or George Faludy live in Toronto, that is when they become intellectual and personal hybrids: Hungarian, Hungarian-Canadian, and Central European or Czech, French-Czech and Central European; of course, such configurations are applicable to a large number of diverse people, whether in Europe or the Americas. It is common knowledge that members of nationalities — ethnic groups in Canada, the USA, or other locations of emigration and/or exile — interact in many aspects when before they would not. Thus, Czechs and Hungarians, for example, discover kinship and the Central European dimension when they are together in Toronto or Berlin. This perspective — what I term "relocated location" — is both an important aspect of the Central European designation, as well as an important force of the construction of the Central European designation. Clearly, the voices of a "relocated location" in the sense I suggest applies to the designation of Central Europe, simply for historical reasons: the wars and revolutions and the economic hardship that was experienced in the region we call Central and East Europe created large waves of exile and emigration to all countries in Western Europe as well as North America (Canada and U.S.), as we know.

In the application of the said fremaowrk, I explore and discuss several selected texts of life writing by Jewish Hungarian women authors whose writing serves as an example for my proposed theoretical framework as applied to migration, diaspora, and ethnic minority writing. But why the specific attention to Jewish Hungarian and/or to Jewish Central European writing (in English)? John Willett, in an editorial entitled "Is There a Central European Culture?" writes that "the elements of a new Central European culture must come from even farther afield than they did before Hitler and Stalin. We certainly cannot expect them to depend on the spontaneous German-Jewish-Yiddish tradition that once seemed to link the comedian Peischacke Burstein in Vilnius with the writer Ettore Schmitz in Trieste: however unforgettable, the source is barred, buried under the masonry of the great concentration camp memorials. But the essence of mid-Europe surely is that its cultural inspiration must come from both East and West, and its role be to test ideas against one another and use the result in its own creativity" (15). The importance and impact of Jewish culture in its varied forms on and in Central Europe is well known (see, for example, Johnston). However, while I understand the cultural importance of Central European Jewry tragic as Willet suggests and as seen and understood because of World War II and the Holocaust, I do not find it "barred" and "buried." First, I understand Central European Jewishness as of a quintessential synthesis and expression of the said Central European culture. Second, life writing and memoirs represent a genre that connects the past and the present and thus it is an advantageous cultural and literary genre to gauge and to understand the problematic at hand, namely Central Europeanness, and third, as it happens, diasporic Jewish Hungarian women's memoir writing has produced some of the most interesting and exciting texts for the said problematic of Central European culture. And the genre of Jewish Hungarian life writing is of relevance for my discussion for another reason. It is curious that much life writing of minority groups, for instance, that of Hungarian Germans reflecting on post-War expulsion often concentrates on "good" memories (see, for example, Murk). It is, then, even more curious that Jewish Hungarian memoirs contain so much positive about life in Hungary before the Holocaust, when, in truth anti-Semitism has been increasing gradually and in intensity in Hungary since before World War I.

In Anglophone North America, life writing is today one of the most prevalent genres and this can be gauged also with regard to Jewish Hungarian women's memoirs. There are, in particular in US-American and Canadian English-language writing many examples of such texts (I should add that the designation "Jewish-Hungarian" is of course in itself problematic: I am certain that most first-generation Jews now living in North America would not readily accept the designation up front, let alone the second-generation. I am using the designation to indicate the cultural and personal background of the writers I am discussing here as per reflection on their own memoir writing). For the present study, I selected Julie Salamon's *The Net of Dreams: A Family's Search for a Rightful Place* (1996), Elaine Kalman Naves's *Journey to Vaja: Reconstructing the World of a Hungarian-Jewish Family* (1996), Susan Rubin Suleiman's *Budapest Diary: In Search of the Motherbook* (1996), Magda Denes's *Castles Burning: A Child's Life in War* (1997), and Judith Kalman's *The County of Birches* (1998).

In a geographical context, Salamon's *The Net of Dreams* is perhaps the most "Central European." Her idea and research of the book began by the impetus of reading, in 1993, about Steven Spielberg's plans to film his *Schindler's List* (Salamon 6) after which she travels to Poland and other areas of East Central Europe such as Huszt, now in the Ukraine, and formerly a town with a substantial Hungarian-speaking population. Salamon's description leading into the history of the mixture of nations is intriguing itself: "This was the land of the *shtetl* — and of Gypsies, Slovaks, Hungarians, and Ukrainians — an ignorant backwater that had been annexed by the USSR after World War II. Now Communism was finished and the place where my parents were from had been reshuffled again. Their birthplace had lost the status of affiliation with Czechoslovakia or the former Austro-Hungarian Empire" (13). What is significant in this brief excerpt is the reference to Czechoslovakia (the interwar period) and the Austro-Hungarian Empire (the period prior to the 1919) and thus the setting of the notion of Central Europe, geographically and culturally. The family history of Julie Salamon stretches across Central and East Central Europe in time, in space, and in cultural parameters. It includes the particularities of their education (*Gymnasium*) and university, their knowledge of languages, and the necessities of manoeuvring from one cultural context to another but altogether being in a Central European space. Salamon's interpretations and explanations of matters and things Central European — be those Slovak, Hungarian, Ruthenian, Jewish, or Czech — extend over much detail. For instance, at one point she explains a specific instance of the usage in Hungarian of the familiar (*te*) and polite (*maga*) forms of address and other forms of address they used such as the Ukrainian-Czech mixture of *zolotik* ("little golden one") in their social and individual contexts (205). Salamon's narrative of memory is concentrated on family and family history and the memory of the horror of the Holocaust runs through it. Yet, the Central European cultural space as well as spaces the family's history and the histories of individual members occupy in the book's narrative involve us as readers not only as historical evidence but also as evidence for a literature of the region.

Elaine Kalman Naves's *Journey to Vaja: Reconstructing the World of a Hungarian-Jewish Family* is the most historical text among the text I am dealing with here. It also has the least mistakes with Hungarian diacritics and the translation of phrases and terms. The Jewish-Hungarian families whose history is told in the book, the Schwarz-Székács, the Weinbergers, the Rochlitz, etc., belonged to that stratum of Jews in Hungary who assimilated and became members of the educated upper-bourgeoisie of the country. In this case, they produced members who were members of the Austro-Hungarian officer corps and upper-government officialdom, landowners, industrialists. One member of the family (Aggie Békés) is also of interest because she earned a doctorate in comparative literature from the University of Debrecen in the 1930s (section of photographs, n.p.). It is well known that Jews in Hungary underwent perhaps the most wide-spread and deepest process of assimilation, for the reason that Kalman Naves describes as "During the forging of Magyar nationalism, they cast their lot wholeheartedly with that of the emerging Magyar nation — only one of the many ethnic groups in the polyglot Austro-Hungarian Empire which included Slovaks, Ukrainians, Slovenes, and many other nationalities. Even the orthodox among Hungarian Jews described themselves with self-conscious pride as *Magyars* of the Israelite faith" (15) and the access of numerous Jewish-Hungarian families to both non-titled nobility and the ranks of the aristocracy is a particular characteristic of Hungarian history which, again, explains much of the said Central European culture and its Jewish aspects (for the Jewish nobility of Hungary, see McCagg; Lukacs 91-93; see also Molnár and Reszler).

Magda Denes's *Castles Burning: A Child's Life in War* is a doubly sad book in view of its author's recent death in 1996 — all other authors of the memoirs under discussion here are alive today. The story of Denes's family is particularly poignant because of her father's act of abandoning his wife and daughter in 1939. The story of this Jewish-Hungarian family, again in the context of its position as educated upper-bourgeoisie, is of particular interest for my argument of Central Europeanness because the story unfolds in "travel." What I mean is the telling of the tale when Magda Denes — after surviving the Holocaust in hiding — flees Hungary in 1946 with her mother and grandmother and how she perceives and experiences life as a refugee with and among all the other nationalities in the refugee camps. The narrative contains much of the self-confidence of the Central European educated. Here is an excerpt: "I always suspected Ervin of having a bit of the prole [proletarian] in him. Anyway, now he wants to emigrate to Palestine with her, and he wants to fight for a Jewish state. I don't even know what that means. Jews are intellectuals, not farmers or soldiers" (147). Magda eventually ends up in New York where she becomes professor of psychoanalysis and psychotherapy at Adelphi University.

Susan Rubin Suleiman's *Budapest Diary: In Search of the Motherbook* is similarly bitter-sweet in many instances of recollections of Budapest life and death during the war and the Holocaust, with a good dose of narcissism in the author's narrative when self-reflective. The book's title itself is intriguing: *Budapest Diary: In Search of the Motherbook* and it is similar to Tibor Fischer's (another second-generation Hungarian) *Under the Frog* (1992, Betty Trask Award of 1992 and shortlisted for the Booker Prize in 1993), in that it contains a translation from the Hungarian. Fischer's un-English *Under the Frog* is a translation of the Hungarian phrase describing when one is in bad circumstances (as in quality of life): *a béka segge alatt* ("under the arse of a frog"). Suleiman's *Motherbook* is a translation of *anyakönyv*, the official name of one's birth certificate in Hungary and a term laden with references of nostalgia and patriotism in Hungarian literature and even in general discourse. Thus, the title of the book sets the scene, the author's search and re-discovery of her Hungarian background and history. In the first chapter, "Prologue: Forgetting Budapest," Suleiman describes her escape from Hungary as a ten year old, in the last months when the border was still open to Czechoslovakia. After stops in Košice and Bratislava — Kassa and Pozsony (the Hungarian names of the cities), and Pressburg (the German name of the city), respectively — the Rubin family of three arrived in Vienna, free. The author then earned a profession and her life with clear distance to her ethnic background in the American melting pot. Although with a brief interest in Hungary during the 1956 Revolution and its aftermath of Hungarian refugees in the United States, it is only in the early 1980s — upon the illness of her mother, her own divorce, and the stress of raising two sons as a single mother — that Zsuzsa (the Hungarian version of her name) again takes to Hungary and her unresolved past. After the 1989 Changes, she is invited to Budapest as a guest professor and she spends an extended period in Hungary. In Budapest — and it is in these chapters where the cultural reading I am interested in is written — Suleiman immerses herself in the intellectual life of scholars, writers, and artists and makes many interesting observations. Her descriptions of life and letters in Budapest is valuable for the North American reader because it is the description of something that does not exist in North America and even in Western European cities it is at best only somewhat similar: it is specifically a Central European situation. Thus, among the many interesting aspects of Central European and, within that, specifically Hungarian scenes, situations, and cultural specifics, some may be of particular interest to the English-speaking North American reader.

In conclusion, the above texts of life writing demonstrate memories and interpretations of migration and diaspora, as well as aspects of ethnicity and they are texts which are explicable best in the context of postulates within the framework of comparative cultural studies in their relevance of diaspora, migration, and ethnic minority writing to literary and culture history — despite or, rather, because of — their in-between relocated location

Note: The above article is a revised version of "An Application of the Systemic and Empirical Framework in Diaspora and Ethnic Studies." *JSchmidt.net: Projekt zu Ehren Siegfried J. Schmidt*. Ed. Achim Barsch, Gebhard Rusch, Reinhold Viehoff, and Friedrich W. Block. Halle: U of Halle-Wittenberg (1999): <http://www.sjschmidt.net/konzepte/texte/totosy1.htm>. Copyright release by Tötösy de Zepetnek.

Works Cited

Ash, Timothy Garton. "Does Central Europe Exist?" 1986. *The Uses of Adversity: Essays on the Fate of Central Europe*. By Timothy Garton Ash. Cambridge: Granta, 1991. 161-91.
Bernheimer, Charles, ed. *Comparative Literature in the Age of Multiculturalism*. Baltimore: The Johns Hopkins UP, 1995.
Bhabha, Homi K. *The Location of Culture*. London: Routledge, 1994.
Castillo, Susan P. *Notes from the Periphery: Marginality in North American Literature and Culture*. Bern: Peter Lang, 1995.
Denes, Magda. *Castles Burning: A Child's Life in War*. New York: Simon &

Schuster, 1997.

Gauss, Karl-Markus. "Why Austria was Out to Lunch during Eastern Enlargement." *Europäische Rundschau: Quarterly for Politics, Economics and Contemporary History*. Special Edition 26 (1998): 113-18.

Gunew, Sneja. *Framing Marginality: Multicultural Literary Studies*. Melbourne: Melbourne UP, 1994.

Jay, Paul. *Contingency Blues: The Search for Foundations in American Criticism*. Madison: The U of Wisconsin P, 1997.

Johnston, William M. *The Austrian Mind*. Berkeley: U of California P, 1972.

Kalman, Judith. *The County of Birches*. Vancouver: Douglas & McIntyre, 1998.

Kalman Naves, Elaine. *Journey to Vaja: Reconstructing the World of a Hungarian-Jewish Family*. Montréal: McGill-Queen's UP, 1996.

Kundera, Milan. "The Tragedy of Central Europe." *The New York Review of Books* (April 1984): 2-15.

Loriggio, Francesco. "History, Literary History, and Ethnic Literature." *Literatures of Lesser Diffusion / Les littératures de moindre diffusion*. Ed. Joseph Pivato, Steven Tötösy de Zepetnek, and Milan V. Dimic. *Canadian Review of Comparative Literature / Revue Canadienne de Littérature Comparée* 16.3-4 (1989): 575-99.

Lukacs, John. *Budapest 1900: A Historical Portrait of a City and Its Culture*. New York: Grove Weidenfeld, 1988.

Malak, Amin. "Ambivalent Affiliations and the Postcolonial Condition: The Fiction of M.G. Vassanji." *World Literature Today* 67.2 (1993): 277-82.

McCagg, William O., Jr. *Jewish Nobles and Geniuses in Modern Hungary*. Boulder: East European Monographs, 1972.

Mohanty, Satya P. *Literary Theory and the Claims of History: Postmodernism, Objectivity, Multicultural Politics*. Ithaca: Cornell UP, 1997.

Molnár, Miklós, and André Reszler, eds. *La Génie de l'Autriche-Hongrie. Etat, société, Culture*. Paris: PU de France, 1989.

Murk, Rosa. *Aber manchmal war es auch schön.... Erinnerungen*. Ed. Bernd Mittenzwei. N.p.: n.p, 1994.

Nemoianu, Virgil. "Learning over Class: The Case of the Central European Ethos." *Cultural Participation: Trends since the Middle Ages*. Ed. Ann Rigney and Douwe Fokkema. Amsterdam: John Benjamins, 1993. 79-107

Newman, Robert S. "The Reader of Exile: Škvorecký's *Engineer of Human Souls*." *The Literature of Emigration and Exile*. Ed. James Whitlark and Wendell Aycock. Lubbock: Texas Tech UP, 1992. 87-104.

Palumbo-Liu, David, ed. *The Ethnic Canon: Histories, Institutions and Interventions*. Minneapolis: U of Minnesota P, 1995.

Paré, François. *Exiguity: Reflections on the Margins of Literature*. Trans. Lin Burman. Waterloo: Wilfrid Laurier UP, 1997.

Rose, Louis. *The Freudian Calling: Early Viennese Psychoanalysis and the Pursuit of Cultural Science*. Detroit: Wayne State UP, 1998.

Salamon, Julie. *The Net of Dreams: A Family's Search for a Rightful Place*. New York: Random House, 1996.

Schmidt, Siegfried J. "Literary Studies from Hermeneutics to Media Culture Studies." *CLCWeb: Comparative Literature and Culture* 12.1 (2010): <http://docs.lib.purdue.edu/clcweb/vol12/iss1/1>.

Siemerling, Winfried, and Katrin Schwenk, eds. *Cultural Difference and the Literary Text: Pluralism and the Limits of Authenticity in North American Literatures*. Iowa City: U of Iowa P, 1996.

Singh, Gurbhagat, ed. *Differential Multilogue: Comparative Literature and National Literatures*. Delhi: Ajanta Publications, 1991.

Suleiman, Susan Rubin. *Budapest Diary: In Search of the Motherbook*. Lincoln: U of Nebraska P, 1996.

Tötösy de Zepetnek, Steven. *Comparative Literature: Theory, Method, Application*. Amsterdam: Rodopi, 1998.

Tötösy de Zepetnek, Steven. "From Comparative Literature Today toward Comparative Cultural Studies." *CLCWeb: Comparative Literature and Culture* 1.3 (1999): <http://docs.lib.purdue.edu/clcweb/vol1/iss3/2>.

Tötösy de Zepetnek, Steven. "From Comparative Literature Today toward Comparative Cultural Studies." *Comparative Literature and Comparative Cultural Studies*. Ed. Steven Tötösy de Zepetnek. West Lafayette: Purdue UP, 2003. 235-67.

Tötösy de Zepetnek, Steven. "Configurations of Postcoloniality and National Identity: Inbetween Peripherality and Narratives of Change." *The Comparatist: Journal of the Southern Comparative Literature Association* 23 (1999): 89-110.

Vasvári, Louise O. "Emigrée Central European Jewish Women's Holocaust Life Writing." *Comparative Central European Holocaust Studies*. Ed. Louise O. Vasvári and Steven Tötösy de Zepetnek. West Lafayette: Purdue UP, 2009. 158-72.

Willett, John. "Is There a Central European Culture?" *Daedalus: Journal of the American Academy of Arts and Sciences*. Special Issue *Eastern Europe — Central Europe — Europe* 119.1 (1990): 1-15.

Author's profile: Steven Tötösy de Zepetnek works in comparative cultural studies and media and communication studies. For lists of his publications see <http://docs.lib.purdue.edu/clcweblibrary/totosycv>. He is editor of the Purdue UP humanities and social sciences quarterly *CLCWeb: Comparative Literature and Culture* <http://docs.lib.purdue.edu/clcweb>, the Purdue UP series of Books in Comparative Cultural Studies, and the Shaker Publisher series of Books in Comparative Culture, Media, and Communication Studies.

Part Two
Identity and Displacement

Cosmopolitanism in Zhu's *Ancient Capital* (*Gudu*)
Yu-chuan Shao

Abstract: In her article "Cosmopolitanism in Zhu's *Ancient Capital* (*Gudu*)" Yu-chuan Shao analyses *Ancient Capital* with Julia Kristeva's concepts in confronting the revival of nationalism in Taiwan. By reading *Ancient Capital* with Kristeva's psychoanalytic rendition of cosmopolitanism, I investigate in my article the theme of catastrophe in Zhu's text. My reading is not only about the minority's anxiety over what Zhu sees as xenophobic nationalism in contemporary Taiwan but as an attempt to envision Taiwan, in the midst of a national mobility, as a cosmopolitan space that accommodates all forms of "foreign-ness." By exploring what Kristeva calls the "encounter with the irreconcilable" I demonstrate the relevance of recognizing the effect of the uncanny toward the Other in our understanding of an ethics of cosmopolitanism.

Introduction

Being "catastrophe bound" (*zai-nan-gan*) is the phrase used by novelist Tienxin Zhu to describe what she sees as the paralysis of nationalism-ridden society in contemporary Taiwan. In her novella *Ancient Capital* (*Gudu*) in which she depicts Taipei as a city suffering havoc caused not only by the impact of globalism but also by political struggle. Zhu voices her anxiety over strained ethnic relations and the shrinkage of cultural and political tolerance that has been plaguing both the private and public spheres of Taiwan since the surge of ethnic nationalism after the end of Martial Law in 1987 and when Taiwan started on the road towards democracy. The melancholic and yet relentless critique of Taiwan's political movements in its post-martial-law era we find in Zhu's fiction may seem rather dubious and unsettling. This is apparent, for example, in the narration of *Ancient Capital* whose protagonist says repeatedly that only through pretending to be a foreigner can she survive the catastrophic situation caused by political inferno. Zhu's intriguing and at once provocative literary expression has led to not only critical acclaim but skeptical remarks about her political intervention and intentions. Some critics assert that the literary device in *Ancient Capital* — viewing Taiwan from the perspective of an outsider, a foreigner — reveals Zhu's ambivalent attitude toward Taiwan as a new national identity (see, e.g., Chen; unless indicated otherwise, all translations are mine).

Is Zhu paranoid in her depiction of Taipei as a city that is being devoured by nationalist frenzy, as various critics point out? Are the critics being fair in relating Zhu's cultural identity to her literary expression, since her recent works often reveal "a deep distrust of any form of politically motivated identification and allegiance" (Yang 161)? In many ways, both Zhu's fiction and the critics who challenge her reflections on social and political phenomena by highlighting her cultural identity as a *wai-sheng-ren* — a term used by native Taiwanese, whose ancestry has been established in Taiwan for hundreds of years — demonstrate Taiwan's political divide caused by the resurgence of nationalism and strained ethnic relations. It seems that the Taiwan discourse of culture is caught up in the same kind of moral and spiritual catastrophe that overwhelms the narrator of *Ancient Capital*. Zhu herself spoke about the issue at hand in an interview by referring to her worry over the paralysis of articulation, that is, the deprivation of criticism about present-day social or political movements in Taiwan because of her Taiwan-Chinese identity (Zhu qtd. in Qiu 148). The issue of nationalism and Zhu's treatment of it is of course a topic of scholars and politicians of many creeds. The concept of "nations without nationalism" is a political concept by psychoanalyst and literary scholar Julia Kristeva and in my article I analyze Zhu's text by applying Kristeva's concept in confronting the revival of nationalism. This concept is an indication of the way Kristeva responds to the nationalist issue which has been plaguing the French society since the 1990s, a time when Europe started to show a surge of populist xenophobia. In her *Nations without Nationalism*, Kristeva argues that at a time of nationalist pretensions and conflicts between nations that consider themselves sacred we should rethink the principles of Enlightenment in order to reevaluate cosmopolitanism. Interestingly, written at a time of ethnic nationalism erupting in Taiwan, Zhu's *Ancient Capital* also hints at the ideals of cosmopolitanism and Zhu, too, refers to the ideals of the Enlightenment to tackle the crises nationalist fever may lead to. By reading *Ancient Capital* with Kristeva's psychoanalytic rendition of cosmopolitanism, I investigate in my article the theme of catastrophe in Zhu's text. My reading is not only about the minority's anxiety over what Zhu sees as xenophobic nationalism in contemporary Taiwan but as an attempt to envision Taiwan, in the midst of a national mobility, as a cosmopolitan space that accommodates all forms of "foreign-ness." By exploring foreign-ness I demonstrate the relevance of recognizing the effect of the uncanny toward the Other in our understanding of an ethics of cosmopolitanism.

The problem of being a "foreigner"

Ancient Capital overwhelms the reader with an impending and omnipresent feeling of catastrophe. "Catastrophe bound" is the word used by the narrator to describe the misery and discontent of living in present-day Taipei, where, in the narrator's view, the government spares no effort to replace the old with the new in the name of progress and where one is doomed to live like a foreigner who can hardly build any emotional bonding to his/her living space by tracing the lived experiences of his/her life. Unsettled by the premonition of catastrophe, which is embodied by a fear of the annihilation of her existential traces, the narrator thus challenges the propaganda of love and identification imposed by the new ruling power: "You just beg for an answer! By whatever means — usually in the name of prosperity, progress or hope and happiness — a city with no intention to preserve the cultural heritage of its people is no difference from an alien place! Are we able to love, cherish, protect or even identify with such an alien city?" (187; see also Lin 64-69). This shadow of catastrophe looms all over the narration and culminates in the breakdown of the narrator, devastated by the unbearable shock of "getting lost" in the city where she was born and has been living for several decades.

Many critics point out that such unbearable catastrophe of dislocation the narrator suffers from symbolizes an identity crisis that the author Zhu and those who bear a similar background have been undergoing in the wake of ethnic nationalism. As Iping Liang notes, "Embedded in Zhu's discontent with Taipei is the deeper discontent with a larger issue: the collective identity of the island" (110; see also Lin). Yet, for some critics, this sense of crisis, expressed in Zhu's provocative tone, can be seen as the manifestation of Zhu's unwillingness to identify with Taiwan's new national identity (see Chen) while other critics warn about the danger of turning such an intricate literary expression into a clean-cut political manifesto in order to reclaim her cultural identity as Taiwan Chinese. Such a defiant gesture can be seen as an act of resistance versus mere nostalgic yearning for a utopian past (Liao 19). Understood in the light of Walter Benjamin's theses on history and subjectivity, the catastrophic state of being that troubles the narrator, as Chaoyang Liao argues, actually points to hope: "Hope here [in the last catastrophic scene] inheres in the drive of history toward incongruities, which always promise to bring about, not poststructuralist revelry in heterogeneity, but the catastrophic, cataclysmic encounter between the subject and its own unfulfilled desires" (22). Hopeful as it may be, such catastrophe bound sentiment points to, I argue, a political and also an existential crisis that can be pinpointed as representing the anger and anxiety of second-generation Chinese in Taiwan over the rule of the so-called Taiwanese Nativists (on this, see, e.g., Lin). Despite the fact such sentiment indeed exposes anxiety, what most critics fail to see is, as Zhu wishes to suggest through her work, the unfavorable marker of "renegade outsiders," the label given to both first-generation Chinese, mainland-born Chinese who arrived in Taiwan with Chiang Kai-shek, and the second generation. As the narrator laments at the beginning of *Ancient Capital*, in the wake of numerous massive political campaigns, people sharing her cultural identity have been plagued with some kind of paranoia as if their social others, those without the renegade label, would always want to check their loyalty to the country: "One campaign speaker thus yells, 'anyone like *You* should kick yourself off and get back to Mainland China'" (167).

The rise of xenophobic sentiment, as Zhu suggests, comes alongside the resurgence of nationalism in Taiwan and the upholding of an anti-Chinese national concept embraced by nationalist politicians. As Taiwan, rather than China, has become the new common denominator in contemporary Taiwan, the anxiety over a still-emerging new national identity — in the name of Taiwan — has escalated the tension between different social groups and thereby spurred more radical actions taken by the nationalists, who regard themselves as natives of Taiwan. Such anxiety and tension has thus led to a defensive hatred or even a persecuting hatred that often arises with the cult of origins. As Kristeva notes, the cult of origins is a reaction of hatred "of those who do not share my origins and who affront me personally, economically, and culturally: I then move back among my own" (*Nations* 2-3). But what is at stake in this cult of origins is not merely about hatred projected onto those different from us; rather, as narrated in Zhu's writing of the world shaken up by an impending catastrophe, the problem of such nationalist cult is more about the harm such xenophobic hatred may do to the social, political, and cultural capabilities of a nation.

In the very beginning of "what of tomorrow's nation," a chapter written specifically for the English version of *Lettre ouverte à Harlem Désir*, Kristeva points out the potential decline of all the civic ideals as a consequence of the cult of origins, be it subjective, sexual, nationalist, or religious. She thus notes: "In years to come it is likely that we could witness a loss of concern for personal freedom, which was one of the essential assets in *the Declaration of the Rights of Man and Citizen*, to the advantage of subjective, sexual, nationalist, and religious protectionism that will freeze evolutionary potentialities of men and women, reducing them to the identification needs of their originary groups" (*Nations* 2). This account of loss, in a distinctive way, gives us a picture of the world that is likely to be shaken by the crises of humanity: a catastrophe of humanity Zhu pictures can be powerful enough to wipe out all collective and individual memories and thereby the possibilities of confronting and recognizing existential differences and singularities simply because they are politically incorrect. Confronting such cultural, political, and personal catastrophe, the narrator of the novella feels devastated by the sense of being like an unwanted foreigner.

Civic ideals in a cosmopolitan city

Similar to Kristeva's reflections on the decline of civic ideals, one predominant concern that looms large in *Ancient Capital* is the question of existential differentiation at a time of national essentialism. It is clear that difference in the midst of us is a constitutive part of our sociality, be it formed by historical realities or mythical reasons, and thus one urgent problem we all have to confront is the problematics of otherness. Otherness is hinted at in the text in numerous provocative responses made by the unsettled narrator, most explicitly stated in allusions to political turnover in both contemporary Japanese and Chinese history. In relating to these historical incidents, Zhu suggests that there can be a benign version of nation building and a better way to treat our political others. As the narrator notes, "Before the day for returning to the island where the political conflict has turned ugly, You suddenly felt there was so much in you and then You started telling your daughter about the stories of how the Meiji emperor and Emperor Kang-xi of the Ching Dynasty treated their political others — those still with unflinching allegiance to the just defeated political regime — not as enemies but as those who were left behind" (176). What these historical moments of power shifts point to is an ideal of cosmopolitanism: the possibility and thereby the prospect of constructing a less oppressive living condition in which people of different or even oppositional identities — a divide caused by historical or political reasons — may learn to accommodate the otherness.

For such a cosmopolitan prospect, Zhu turns to Osaka, a Japanese city where, in the narrator's view, the past and the present have reconciled with each other perfectly, and presents the city as an exemplar of a cosmopolitan space where personal freedom and existential differences can be accommodated. As a foreigner in such a cosmopolitan space, the narrator feels at home with the foreignness of herself and with that of a foreign country. At a café in the city center, the narrator enjoys the freedom of being different, being foreign: "Your language does not cause any sort of disturbance, or, to put it more specifically, no one shows any sign of being disturbed ... But you really appreciate such a state of freedom, in which people have learned to live with the presence of others" (182-83). Such a space of freedom also demonstrates the kind of cosmopolitan ideals that Kristeva views as the wealth of the Enlightenment: Montesquieu's concept of the nation, Kristeva notes, can be "affirmed as a space of freedom" and at once "dissolved in its own identity, eventually appearing as a texture of many singularities" (*Nations* 32). Apparently, by turning a Japanese city into a space accommodating all forms of singularities and differences, in contrast to a nationalist space hostile to differences, Zhu demonstrates the same line of thought as cosmopolitan thinkers such as Kristeva. Kristeva declares her position when facing her country's crisis of national identity: "A rare species, perhaps on the verge of extinction in a time of renewed nationalism: I am a cosmopolitan" (*Nations* 15). In *Nations without Nationalism*, Kristeva reiterates the political and ethical significance of maintaining the principle of universality. As revealed in her analysis of the tension between nationalism and cosmopolitanism at various historical times, such upholding of the concept of universality, of "a symbolic dignity for the whole of mankind," appears to be as "a rampart against a nationalist, regionalist and religious fragmentation" (*Nations* 27). But, as Kristeva suggests, maintaining such a universal principle of humanity, as distinct from the historical realities of nation and citizenship, does not aim to downplay historical realities or other forms of particularities. Rather, such cosmopolitan ideals may help to open possibilities of tackling the confrontations that emanate from the perpetuation of particularities.

In the light of cosmopolitanism, the crisis of national identity — as often caused by national and religious conflicts, immigration, and racism — is also a crisis in civilization and humanity. Such a crisis, as we see in Kristeva's analysis, reveals a political and at once an ethical crisis in how our capacity to accommodate otherness can be undermined by the alluring power of nationalist sentimentality, by the worship of *Volksgeist* ("national spirit") — what Kristeva calls "a romantic withdrawal into the mystique of the past, into the people's character, or into the individual and national genius" (*Strangers* 177). Seeing the affinity between present-day nationalism and the concept of *Volksgeist* as formulated by German romantics such as Herder, Kristeva calls our attention to the civic ideals upheld as the basis of Montesquieu's idea of nation, which, as Kristeva points out, brings together the national and the cosmopolitan without erasing national boundaries or historical realities. But what is at issue in the midst of national mobility, nevertheless, lies in our capacity to see the limits of nationalism and the necessity of acknowledging foreignness. As Kristeva contends, this is a capacity that has already been revealed to us in maintaining the distinction between human beings and citizens, between the national and the cosmopolitan. In his cosmopolitanism, Kristeva notes, Montesquieu "protected the rights of man beyond the rights of the citizen, concerned as he was to protect 'privacy,' 'weakness,' and 'shyness,' so that homogeneous, uniform sociality would not erase them" (*Nations* 28).

Given similar concerns over such a crisis in humanity, *Ancient Capital* exposes all manifestations of existential difference that can be found in the city dwellers' memories of their lived experiences — that is, to use Montesquieu's words, the privacy, weakness, and shyness of individuals — so as to defy the oppressive essentialism of nationalist ideology. In a defiant manner, Zhu challenges the kind of xenophobic nationalist sentiment for such xenophobia tends to undermine the democratic capabilities of a cosmopolitan cityscape and cause a devastating impact on both the public and private spheres. Confronted with such labels as "politically backward," "unpatriotic," or "foreigner" often attached to descendants of Mainland Chinese, the narrator thus questions the new ruling power's project of restructuring, which, in her view, is grounded in the ideology of nativism and nationalism: "Why would people want to stay here if this so-called *homeland* has destroyed everything they may cling to? The new ruling party must be aware of that so they start propagandizing sense of community, asking people to show more allegiance to the new nation, their native land and the new ruling party that represents the authenticity of native culture" (199). With reference to the diversity of the flora planted all around Taiwan at different historical points by immigrants, Zhu gives us a national concept that brings together the national and the cosmopolitan as we see in Montesquieu's cosmopolitanism. In this manner, Zhu's narrator leads us to see such a cosmopolitan space composed of plants of all sorts that reveal the planters' love and memory of their respective homelands.

The encounter with strangeness

As suggested in both *Strangers to Ourselves* and *Nations without Nationalism*, the ethical and political implications we may find in Kristeva's ethics of cosmopolitanism cannot be addressed without being formulated in psychoanalytic terms. As Kristeva suggests in her book *Nations without Nationalism*, the development of the concept of universality — starting in Stoicism — continued to make progress and "took on a new orientation with the Freudian discovery of our intrinsic difference" (21). In *Strangers to Ourselves*, Kristeva has already pointed out the political and ethical significance of the Freudian breakthrough: "With Freud indeed, foreignness, an uncanny one, creeps into the tranquility of reason itself, and, without being restricted to madness, beauty, or faith anymore than to ethnicity or race, irrigates our very speaking-being, estranged by other logics, including the heterogeneity of biology" (170). Drawing on both the Enlightenment's civic ideals and the Freudian discovery of strangeness as the unconscious, Kristeva's cosmopolitan thinking aims to address the unconscious of nationalism — the symptom that the foreigner provokes — and the unconscious of personal and national identity.

Kristeva's psychoanalytic rendition of cosmopolitanism has shed a new light on the way we may approach the kind of symptomatic and provocative confessional narrative as narrated in *Ancient Capital*. Afflicted with the burden of reclaiming and redefining her personal, cultural, and political identity, the narrator, by assuming a dual identity of a resident and a foreigner, is thrown into an existential turmoil and thereby a psychoanalytic journey into the encounter with otherness — the strangeness of herself and of the other. This tale of encountering the other can be readily taken as evidence showing Zhu's unwillingness to identify with Taiwan's new national identity and her condemnatory view of the pro-Taiwan-Independence ruling power (see Chen). But, through the mapping of Taipei Zhu aims to expose the troubled mind of second-generation Chinese and expose the process of struggling with otherness and the importance of encountering otherness / strangeness so as to open up the possibility of recognizing the causes of the uncanny. As the uncanny affect one may feel about social others can be taken to mean "politically incorrect" by nationalist politicians, Zhu challenges and complicates our limited perception of otherness through the narrator's double vision: whereas the narrator laments about the strangeness of "new" alleys and streets reorganized by the new ruling powers, she starts mumbling on and on about the "old" looks of the city streets and the strangeness of the traces left by the old ruling powers:

No matter whether the bull-eyed windows get blurry or not, or whether we may still see big-leaved or small-leaved mulberry trees ... all these old houses have one thing in common. That is, on their doors, lacquered or not, are marked by chalk "united, Mainland, Chinese, or China" but never "Taiwan" There is no exception throughout the entire alley. And suddenly you just cannot but think of one story in *The Arabian Nights*, in which one's life can be either spared or taken away by the right marking on one's door — when the time comes. (187)

As if being prompted by the urge to know the truth of strangeness/foreignness, the narrator, undertaking a journey into memory lane, digs out all forms of strangeness/foreignness caused either by the mediation of time or by the maneuvers of political power as an attempt to restore the complexity of history which tends to be simplified or even distorted by the ruling party.

It is through journeying into the complexity of history we can truly see the possibility of opening up an ethical dimension of strained social and political relations and thereby the meaning of thinking toward an ethics of cosmopolitanism. As Kriteva notes, "Psychoanalysis is then experienced as a journey into the strangeness of the other and of oneself, toward an ethics of respect for the irreconcilable. How could one tolerate a foreigner if one did not know one was a stranger to oneself?" (*Strangers* 182). In *Ancient Capital* the encounter with otherness — the strangeness of the other and of oneself — evokes the most devastated and catastrophic reaction to the difficulty one may have in situating him/herself with respect to the other when one gets caught in projections of identification. Catastrophic as it may be, such a hysterical and yet conscientious encounter with otherness, as Zhu suggests, may help set us free from a rigid self-other boundary, from an immobilized personal and national identity, and from a destructive resentment toward the other.

Wandering through the strangeness of the city streets, Zhu's narrator not only confronts the strangeness of the other and of oneself but discloses the entangled relationship between the sense of strangeness and the intervention of power struggle. In a provocative tone, the narrator lays bare the way the uncanny we project onto our social others is bound up with the alienating force of the political regime. And thus Zhu challenges the political incorrectness of her cultural identity and also the political correctness of the new national identity:

You envy those who were never silly enough to line up for the birthday buns of the leader of the old ruling party (as you may recall, there seemed to be some in class), never silly enough to be moved and brainwashed by the education of patriotism of the old days ... so they could be spared the pain of trying to keep one's cultural and political integrity in later days after the old power is being replaced by the new. And then now — twenty years from then — some politically correct writers can always find for them a couple of relatives who happen to be the victims of the 228 Event ... You just want to know how they could side with the ideology of the new ruling party at such an early age! (214-15)

In the context of Freud's notion of the uncanny, strangeness experienced by the narrator can be related to anxiety of castration, the subject's anxiety of being negated, crushed by the other, as she is anxiously concerned that her part of history tends to be disregarded or even twisted by the new powers. But, what is at issue here is not only to see the strangeness of the social, political other but to recognize our own strangeness — our unconscious that defines our strangeness and thereby demarcates the strangeness of the other. As Kristeva contends, through the concept of the uncanny, Freud teaches us how to detect foreignness in ourselves: "When we flee from or struggle against the foreigner, we are fighting our unconscious — that improper facet of our impossible own and proper" (*Strangers* 191). Seen through the lens of the uncanny, the provocative act of Zhu's narrator can thus be understood as an attempt to enact the possibility of recognizing the unconscious — the strangeness of the other and of oneself — to use Kristeva's words.

In their distinctive ways, both Kristeva and Zhu present how nationalism may "displace emotions which belong to our personal lives onto political life" and thus lead to the disappearance of the public sphere (Fine 154). Moreover, both writers bring us important insights into why the problem of foreigners and the uncanny toward the other have to be incorporated into our analysis of the tension between nationalism and cosmopolitanism. Confronting the rise of ethnic nationalism, both writers ask us to think toward the possibility of reconciling difference and foreignness while retaining subjectivity and particularity. As Kristeva notes, "The ethics of psychoanalysis implies a politics: it would involve a cosmopolitanism of a new sort that ... might work for a mankind whose solidarity is founded on the consciousness of its unconscious — desiring, destructive, fearful, empty, impossible" (*Strangers* 192). As narrated in *Ancient Capital*, who has difficulty integrating all denominators given by the new era or the new political regime, the problem of nationalism can truly be confronted when we move closer to the crux of foreignness and that of nationalism, that is, to the unconscious truth of the other and of oneself. At the moment of encountering such unconscious truth, such catastrophic burden, we may get to hear the central question posed by both writers: when facing the strangeness of the other, would we confront the strangeness of our own and try to accommodate strangeness as such? Or, the only answer left for us is "We don't want you here since you don't belong!"

Works Cited

Benjamin, Walter. *Illuminations*. Trans. Harry Zohn. Ed. Hannah Arendt. New York: Schoken, 1968.
Fine, Robert. "Benign Nationalism? The Limits of the Civic Ideal." *People, Nation and State: The Meaning of Ethnicity and Nationalism*. Ed. Edward Mortimer and Robert Fine. New York: I.B. Tauris, 1999. 149-61.
Kristeva, Julia. *Strangers to Ourselves*. Trans. Leon S. Roudiez. New York: Columbia UP, 1991.
Kristeva, Julia. *Nations without Nationalism*. Trans. Leon S. Roudiez. New York: Columbia UP, 1993.
Liang, Iping. "Taipei and Its Discontents: fin-de-siècle Mappings of Taipei in *Gudu* and *Taipei 100*." *Tamkang Review* 31.2 (2000): 103-29.
Lin, Pei-Yin. "Nativist Rhetoric in Contemporary Taiwan." *Cultural Discourse in Taiwan*. Ed. Chin-Chuan Cheng, I-Chun Wang, and Steven Tötösy de Zepetnek. Kaohsiung: National Sun Yat-sen U, Humanities and Social Sciences Series, 2009.
Chen, Yihua. "Forever a Stranger: On Tienxin Zhu's *Gudu*." Taipei: Fujen U, 1998. n.p.
Liao, Chaoyang. "Hope and Disaster: Notes on Politics in Light of *Gudu*" ("Zai-nan yu xi-wang. Cong *Gudu* yu 'Xie-se-bian-fu jiang-lin te cheng-shi' kan zheng-zhi"). *Taiwan: A Radical Quarterly in Social Studies* 43 (2001): 1-39.
Qiu, Guifen. *Dialogues of/with Women: Conversations with Contemporary Taiwan Women Writers* (Bu/tung-guo nu-ren gua-zao. Fang-tan dang-dai Taiwan nu-zuo-jia). Taipei: Yuan-zun, 1998.
Yang, Zhao. *Literature, Society and Historical Imagination: Notes on Literature in Post-war Taiwan* (Wen-xue, she-hui yu li-shi-xiang-xiang. Zhan-hou wen-xue-shi san-lun). Taipei: Lian-he wen-xue, 1995.
Zhu, Tienxin. *Gudu*. Taipei: Mai-tian, 1997.

Author's profile: Yu-chuan Shao teaches literature and cultural studies at National Taiwan Normal University. Her recent publications include the articles "Curse or Blessing from the Empires: The Conflict between Individuality and Collectivity *in A Portrait of the Artist as a Young Man*" (2008) and "The Double Consciousness of Cultural Pariahs: Fantasy, Trauma, and Black Identity in Toni Morrison's *Tar Baby*" (2006). Currently, she is working on studies on the issues of modernity and cultural identity in postcolonial literature.

British Muslims and Limits of Multiculturalism in Kureishi's *The Black Album*
Shao-Ming Kung

Abstract: In his article "British Muslims and Limits of Multiculturalism in Kureishi's *The Black Album*" Shao-Ming Kung discusses the novel with regard to English national identity, multiculturalism, and the British Muslim community. Drawing on postcolonial theories of nationalism, ethnicity, and diaspora, along with Hanif Kureishi's concept of "effective multiculturalism," Kung discusses how Kureishi's text copes with the problems of British Muslim alienation and their appeal to radicalism. Most critics agree that in presenting a conflict between Western liberalism and Islamic fundamentalism, Kureishi's novel marginalized this already marginalized group. Kung argues that despite his critique of radical forms of the "fundamentalists," Kureishi has shown how the rise of radical Islamism represents a politico-religious resistance against British racism. Predicting the events of the 2005 London bombings, Kureishi's novel deserves our reconsideration of the civil right of British Muslims and a renewed configuration of Englishness in the multi-ethnic context.

Ashley Dawson notes that celebrations of Britain's hybridity tend to "highlight the cultural impact of Black and Asian Britons while ignoring the enduring obstacles they face" (26). Indeed, the effect of racial discourse is still evident in the minds of both white Britons and assimilated immigrants, while postnational violence embodied explicitly by the rise of Muslim fundamentalism brings to light the limits of the British government's multicultural policy. A number of questions thus deserve our attention: what does it mean to be British? To what extent does the concept of Englishness need to be revised? And what is wrong with official British policies of multiculturalism, especially with public discourse fluctuating between tolerance for racial difference and hostile attitudes toward immigrants? How should we re-examine the relationship between Englishness and multiculturalism in the context of global diasporas, especially since the 7 July 2005 bombings in London by British Muslims?

In my study, I explore the issue of rethinking English national identity through the policy of British multiculturalism towards the Muslim community in Hanif Kureishi's 1995 *The Black Album*. Drawing on postcolonial theories of nationalism, ethnicity, and diaspora along with Kureishi's concept of "effective multiculturalism," I discuss how Kureishi narrates problems of alienation and British Muslim's appeal to radicalism. Most critics agree that in presenting a conflict between Western liberalism and Islamic fundamentalism, Kureishi's novel further marginalizes this already marginalized group, while "re-inscribing dominant liberalism as the norm" (Ranasinha 239). I argue that despite his critique of radical forms of the "fundamentalists," Kureishi has shown how the rise of radical Islamism amongst young Muslims expresses a politico-religious resistance against British racism. Not only does Kureishi modify the stereotypical representation of British Muslim groups by exposing its complexity and heterogeneity; he also challenges the seemingly benevolent liberalism embodied by the protagonist's white lecturer/lover, Deedee Osgood, whose multiculturalism and sexual hedonism are problematized. Predicting the events of 7 July 2005 London bombings, Kureishi's novel deserves our reconsideration of the civil rights of British Muslims and a renewed configuration of Englishness in a multi-ethnic context.

Englishness, multiculturalism, and British Muslims

In a speech on new English identity in Britain, David Blunkett remarked that the Britons now live in an age of migration and increased international interdependence. Questions of national identity therefore rise to the fore: is it more important "to articulate a shared sense of national identity in conditions of flux and change?" and if so, how can we "reconcile this with diversity, openness and pluralism of belief and practice?" (2). And so what does this mean for the English? Is a "renewed sense of Englishness" (Blunkett 2) an important component of English national identity?

One well-used theoretical perspective of an understanding the way in which national identity is constructed is Benedict Anderson's concept of the nation as an "imagined community" (6) in which the nation is conceived as both imaginary and as a shared "comradeship" (7). Accepting Anderson's model for the moment, the imagined status of the nation has two consequences. Firstly, the fact that it is difficult to examine objectively an imaginative construct means that it can be manipulated to produce a powerful ideological discourse for a disparate group of people. Secondly, because it is non-fixed, it is open to varying interpretations and claims. Based on Anderson's model, we can assume that within each nation at any moment in history, there are always "competing versions of the nation, each of which combine social, geographical and historical images" (Bentley 485).

In *Border Dialogues*, Iain Chambers proposes that there are two versions of "Englishness." The first one is "Anglo-centric, frequently conservative, backward-looking, and increasingly located in a frozen and largely stereotyped idea of the national, that is, English culture"

(27). The other is "ex-centric, open-ended, and multi-ethnic" (27). In Chambers's formulation, Englishness has been, conventionally, understood as representing a common culture while remaining aloof from historical or demographic divergencies and differences. Likewise, John McLeod emphasizes that post-war immigration to Britain resulted in "a new multicultural English population as well as triggering myths of an embattled national identity which turned increasingly to race and heterosexuality as the prime marker of legitimacy and belonging" (3). Paul Langford stresses the historically "mongrel nature" of the English while acknowledging that the creation of a self-consciously multiracial society "might have startled many who sought to summarize the English character between the mid-seventeenth and mid-nineteenth century" (318). In their analysis of contemporary concept of Englishness, both Jeremy Paxman and Roger Scruton highlight the changed nature of Englishness for the contemporary world and although neither of them mentions multiculturalism outright, the issue hovers implicitly around their writing on the subject.

In fact, contemporary England and Englishness is experiencing a period of transformation. And the debate on Englishness occurs parallel with the discourse about multiculturalism. We may say that what the discourse of multiculturalism does is to "pluralize Anderson's notion of community" (Bentley 485). This view indicates that contemporary England is identified more accurately as an amalgamation of different social and cultural communities, each of which is engaged in negotiating the larger grouping that constitutes the nation. Rather than two poles excluding each other, Englishness and multiculturalism can be conceived as having a "dialectical relationship," which sometimes appears as an opposition while at other times overlapping and even mutually supportive. Peter Ackroyd, for example, manages to incorporate both positions in close proximity. In the conclusion to *Albion: The Origin of the English Imagination* he claims that: "Englishness is the principle of diversity itself. In English literature, music and painting, heterogeneity becomes the form and type of art. This condition reflects both a mixed language comprised of many different elements and a mixed culture comprised of many different races" (448). Similarly, Roger Scruton writes that "the multicultural and multiethnic make-up of contemporary England has replaced any traditional, racially homogenous model" (244).

Among Western societies Britain has by far the largest population where South Asian Muslims have settled permanently. British Muslims are a diverse and a vibrant community and they form an essential part of Britain's multi-ethnic, multi-cultural society. However, despite strenuous attempts to accommodate its Muslim population and assist the emergence of a religiously pluralist society, Britain still becomes the target of violence by Islamic fundamentalists. As Judith M. Brown points out, one of the core problems in the relationship of South Asian Muslims with wider British society and the state, clearly manifest in the wake of 7 July, is the considerable "ignorance on the part of most Britons and their political leaders about the inner dynamics and problems of the various British Muslim communities" (143), and "the failure of liberal multiculturalism to enable both meaningful discussion between groups and the emergence of minority leaders who can really 'speak for' the great diversity of British Islam" (144). Moreover, despite the fact that England is becoming a multicultural and multiethnic society, the legacy of colonial racism still exits and its effects have a great impact on the remaking of English national identity.

In *Multicultural Politics*, Tariq Modood defines "cultural racism" as the forms of prejudice that exclude and racialize culturally different ethnic minorities. Modood argues that Britain's shifting racialized boundaries are beginning to include certain culturally assimilated South Asian and African Caribbean (middle-class) values, but continue to exclude and racialize culturally "different" Asians, Arabs, and non-white Muslims. Modood demonstrates that Britain's South Asian Muslims, particularly its Pakistani and Bangladeshi communities, are the most alienated, "socially deprived and racially harassed group" (80). Modood examines why Muslims are portrayed as a "radical assault" upon British values, a threat to the state and an enemy to good race relations and finds that cultural racism is particularly aggressive towards minorities "sufficiently numerous to reproduce [themselves] as a community" (80). It is hostile to communities with a distinctive and cohesive value system, which can be perceived as an alternative and possible challenge, to the "norm" and to those who wish to maintain and assert their cultural distinctiveness in public. British Muslims are perceived as the minority most resistant to assimilation. British Muslims' mass protests against Salman Rushdie's *The Satanic Verses* provided a focal point for anti-Muslim racism. Modood makes the important point that discourses that regard Muslims as a problem or a threat are "not confined to an extreme fringe, popular prejudice or the right wing … they can be implicit or explicit in both elite and progressive discourses" (81-82).

After 9/11, and certainly after 7/7, a whole host of factors have impacted negatively on British Muslims. These racial and ethnic profiling in the criminal justice system and civil society debates around culture that place South Asian Muslims at its heart. In other words, British Muslims are now in danger of being positioned as "the enemy within," whereas the multiculturalist credo of valuing and protecting cultural diversity is countered by a renewed call for assimilation/integration or for a immigration control altogether. As Tahir Abbas indicates, all attempts to make multiculturalism work in the British case have been "fraught with ambiguities, inconsistencies, challenges and political leanings, all impacted by present politics and collective memory" (289). Nevertheless, how to deal with the proliferation of ethnic and cultural differences within Britain as national borders become increasingly porous has become increasing urgent and complex.

British racism and the flaws of multicultural policy are what make Hanif Kureishi's novels so powerful. The title of the novel is itself a mark of racial divide: according to Bart Moore-Gilbert Prince's *Black Album* from which Kureishi's novel takes its title is itself a reference to the Beatles' *White Album* (115). In moving from the "White Album" to the "Black Album" Kureishi not only focuses attention on an alternative music tradition but also offers us a particular model of identity that interrogates English culture. In the light of the 7 July bombings, questions of rethinking Englishness can be framed in terms of their possible effect on how Britain, and particularly its government, conceives of issues of English identity. In his writings of South Asians in Britain, Englishness is increasingly approached through a second-generation diaspora sensibility. While *The Buddha of Suburbia* stresses on Karim Amir's fluid hybridity between center and margin, *The Black Album* engages more openly with the debates around Englishness and multiculturalism and attempts to offer a reframed model of national identity. Englishness is both "interrogated and opened up" (Stein 142) and the novel's message about the limits of multiculturalism as well as the dangers of British Muslim violence demand our reconsideration. But as Susie Thomas points out, *The Black Album* raises the question of a writer's responsibility to "combat negative stereotyping, especially during a time of rising Muslimophobia" (103). This need to reappraise Kureishi's novel is imperative for us to recognize not only its place within a history of social protest literature but also the power of its own social comment on racism as well as the importance of re-writing Englishness in the context of multiethnic Britain.

"The Brown Man's Burden" and racism in *The Black Album*

Kureishi's novel offers a particular portrait of alienation facing British-born ethnic populations. Shahid Hasan, the novel's protagonist, is a South Asian British Muslim torn between two opposing forces, Western liberalism/multiculturalism and Islamic fundamentalism. Under the shadow of racism and racist discourses since Enoch Powell's "rivers of blood" speech and Thatcherite anxieties about the nation being "swamped" by "people of a different culture" British Muslims, despite their politico-economic integration into the public sphere, have long been excluded as alienated subjects outside the national community (see Thatcher). As Shahid notes, in Britain Muslims are "third-class citizens, even lower than the white working class" (209) and that racist violence was on the increase. He fears that his father, who expects future generations to be accepted as English, may have been deluded: "We haven't been! We're not equal!" (209). While his parents still resist giving up their belief in the immigrant's ideal of England as a land of welcome and opportunity, despite the reality falling short of their expectations, Shahid has recognized the fact beneath the "brown man's burden": "However far we go, we'll always be underneath" (209). In characters such a Jump, the stereotypical Orientalist view of British Muslims is clearly and still prominent: "You will slit the throats of us infidels as we sleep. Or convert us. Soon books and … and … bacon will be banned. Isn't that what you people want?" (191).

The specter of racial violence, in the form of right-wing racism, is also present in the novel: "The family had been harried — stared at, spat on, called 'Paki scum' for months, and finally attacked. The husband had been smashed over the head with a bottle and taken to hospital. The wife had been punched. Lighted matches had been pushed through the letter-box. At all hours the bell had been rung and the culprits said they would return to slaughter the children" (90). Certainly, a racist climate curtails the potential for an affiliation of Asian Muslims with English culture. Shahid also notes that British racism is not only seen as an external force; it can become internalized and hence even harder to tackle. The influence of "internalized racism" not only drives Shahid to self-hatred — he confesses to "becoming a monster" (11) and to wanting "to be a racist" (*Black Album* 11) at the novel's opening: "Why can't I be a racist like everyone else? Why do I have to miss out on that privilege? … Why can't I swagger around pissing on others for being inferior? I began to turn into one of them" (11). With his mind invaded by "killing-nigger fantasies," Shahid hopes to become a white racist so that he could mock at his Muslim community rather than being alienated in the society. However, despite his ambivalent desire for "flirting with white racism," Shahid is persuaded by his Asian roommate, Chad, to give up the thought and try an alternative choice — that is, turning to radical fundamentalism led by Riaz's group. Like Shahid suffering from second-generation identity crisis, Trevor Buss alias Chad had been adopted and his "soul got lost in translation" (107), as Deedee Osgood, Shahid's white college instructor, puts it. Confronted with the effortless belonging of the white children with whom he grew up, Chad found it difficult to belong. White Englishness is experienced as an ethnicity which denigrates Trevor's affiliation: "church bells" and "English country cottages and ordinary English people ... the whole Orwellian idea of England" signaled exclusion to the boy (106). In England people mistook him habitually for a street robber. However, when asking for salt in Southall, he was mocked for his accent despite Urdu language classes. Even in Pakistan they "looked at him even more strangely. Why should he be able to fit into a third World theocracy?" (107). He has tried the Labor Party before Riaz's gang, but he found them too racist. Alienated both within and outside the community, Trevor is unable forge affiliations in the white countryside, nor in Asian Southall, nor in Pakistan. Consequently, he leaves his family at an early age, changes his name to Chad, and his life is saved when he is converted into one of Riaz's "spiritual brothers." His anger over this experience of exclusion causes him to reject any claim to Britishness from which he perceives himself to be excluded as a "Paki," the demonized racial other of white Britain. This rejection by British racism is coupled with an equally powerful embrace of Islamic identity — a transformative process in which Chad asserts his identity as, "No more Paki. Me a Muslim" (128).

An important function of Chad's and Shahid's involvement with Islam in the novel is to protect a Bengali family from the racist white working class, which extends beyond pejorative name calling into physical assaults. They encounter a woman on an East London council estate, whose hatred is virulent in her verbal assaults: "'Paki! Paki! Paki!' She screamed. Her body had become an arched limb of hatred with a livid opening at the tip, spewing curses. 'You stolen our jobs! Taken our housing! Paki got everything! Give it back and go back home!'" (139). For the white working classes their own anger over deprived conditions is focused against perceived racial otherness — Muslim immigrants from Pakistan. This aggression is manifested within an economic framework in which race becomes a focal point of the white working classes own economic disenfranchisement.

Both Chad and Shahid experience their own otherness and Kureishi suggests that the alienation Shahid, Chad, and "the brothers" experience at the hands of a racist society potentially drives them into radical Islamic groups that counter non-belonging and racism with mutual support and belief. Chad functions in the novel as "Shahid's alter ego," a dangerous warning of what Shahid would become if he fails to come to terms with what it means to be a British Muslim. Nevertheless, in spite of its monolithic ideology, Islamic fundamentalism does provide an alternative to diasporic identity in post-imperial Britain.

The revival of Islamic fundamentalism

For Kureishi, it is the experience of racism and the barriers for inclusion in British national identity that provides the impetus for Muslim characters to seek refuge in the collective identity of Islam. The British-born generation realizes the degree to which their parents, despite their attempts at assimilation, remain rejected by the host society and feel themselves also rejected. In turn, some of them renounce the "path of assimilation" and practice a "spiritual return" to Islam (Stein 125). In other words, it is precisely the intolerance of the host society towards its "Others" which generates the physical and ideological resistance in the form of fundamentalist activity.

Kureishi's representation of Muslim "fundamentalist" violence makes it clear that such threats do not spring from nowhere, but are instead reactions born out of the specific ideological circumstances in the transnational context. In a way that echoes reactions to the Iraq war and their implication in terrorist activity, Riaz's gang see themselves as part of an international solidarity, declaring: "We fight for our people who are being tortured in Palestine, Afghanistan, Kashmir" (82). Their involvement in radical activities is part of a growing Muslim international consciousness and cannot be separated from conflicts involving other Muslim populations, and the role of Britain in these conflicts. But more than this, Kureishi suggests that it is racism that young British Muslims are facing and that is the root cause for violent fundamentalism. This alternative rendering of Islam is at its height in Kureishi's description of the London mosque. Here Kureishi provides an image of Islam not as representative of essentialism, but of diversity:

Arranged on three floors, the rooms of the mosque were as big as tennis courts. Men of so many types and nationalities — Tunisians, Indians, Algerians, Scots, French — gathered there, chatting in the entrance, where they removed their shoes and then retired to wash, that it would have been difficult, without prior knowledge, to tell which country the mosque was in. Here race and class barriers had been suspended. There were businessmen in expensive suits, others in London Underground and Post Office uniforms; bowed old men in salwar kamiz fiddled with beads. Chic lads with ponytails, working in computers, exchanged business cards with young men in suits. Forty Ethiopians sat to one side of one room, addressed by one of their number in robes … There were dozens of languages. Strangers spoke to one another. The atmosphere was uncompetitive, peaceful, meditative. (131-32)

Here the mosque defines the hybrid nature of Islam's adherents. Instead of reinforcing the stereotypical portraits of British Asian Muslims, Kureishi's text offers us a complex and insightful portrayal, capturing the Islamic model of community wherein all people are united, across race or culture, before God.

It is significant to recognize that the men attracted to Riaz's talks in the East End mosques are not extremists or recently arrived immigrants, but "local cockney Asians" (80). The choice of a term such as "cockney" is not incidental. By placing these men in the East End, the heartland of London's skinhead national front membership, we can trace a direct connection between the attraction of Riaz and the oppression faced by these young men in their lives outside the mosques. Furthermore, Riaz's understanding of Islam can hardly be thought of as traditional, despite its attempt to cast itself as such. In his lectures entitled "Rave to the Grave?" and "Adam and Eve not Adam and Steve," Riaz offers a contemporary understanding of Islam, one that attempts to redraw the boundaries of tradition in the British diasporic context: "We're not blasted Christians … We don't turn the other cheek. We will fight for our people who are being tortured in Palestine, Afghanistan, Kashmir! War has been declared against us. But we are armed" (82). Shahid does not involve himself with radical Islamic activity, nor is he totally assimilated into Western liberal multiculturalism. Towards the end of the novel, Shahid realizes that even beneath Deedee's liberal education white elitist arrogance is hidden.

Liberal multiculturalism, its vision, and its limits

In Kureishi's *The Black Album*, liberal multiculturalism is both celebrated and criticized. While Deedee Osgood, Shahid's literature and cultural studies teacher offers him an alternative education by studying colonial and postcolonial canons, Andrew Brownlow applies

Eurocentric Marxism to tackling the marginalization of Muslim diasporas in Britain. In their respective concerns for minority identities, both characters appear radical and democratic. Yet Kureishi's text suggests that their apparently progressive views replicate the positions taken up by the white elitist supremacy, a racist pride that curtails a transnational interaction between the white and Muslim communities.

Initially, Shahid is drawn to his white liberal English instructor who teaches him in the ways of openness and free expression. She adjusts the traditional syllabus of English studies to make it reflect more the experience of the various kinds of historically marginalized constituencies. To make explicit the ethnocentric assumptions of the established canon and to emphasize the historical links between metropolitan culture and the histories of imperialism, she offers a "course on colonialism and literature" which leaves Shahid, for one, "in a fog of inchoate anger and illumination" (25). Thus she is keen on extending the syllabus to incorporate more immigrant writings and popular fiction. She even introduces aspects of popular music, especially "black" popular music such as Prince's *Black Album*, into her teaching. At one point, Deedee identifies herself explicitly as a "liberal" and her pedagogical politics is manifested in the conduct of her private life including sexual games in which Shahid experiences a love affair. However, Shahid holds some doubts about Deedee's attempt to tilt English studies in the direction of "cultural studies" as well as her problematic mentorship which leads only to empty sensuality of postmodern Western culture. Later in the text, Shahid reconsiders this issue from a somewhat different angle, which connects it directly with Kureishi's broader enquiry into the social potential of the traditional "high" cultural canon in the context of modern multicultural Britain: "He didn't always appreciate being played Madonna or George Clinton in class, or offered a lecture on the history of funk as if it were somehow more 'him' than Fathers and Sons. Any art could become 'his,' if its value is demonstrated" (112). From one perspective, Shahid's response might be taken as an affirmation of a form of humanist universalism. Nonetheless, Shahid is undoubtedly right to wonder whether Deedee's strategy does not itself embody — albeit unconsciously — a subtle new form of exclusion, rather than empowerment, of the racial minorities on whose behalf to act she seems so interested. Shahid's uneasy response reflects the deeply troubled tone of the novel's larger inquiry into the paradoxes of metropolitan liberalism's efforts to promote anti-racist initiatives which might foster a greater sense of unity and commonality in national life. When Deedee forgets her own sympathetic anti-racism and attacks the authenticity of religion and its value as "culture," however, Shahid explodes angrily, invoking the specter of racism implicit in her liberalist ideology. As Chad complains, Deedee's intervention as both feminist and liberal is by no means unproblematic: "Would I dare hide a member of Osgood's family in my house and fill her with propaganda? If I did, what accusations? Terrorist! Fanatic! We can never win. The imperialist idea hasn't died" (191). The deep ambiguities surrounding Deedee's benevolence in this instance derive in part from the fact that, as a white feminist, Deedee is also profiting from the predicament she is attempting to alleviate. From the outset of the novel, questions are raised about the integrity of her attitudes towards the racial. Her attempt to disrupt Riaz's protest against the offending text — one assumes it is *The Satanic Verses* although it is never identified as such — it is she who calls the police to stop the Muslim students and thus contradicts the strong line she has taken against censorship in her classes on Plato and Orwell.

On the other hand, Andrew Brownlow, Deedee's husband, represents a quite different version of metropolitan anti-racism. Rather than promoting assimilation, his approach is organized ostensibly by the principle of respect for cultural difference. In his solidarity with Riaz's desire to defend his own Muslim culture, Brownlow ends by risking his career and he acts throughout with a kind of "mad honesty" (203) which Shahid finds beguiling. On closer inspection, however, Brownlow's cultural relativism is no more satisfactory, or less self-interested, than Deedee's unwitting endorsement of an "assimilationist" model of relations between dominant and minority cultures. As Shahid points out, Brownlow's support for book burning contradicts his opposition to censorship (which was a big factor in his activism in 1960s), as does Deedee's intervention on the other side. His misrecognition of Shahid at the end of the text also implies that to Brownlow, stereotypically, all members of the ethnic minorities are "looking the same." Furthermore, Brownlow's advocacy of a master-narrative of "Reason" — which Riaz contextualizes as the "reason" of "a minority who live in northern Europe" (82) — leads him at times to represent his ally as a "slave of superstition." Such positions conflict radically with Brownlow's commitment to respect cultural difference. In this light, Brownlow's conception of cultural difference slides all too easily into the coercive demand for "authenticity" or "cultural purity" on the part of minorities of the kind evident in one character's disgust at Shahid's attempt to situate himself in a "hybrid" position, "in-between" cultures: "I thought you loved Asian people" (162), says Shahid and then receives the reply that "Not when they get fucking Westernized. You all wanna be like us now. It's the wrong turnin" (162). Besides Brownlow, Kureishi also introduces another character, Councillor Rudder, a socialist politician, to deal with social tensions and their implication on the rising frustrations of Muslim youths. Ironically, he is simply interested in the position until the Labor party is re-elected (179). There is thus in Kureishi's comment on Tony Blair a precedent within *The Black Album* itself that sees left wing politicians as failing to offer an effective counter-ideology to capitalism and its racist manifestations.

In the characters of Deedee and Brownlow, Kureishi interrogates white assumptions of liberal education, exposes the limits of British liberal multiculturalism, and warns against the appropriations of racial otherness that undermine liberal politics. Although Shahid is illuminated by Deedee's liberal pedagogy to explore "innumerable ways of being in the world" (274), the essentialist English identity offered by his white instructor — whose apologies must be made for "taking him [Shahid] to places where there were only white people" (66) — reveals the implicit limitations of her version of liberal anti-racism. In turn, Brownlow argues against racial antagonism and cultural rivalries which surround him: "Liberalism cannot survive these forces" (180). In such a divided social context Kureishi's novel suggests that the ideologies of "Englishness" underlying the traditional conception of "humane education" to which Brownlow and Deedee are devoted in the end requires radical revision.

Ethnic conflicts and the crisis of English national identity

In the wake of the event of 7 July London bombings, Kureishi's novel reads as prescient and prophetic. While the bombers of July 7 were not from London, those who attempted a second series of failed bombings on 21 July were. Yet in reference to both events, focused on British Muslim violence, Kureishi's story still seems a prophetic warning of the threat to London from members of fundamentalist groups. At several points in the novel before its explosive conclusion, real acts of violence and destruction centered about London are presented. These activities are central to the novel's representation of the relationship between identity and anti-social behavior.

The first act of violence in the novel occurs when a bomb has "exploded on the main concourse of Victorian Station" (101; in fact, this event refers, as Sara Upstone points out, to the IRA bombings in London in 1991, although the novel is set in 1989). Moving through London after the event, Shahid observes that the British media "merely showed the blood-soiled faces and accounts of passers-by of the blast" (102) while other Britons around him expressed their confusion and anger towards "the lurked armies of resentment" (103). Here the violence is constructed carefully as unnamed, so as to stand as a haunting specter of the danger posed to the city by extremism in all its forms: "But which faction was it? Which underground group? Which war, cause or grievance was being demonstrated? The world was full of seething causes which required vengeance — that at least was known" (103). On the other hand, the event is represented in such a way as to read as Kureishi's apocalyptic warning of what might happen in London in the future if racial tensions are not addressed.

The most notorious scene of violence in the novel is the public book burning of Rushdie's *The Satanic Verses* Kureishi only alludes to. Infuriated by the writer's blasphemous rewriting of the *Koran* and of the prophet Mohammad, Riaz's gang of young Muslim fundamentalists decided to burn the book on campus. Although the flames there "had been no catastrophe and no immediate victims" (226), Deedee felt ashamed and started to criticize their absurdity. While the college principal dared not to stop the book burners for fear of accusation of racism, Deedee held a copy of Rushdie's novel and tried to make an open discussion in the class: "What sort of people burn books ... I'd heard books were on the way out. I never imagined they'd be replaced by vegetables" (210), says Deedee to Shahid. As Kenneth C. Kaleta points out, the conflict between fundamentalism and western progress in Kureishi's novel reflects the writer's "opinion of the censorship of the book and his refusal to accept terrorism" (137). Unfortunately Deedee's effort to defend the freedom of speech has been further thwarted by her young Muslims students, who sack her house, force her into hiding, and even exclude Shahid from their community. As the situation with Riaz's gang escalates, "another bombing in the City" (227) sets the scene for the final petrol bomb attack on the bookshop and its tragic consequences. Disappointed by Brownlow's defeatism and hypocrisy, but equally disgusted with Riaz, Shahid chooses to side with Deedee, and plays a crucial part in protecting her from the wrath of Riaz's followers. But the reconciliation between the lovers at the end of the novel is provisional, the clear implication being that their relationship must be renegotiated on a day-to-day basis.

Whereas the official reaction to the 7 July bombing suggested shock and disbelief at the level of alienation felt by some young male British Muslims, Kureishi's novel documents this alienation plainly and uncompromisingly. Kureishi emphasizes the naivety of any suggestion that being born in Britain results naturally in belonging. Uncle Asif has warned Shahid's brother Chilli that "it's easy for people, especially if they're young ... to forget we've barely arrived over in England. It takes several generations to become accustomed to a place" (54).

In his essay "Carnival of Culture" Kureishi proposes to render multiculturalism as a political solution, rather than an abstract or under-developed concept and a critical perspective crucial to our reading of *The Black Album*: "Religions may be illusions ... but these are important and profound illusions. But they will modify as they come into contact with other ideas. This is what an effective multiculturalism is: not a superficial exchange of festivals and food, but a robust and committed exchange of ideas — a conflict which is worth enduring, rather than a war" (100). Unlike multiculturalism which values and protects cultural diversity, Kureishi's concept of "effective multiculturalism" is a modified one, which relies upon an interactive exchange between white Britons and Muslim groups. Moreover, as Kureishi claims in "The Rainbow Sign, "it is the British who have to make these adjustments. It is the British, the white British, who have to learn that being British isn't what it was. Now it is a more complex thing, involving new elements" (55). Instead of sticking to a racially monolithic definition of Englishness, Kureishi suggests that a more "tolerant, multi-faceted Englishness" — one that includes the possibility of strong religious faith and recognizes the needs and political concerns of its Muslims subjects — is needed if further violence is to be prevented.

Conclusion

Contrary to Ruvani Ranasinha's comment that Kureishi "homogenizes the Muslim community, concealing its broad diversity of faith and practice" (89), I argue that Kureishi in fact understands this fundamentalism very well. He also recognizes the potential consequences of fundamentalist violence. However, by challenging the stereotypical representation of British Muslims with a complex and insightful portrayal, Kureishi's novel highlights the heterogeneity of British Muslims, represents prophetically the limits of white liberal multiculturalism, and reveals the tensions bred by intolerance and their dangers. Denouncing them as "infidels within" or enforcing them into integration will reinforce an unending "war on terror" or a "clash between civilizations." To get rid of the specter of racism and fundamentalist violence, an effective multicultural policy towards those marginalized groups has to be developed and implemented; above all, there is the need to pluralize the English national community into a more tolerant, multi-ethnic one.

Works Cited

Abbas, Tahir. "Muslim Minorities in Britain: Integration, Multiculturalism and Radicalism in the Post-7/7 Period." *Journal of Intercultural Studies* 28.3 (2007): 287-300.
Ackroyd, Peter. *Albion: The Origins of the English Imagination*. London: Chatto and Windus, 2002.
Bentley, Nick. "Re-writing Englishness: Imagining the Nation in Julian Barnes's *England, England* and Zadie Smith's *White Teeth*." *Textual Practice* 21.3 (2007): 483-504.
Brown, Judith M. *Global South Asians*. Cambridge: Cambridge UP, 2006.
Chambers, Iain. *Border Dialogues: Journeys in Postmodernity*. London: Routledge, 1990.
Dawson, Ashley. *Mongrel Nation: Diasporic Culture and the Making of Postcolonial Britain*. Ann Arbor: U of Michigan P, 2007.
Hammond, Andrew. "The Hybrid State: Hanif Kureishi and Thatcher's Britain." *Reconstructing Hybridity: Post-colonial Studies in Transition*. Ed. Joel Kuortti and Jopi Nyman. Amsterdam: Rodopi, 2007. 221-40.
Kaleta, Kenneth C. *Hanif Kureishi: Postcolonial Storyteller*. Austin: U of Texas P, 1998.
Kureishi, Hanif. *The Black Album*. New York: Scribner, 1996.
Kureishi, Hanif. "The Rainbow Sign." *Dreaming and Scheming: Reflections on Writing and Politics*. By Hanif Kureishi. London: Faber and Faber, 2002. 25-56.
Kureishi, Hanif. "The Carnival of Culture." *The Word and the Bomb*. By Hanif Kureishi. London: Faber and Faber, 2005. 95-100.
Langford, Paul. *Englishness Identified: Manners and Character 1650–1850*. Oxford: Oxford UP, 2000.
Moore-Gilbert, Bart. *Hanif Kureishi*. Manchester: Manchester UP, 2001.
McLeod, John, and David Rogers, eds. *The Revision of Englishness*. Manchester: Manchester UP, 2004.
Paxman, Jeremy. *The English: A Portrait of a People*. London: Michael Joseph, 1998.
Ranasinha, Ruvani. *Hanif Kureishi*. Tavistock: Northcote House, 2002.
Scruton, Roger. *England: An Elegy*. London: Chatto and Windus, 2000.
Stein, Mark. *Black British Literature: Novels of Transformation*. Columbus: Ohio State UP, 2004.
Thatcher, Margaret. BBC Panorama Interview. *Intercom: A Newsletter* (May 1978): 2-3.
Thomas, Susie, ed. *Hanif Kureishi*. New York: Palgrave Macmillan, 2005.
Upstone, Sara. "A Question of Black or White: Returning to Hanif Kureishi's *The Black Album*." *Postcolonial Text* 4.1 (2008): 1-24.

Author's profile: Shao-Ming Kung teaches literature at National Taiwan University. In research his interests include twentieth-century British and

US-American literature, postcolonial studies, and magical realism. His publications include the articles "Global Hybridization and Diasporic Subjects in Salman Rushdie's *The Satanic Verses*," *Tamkang Review* (2003) and "Names and Cultural Translation in Jhumpa Lahiri's *The Namesake*," *Translation Quarterly* (2009).

(Im)migration and Cultural Diasporization in Garcia's *Monkey Hunting*
Jade Tsui-yu Lee

Abstract: In her article "(Im)migration and Cultural Disporization in Garcia's *Monkey Hunting*" Jade Tsui-yu Lee examines how Chinese ethnicities have been diasporized and hybridized across time and place in literary imagination and reconsiders "home" as a provisional and contested construct. Lee analyzes the Cuban American novelist's 2003 novel *Monkey Hunting* in light of the above hypotheses. Garcia depicts diaspora experiences of a Chinese migrant, Chen Pan (inspired by the legendary Chinese monkey trickster Sun Wu-kong and his allegorical journey to the West). Garcia's text encapsulates "cut-and-mix" national, cultural, and gender identities which problematize questions of totalizing, essential authenticity, ethnicity, and origin. In its representation of Chen Pan's departure from Amoi (Xiamen, Mainland China) and his indentured servitude on a Cuban plantation and the subsequent unraveling of a four-generation family saga, *Monkey Hunting* showcases the process of "diasporization" and the re-conceptualization of home as a dwelling place.

Introduction

The millions of refugees, expatriates, and emigrants who have left their home countries in search of new opportunities in recent decades necessitate a rethinking of nationalism, thus in light of migration and diaspora conditions and experiences. In this article I examine how Chinese ethnicities have been diasporized and hybridized across time and place in literary imagination, and reconsider the concepts of "home" as a provisional, contested construct. I analyze Cuban American novelist Cristina Garcia's 2003 novel *Monkey Hunting* in light of the above hypotheses. Garcia depicts the diaspora experiences of a Chinese migrant, Chen Pan (inspired by the legendary Chinese monkey trickster Sun Wu-kong and his allegorical journey to the West). Garcia's text encapsulates "cut-and-mix" national, cultural and gender identities, which problematizes questions of totalizing, essential authenticity, ethnicity and origin. In its representation of Chen Pan's departure from Amoi (Xiamen) China and his indentured servitude on a Cuban plantation, and the subsequent unraveling of a four-generation family saga, *Monkey Hunting* showcases the process of "diasporization" and the re-conceptualization of home as a dwelling place.

Journey in/to the West

The image of "home" is by nature paradoxical — etymologically and conceptually: "Home" in old English, *ham*, is akin to the Old High German *heim* [*Heim*] and stems from the Greek for "village," "base" and "abode" (*Webster's Dictionary*); the Chinese ideogram for home portrays a pig beneath the roof of a house, connoting domestication, plenty, and a combined sense of dynamism and tranquility — juxtaposing a feeling of intensity alongside the general perception of home as a pacific locale. In this vein, as Iain Chambers notes, home should be understood as "a mobile habitat, as a mode of inhabiting time and space not as though it were a fixed and closed structure" (4). Extending Chamber's "motile" description, viewing home within a diasporic context — by definition an itinerant, unstable perspective — entails a complicated set of psychodynamic mechanisms, including forgetting and remembering of home(land), homecoming, homemaking, and desire for home. Combining these various ideas, a disaporic mapping of home is activated en route and in trajectory, with the act of "homing" (that is, "to navigate toward a point," and also "to bring or provide with a home") requiring endless negotiation and compromise, and an undoing of the points of departure and arrival. Seen in these light, "home" in diaspora, with its interrelated experiences of loss of origin and return to roots, can be redefined as "homing," a continuous search for and approximation of a "home base" in both imagination and practice.

Monkey Hunting exemplifies diasporic homing by way of travel and migration. The novel traces the migratory experiences of Chen Pan and his offspring across four generations in multiple times and places: Havana from 1857-1868, 1899, and 1917; New York in 1968; Shanghai in 1924 and 1939; and Saigon in 1969 and 1970. The stories revolve around four protagonists: Chen Pan, his son Lorenzo Chen, Pan's granddaughter Chen Fang, and Pan's great-great-grandson Domingo Chen. Spanning more than one hundred years, the novel begins in Amoy (Xiamen), China, in 1857, where the young Chen Pan signs a contract to work as an overseas field worker, believing that he will return home a rich man (the classic picture of the Chinese "sojourner" of the nineteenth century). He finds, however, that he has been deceived, and is taken into slavery in Cuba. After long, harsh labor on a Cuban plantation, Chen Pan escapes and survives alone, wandering in the jungle for years. Later, he manages to open a second-hand antique shop after he saves a count, who offers Pan financial aid and freedom in gratitude. Pan marries Lucrecia, a mulatto ex-slave, who bears him three children. Called by the natives *un chino aplatanado* — a Chinese transplant — Pan finds it easier "to be Cuban than to try to become

Chinese again" (245). In contrast, his young wife considers herself Chinese: "She was Chinese in her liver, Chinese in her heart" (138).

The book's title and epigraph allude to the Chinese myth of the Monkey King, Sun Wu-kong, who stole the Divine Empress's Peach, and was able to transform himself into a veritable army of monkey helpers. Garcia has noted that by alluding to this myth she hopes to address "the notion of immortality, how legacies get passed on from generation to generation, and how we're always beholden to our origins" (Garcia qtd. in Brown 260). Intertextually, the novel echoes Maxine Hong Kingston's 1990 novel *Tripmaster Monkey: His Fake Book*. In Kingston's novel, the fifth-generation Asian American protagonist Wittman Ah Sing, a Berkeley graduate, playwright, actor, and parody of Walt Whitman, undertakes a journey not "to" but "in" the West. Claiming himself "the present-day U.S.A. incarnation of the King of the monkeys," Ah Sing embarks on a journey seeking his cultural identity. Swinging from English and US-American canonical writers and a distinct Chinese heritage, Ah Sing attempts to find his own situatedness in San Francisco and the Bay Area. His image/imagination of self is a bricolage of Whitman singing (Wittman Ah "Sing") and Bret Hart/Mark Twain's "heathen Ah sin" (I sin/I sing). Wittman Ah Sing, the name itself a partial re-presentation and repetition in Homi Bhabha's words, a "Wittman" instead of "Whitman" and "Ah Sing" instead of "I sing in Whitman's Song of Myself," suggests the protagonist's quintessential mimicry. Through his voice Wit Man/Aaaaaieeeeee/Ah/IIIIII III/I Sing, Kingston creates a "postmodern representation of 'China man,'" which becomes "a very complex aesthetic object, many-façaded, all-inclusive, and pluralistic" (Wang 101).

If Kingston's *Tripmaster Monkey* stands for mimicry and transgression, Garcia's monkey-like protagonist is less comical, if no less critical. Centered in these Chinese-box, *mise-en-abyme* narratives is an allusion and reference to the sixteenth-century Chinese folk classic *The Journey to the West*, authored by Wu Cheng-en. Coincidentally, both novels take on the motif of an allegorical journey, stressing the Master Monkey's skills of bodily transformation and tactical adaptation into his surroundings. In Wu's account, the cunning, resourceful but irrepressible trickster Monkey accompanies a young priest along with two other disciples on a journey to "the West" (India) in order to retrieve a sacred scripture. The journey, although aiming at canonicity in its recuperation the Buddhist classics, stresses the adventures themselves. Both Kingston and Garcia draw on the allegorical journey to the West to metaphorize their protagonists' search for cultural roots. This search for roots may now be seen, however, as a given "routing." In a 2003 interview, Garcia described some of the themes in *Monkey Hunting* and other of her works: "For me, each book embroiders the themes and obsessions that drove me to write in the first place. The characters may be different, the settings and times and particulars may vary wildly but the bigger questions of where do we belong and how do we negotiate our identities between and among cultures is what keeps me going" (17). The multiple and fragmented narratives of *Monkey Hunting*, set against a rich historical backdrop, evince such struggles to negotiate identity, belonging, and the search for an abiding place or "home."

Home and cultural roots/routes

If in Wu's tale the four travelers' search can be seen as a search for legitimacy, in Kingston's and Garcia's texts the protagonists' journeys justify Wittman Ah Sing's and Chen Pan's political engagement and legitimize their voices and situational, narrative positions. Historically put, the British Emancipation Act was passed in 1833, and was followed by a six-year period of apprenticeship lasting until 1838. Slaves were emancipated in French colonies in 1848, while Dutch Caribbean slaves were freed in 1863. Slaves were freed in 1873 in Puerto Rico and in 1886 in Cuba (see Richardson 70). As a result of slave emancipation and subsequent apprenticeship, Caribbean planters in the nineteenth century were faced with a diminishing labor force. To replenish the labor shortage, indentured laborers were introduced first from India and then from China. It is estimated that between 1848 and 1874, 125,000 Chinese contract laborers were shipped to Cuba. These indentured laborers may have left their homelands with high hopes, but they found that "Once landed, they were offered for sale as though they were slaves" (Richardson 75). As Bonham C. Richardson notes, Chinese plantation workers "lived in crude housing, labored long hours, and were treated with the same rough anonymity that always had been accorded the region's black slaves" (76).

   Garcia — who has no Chinese ancestry — has shown a keen interest in exploring the history of early Chinese settlers in Cuba. Four wars serve as the backdrop of *Monkey Hunting*: The Chinese Revolution, the Cuban War of Independence, the Cultural Revolution in China, and the Vietnam War. With these historical events as background, Garcia's political aim is to highlight the lives and ambitions of Chinese Cubans. She has claimed that Chinese people have never been given appropriate credit for what they have added to Cuban life and history, including their contributions to the island's plantocracy and their roles in its War of Independence (see Garcia in Brown 260). With this in mind, various layers of historical events are interwoven into the narrative of Chen Pan's life in *Monkey Hunting*. As Chen Pan recalls, Cuban President Mario Garcia Menocal in 1917 passed a law allowing more Chinese immigrants to be introduced into Cuba during the war and the following two years, as the Cuban government predicted the rise of a lucrative sugar market. Thus Cuba again brought in boatloads of Chinese to work on the sugar fields. According to Walton Look Lai, the number the Chinese agricultural laborers imported between 1917 and 1921 in a special program reached 12,000 and another 5,000 were introduced in the 1920s and 1930s (Look Lai 17). The narrator in *Monkey Hunting* pinpoints the unfair conditions imposed on the Chinese workers, remarking, "Chen Pan knew it was only a matter of time before the Chinese no longer would be welcomed in Cuba. In times of economic necessity, they were usually the first scapegoats. This infuriated Chen Pan because thousands of chinos had fought hard for the country's independence. During the Ten Years' War they'd taken up machetes, fought under Calixto Garcia, Napoleon Arango, all the great leaders" (246).

In the novel the Chinos who participated in the war are portrayed in a heroic light. Unlike those *criollos* (Creoles) "who swelled the ranks after news of a victory and disappeared when the losses began to mount," chinos "fought everywhere in the eastern provinces … When they were captured, they pretended to speak no Spanish, but not a single one ever surrendered or betrayed the Cuban cause" (246-47). Garcia has noted that her book is "ultimately a 120-year dialogue between Cuba and Asia" (Garcia qtd. in Brown 259), and to write the book she was concerned with her ability to "do [Chen Pan's] story justice and with authenticity" (Garcia qtd. in Brown 258-9). Much to her surprise, Garcia in the course of writing discovered that nineteenth-century Cuban economy was founded and fueled by enslavement of Africans, Chinese, and others. However, the Chinese laborers' contribution has been unduly neglected and even rendered invisible: "It's disturbing how the island's vibrant culture was forged under such brutality. Now it's never far from my thoughts when I think and write about Cuba. I also was surprised to learn that the Chinese participated in the various wars for independence. They very quickly took on the nationalist cause and fought as long and hard for Cuban independence as anybody. There were many Chinese war heroes" (Garcia qtd. Brown 259-60).

Garcia's reference to the Chinos as war heroes recalls the Monkey Master's features — forced exile and obligation to obtain the scripture, initial impudence and later loyalty to his Master. The superimposition of the Monkey trickster, Chen Pan and other Chinos shows how cultural icons can be motivated, transposed, and transported even in a foreign land. In the dissemination and cross-fertilization of images of heroic warriors, dialogues between the two different worlds are made possible. Chen Pan becomes a prototype of the Chinese inhabitants residing in the Caribbean region, and settling into commercial trade. In a 1945 work, Creole writer Jean de Boissière depicted the early Chinese settlers in Trinidad as follows:

[The Chinese] came as indentured labourers, or coolies. There were no women among them so that their descendants today range from mixtures nearly pure white to nearly pure negro. Their Chinese identity was depleted, and they merged into the potpourri that is Caribbean/West Indian culture. This was not only due to the fact that there were no women of their own race that would have enabled them to maintain racial purity, but also the inadaptability of the Chinese workers to the tropical climate and agricultural working conditions of the West Indies. Because most of them had come from commercial cities on the Chinese seacoast, they were most comfortable in energetic trading environments, and less at ease in the labouring classes to which they had been transplanted. As this became apparent, planters concentrated on employing more pliable Hindus, which left the Chinese of this first wave of immigration to meld into Trinidad's mixture of class and culture. (Boissière qtd. in Look Lai 274)

Physically robust and shrewd, Chen Pan is depicted as good at farming, though also a risk-taking and sharp-witted man. On the dangerous sea voyage to the Americas and living in the harsh conditions of plantation life he proves himself eminently adaptable. Most of the Chinese countrymen working on Cuban plantations were farmers at home as well and they suffer from homesickness and the nostalgia for the land in which they had enjoyed the "quiet pleasure of working the soil" (81). Chen Pan, the son of a failed poet, is different and has since childhood been interested in poetry. Chen Pan prefers books to the hoe, which suits him for work in Havana as a trader, and ultimately he is "most grateful to Cuba" that he is able "to be freed, at last, from the harsh cycles of the land" (81). Metaphorically, what Chen Pan brought from China is a seed for new cultural cultivation, and his marriage to a pregnant mulatto slave, considered a mad impulse by the other Chinese, advances his fusion with Caribbean life. Little by little, he acquires the skills needed to survive his many trials: the brutality of life on the plantations, his lone excursion into the forest where he fights his mother's haunting curse, the battles against the Spaniards, and finally the daily routines running a second-hand antique shop in Havana. He has found a home for himself in Havana and although he "never understood what the sight of Havana, with its seductive curve of coast, stirred in him," he knew that "from the moment he arrived, he knew it was where he belonged" (62) and thus is former Chinese life fades away. In an interview, Scott Shibuya Brown asked Garcia whether Chen Pan is "a Chinese man in Cuba, a Chinese-Cuban, or ... simply part of the mix of Cuban people" in (Brown 261). Garcia answered, "At the end of the book, Chen Pan talks about belonging neither to China nor to Cuba entirely. He's lost most of his Chinese and yet his Spanish is still quite fractured and heavily accented. He belongs somewhere between both worlds, but probably a little closer to Cuba. In the end, I think he gave his heart to Cuba (partly through the love of his wife) and that's where his legacy remains" (Garcia qtd. in Brown 262). With connections to both worlds, Chen Pan fashions a hybrid identity, the realization of homing desires and his negotiations with different cultural sources and actors. In his continuous negotiation and affirmation of diasporic identities:

After the cane was cut and ground, the days were filled with lesser tasks — repairing tools, weeding the dormant fields, reseeding them in the intervals between the rains. A few Chinese adopted Spanish names, cut off their queues, [long braided hair] adapted their palates to the local food. They took the names of wealthy Cubans, hoping to achieve the same prosperity. Yu Ming-hsing became Esteban Sarinana. Li Chao-Chun renamed himself Perfecto Diaz and slicked his hair back with perfumed oil. Thickheaded Kuo Chan insisted on being called Juan-Juan Capote. "Why Juan-Juan?" Chen Pan asked him, to which he replied, "Twice as much luck." (36)

Like most Chinese workers, Chen Pan cuts off his queue upon his arrival on the plantation, tries hard to learn Spanish although in the beginning the language is incomprehensible to him: "Spanish sounded like so much noise to him. Firecrackers set off on New Year's Day. There was no bend in the sounds, no ups or downs, just rat-tat-tat-tat-tat. Like that. Tra-ba-jo, tra-ba-jo" (26). He also endeavors to imitate the manners and language of the locals. Homi Bhabha's concept of "colonial mimicry" explains why Chen Pan's personal struggle is characteristic of a transcultural encounter. His desire for "a reformed, recognized other" makes him a subject in a dominating "partial re-presentation" which is "almost the same" but "never quite white" (Bhabha 85). The result of such partially successful mimicry is ambivalence toward the dominant power.

Although submissive to the oppressors, Chen Pan and other slave workers have deep hatred for the overseers who whip them for "any small wrong — if they slowed down or spoke their own language or dared to protest" (27). Chen Pan finds the coerced silence particularly insufferable and he finds psychological shelter in an imagined landscape of the island: "No matter that he was stuck on this devil island surrounded by mangroves and flesh hungry sharks, that his arm often dropped in mid-swing from pure exhaustion. He imagined the breezes as fresh breaths from the sea, coaxing boats along the horizon, their sails puffed up and purposeful" (28). He does not find solace in memories of his father but in the breeze from the sea in which he finds the consoling power to alleviate his misery — a home to be. The conception of home is thus given a volatility, accentuated by the characters' dismissal of cultural/bloodline purity, their long search for belongingness, and their homing instinct.

The continuous search for home can be explicated with Stuart Hall's remarks about African Americans: "This is our 'long journey' home … These symbolic journeys are necessary for us all – and necessarily circular. This is the Africa we must return to — but 'by another route': what Africa has become in the new World, what we have made of 'Africa': 'Africa' as we retell it through politics, memory, and desire" ("Cultural Identity and Diaspora" 242). In *Monkey Hunting*, Domingo, the fourth- generation of Chen Pan's family, is a Mulatto of Chinese and African ancestry. Born in Cuba with a Chinese look, he migrates to New York with his "Papi," a revolutionary activist who has been sent to a psychiatric hospital because of his refusal to help with the intelligence agencies. He later commits suicide by flinging himself in front of a southbound train (southward and homeward, symbolically). Respect to dead ancestors has become his ingrained belief, as Domingo has been told by his father that neglect of ancestors is the worst sin (106). Carrying the spectacles of Chen Pan, his great-grandfather, as a charm, Domingo has inherited his ancestor's characteristics and becomes a warrior. Although a Cuban native, Domingo joins the U.S. army and is sent to Vietnam. Ironically, his Asian outlook often disturbs his comrades, but it is also a good camouflage in the Vietnamese jungles. He claims to have been attacked by a group of albino monkeys in the jungle, his jacket stripped from him, and his rifle stolen, although miraculously the pair of spectacles owned by Chen Pan (metaphorically, Chen Pan's prospects and legacies) are intact. His stories are not believed by his commanding officer, as the so-called "white" monkeys are nowhere to be found. His encounter with the "white monkeys" may have been a fantasy; but his wounds nevertheless are real and have left a "tattoo" scarred on his shoulder. Afterwards, he falls in love with a Vietnamese prostitute, Tham Thanh Lan, whose body reminds him of the Cuba he remembers as a young boy, as if it "stored everything its flesh" (162). Metaphorically, Domingo finds a home in Tham Thanh Lan's serene body, which echoes the title of the novel's second part: traveling with the flesh. A "reincarnated" home is thus materialized in Domingo's circular migration and in the doing and undoing of a home base, and reactivated in the sense of the trajectory, the detour and the approximation of a home.

Toward the end of the story, when Chen Pan looks back on his lifetime, he has the following reflections on the question of his own identity: "After so many years in Cuba, Chen Pan had forgotten much of his Chinese. He mixed his talk with words from here and words from there until he spoke no true language at all. There were only a few people left in Havana with whom he could comfortably communicate. Long ago he'd lived in China, known all its customs and manners. How useless these had been outside their own geography! Still, it was easier for him to be Cuban than to try to become Chinese again" (245). This is perhaps not an "either-or" but a "both-and" statement. Garcia's novel exemplifies a "contact zone" proposed by Mary Louise Pratt in her *Imperial Eyes: Travel Writing and Transculturation* where she examines European travel writing since 1750. Pratt contends that a "contact zone" occurs as a space of encounters where "disparate cultures meet, clash and grapple with each other, often in highly asymmetrical relations of domination and subordination" (4). According to Pratt, the contact zone is the social place where subjects are constituted in and by their relations to each other which is often characterized by asymmetrical relations of power, and the relations include "copresence, interaction, interlocking understandings and practices" (7). It seems also apt to refer to Pratt's use of "transculturation," a term she adopts from the Cuban sociologist Fernando Ortiz, suggesting the phenomenon in which how "subordinated or marginal groups select and invent from materials transmitted to them by a dominant or metropolitan culture" (6). Transculturation is a phenomenon of the contact zone, as Pratt argues, in which one culture enhances its own group by borrowing or inventing materials from the dominant group.

Chen Pan's tale not only reveals the above suggested "contact" perspective and a prototype of transculturation, but also exemplifies how the "Western" eyes construct and shape the subordinated others. Garcia herself admits that "it was extremely difficult" to write about Chinese history and Chinese characters (Garcia qtd. in Brown 258). Having no Chinese background and no prior knowledge, Garcia had to work hard to familiarize herself with Chinese history, culture, and poetry before she began to write. While writing, she tried "to enter the bloodstream of Chen Pan to know him slowly and painfully but ultimately in a deep and satisfying way" (Garcia qtd. in Brown 258). Garcia often questions herself with authenticity or whether she has done Chen Pan's story justice (Garcia qtd. in Brown 258-59). After she finished the manuscript, she consulted "several experts just to make sure [she'd] gotten it right" (Garcia qtd. in Brown 259). Even so, arguably, many passages in the novel can be questioned about their authenticity from the readers' viewpoints. For instance, in the prologue in which Garcia describes Chen Pan's life in China before his ship voyage, he is described to be invited for having tea which "was hot and heavily sugared" (4). Considering that the setting is Amoy in Southern China, it is quite unusual for people living in the area to have tea with sugar, something not common there. It is also hard to imagine that a poverty stricken area such as Amoy in the mid-nineteenth century would take sugar, a luxury, into tea drinking. Later on, when the sea voyage is introduced, it is described that "the men got beef jerky and rice gruel to eat" (9). Again, as is known, beef jerky is not commonly found in southern Chinese food preparation, as water buffalos were (and still are in some cases) considered an important livestock in helping the fieldwork. In southern Chinese cuisine, beef dishes were only developed more recently in the twentieth century. Instead of beef, perhaps marinated pork jerky or salted fish have been more known dishes for long preservation. In addition, another episode that is particularly intriguing is how Chen Pan's mother is described. The narrator notes that "Chen Pan's mother ridiculed her husband as she hobbled from room to room on her lotus feet ... Chen Pan's mother was from a family of well-to-do farmers, and far from beautiful. She knew little poetry, but used to repeat the same line to nettle her improvident husband: Poets mostly starve to death embracing empty mountains" (11). Conventionally, Chinese women would have their feet bound to meet the required custom, especially those from well-to-do families. However, farmers and the poor would generally ignore the practice as they need helping hands including male and female children. Hence, Chen Pan's mother becomes a mystery as she is described to come from a well-to-do family and thus with bound feet. However, she is also said to be ignorant and rustic which make her bound feet improbable.

The above examples encapsulate the reinvention of "China," "Cuba," and "America" by a Cuban writer who implements processes of transculturation. To a large extent, Garcia's novel recalls also the award-winning novel written by the Chinese American novelist Shawn Wong, *Homebase*. The 1979 novel recounts the history of four generations of a Chinese American family. The novel's protagonist, Rainsford Chan, a fourth-generation Chinese growing up in the 1950s and 1960s, who "interacts" to tell the family's history with his ancestors who helped build the U.S. by constructing the railroad and sometimes his ancestors appear as narrators. In *Monkey Hunting* and *Homebase* the identity of the cultural group is hybridized and loaded with various cultural layers. In this respect, both novels correspond to Hall's concept of diasporization. Hall comments that "The diaspora experience as I intend it here is defined, not by essence or purity, but by the recognition of a necessary heterogeneity and diversity; by a conception of 'identity' which lives with and through, not despite, difference; by hybridity. Diaspora identities are those which are constantly producing and reproducing themselves anew, through transformation and difference" ("Cultural Identity and Diaspora" 244). The characters in *Monkey Hunting* demonstrate the experience of diaspora as "the process of unsettling, recombination, hybridization and 'cut-and-mix' — in short, the process of cultural diaspora-ization" (Hall, "New Ethnicities" 447).

In the article at hand I reconsider the conception of home in terms of trajectories of (im)migration, overlapping, and border-crossing and examine diasporic experiences represented as hybridized, ever-evolving processes. Amid the cross-fertilization of diasporic roots/routes, the (im)migrant groups are able to map out a "home base," however transient and provisional, which provides them with sources of comfort and life energies, and most importantly, act as a relay station in their (im)migrant landscapes. Again, to borrow from Hall, one can argue that the Chinese (im)migrants are the "product of a diasporic consciousness, that is, the product of several interlocking histories and cultures, belonging at the same time to several 'homes' — and thus to no particular home" ("Culture, Community, Nation" 362).

Works Cited

Bhabha, Homi. "Of Mimicry and Man: The Ambivalence of Colonial Discourse." *The Location of Culture*. By Homi Bhabha. London: Routledge, 1994. 85-92.

Brown, Scott Shibuya. "A Conversation with Cristina Garcia." *Monkey Hunting*. By Cristina Garcia. New York: Ballantine Books, 2004. 257-66.

Chambers, Iain. *Migrancy, Culture, Identity*. London: Routledge, 1995.

Garcia, Cristina. *Monkey Hunting*. New York: Ballantine Books, 2003.

Garcia, Cristina. "Interview: Cristina Garcia's Search for Origins." *Criticas* 3 (2003): 10-17.

Hall, Stuart. "New Ethnicities." *Stuart Hall: Critical Dialogues in Cultural Studies*. Ed. David Morley and Kuan-Hsing Chen. London: Routledge, 1996. 441-49.

Hall, Stuart. "Culture, Community, Nation" *Cultural Studies* 7.3 (1993): 349-63.

Hall, Stuart. "Cultural Identity and Diaspora." *Theorizing Diaspora*, Ed. Jana Evans Braziel and Anita Mannur. Malden: Blackwell, 2006. 233-46.

Kingston, Maxine Hone. *Tripmaster Monkey: His Fake Book*. New York: Vintage, 1990.

Look Lai, Walton. *The Chinese in the West Indies. 1806-1995: A Documentary History*. Kingston: UP of West Indies, 1998.

Pratt, May Louise. *Imperial Eyes: Travel Writing and Transculturation*. London & New York: Routledge, 1998.

Richardson, Bonham C. *The Caribbean in the Wider World, 1492-1992*. New York: Cambridge UP, 1992.

Wang, Jennie. "Tripmaster Monkey: Kingston's Postmodern Representation of a New 'China Man'." *MELUS: The Society for the Study of the Multi-Ethnic Literature of the United States* 20.1 (1995): 101-14.

Wong, Shwan. *Homebase*. Oakland: Bookpeople, 1979.

Author's profile: Jade Tsui-yu Lee teaches English and US-American literature at National Kaohsiung Normal University where she is also director for the Program in International Cooperation. Her interests in research include postcolonial fiction, cultural studies, and ethnic studies and her recent publications include "Transcultural Hospitality: Transactions with the Alien in Brian Castro's *Birds of Passage* and *After China*," *ChungWai Literary Monthly* (2006) and "A Moveable Feast": Life Writings/Narrations in Monique Truong's *The Book of Salt*," *Review of English and American Literature* (2009).

Documentary Photography of the Internment of Japanese Americans
Hsiu-chuan Lee

Abstract: In his article "Documentary Photography of the Internment of Japanese Americans" Hsiu-chuan Lee presents a re-reading of popular documentary photography on the Japanese American internment. Through an analysis of Ansel Adams's Manzanar photographic collection, *Born Free and Equal* (1944) and Carl Mydans's photography for *Life* magazine's 1944 feature article on the Tule Lake Relocation Center, Lee reads the internment as an event through which U.S. domesticity and the country's complicated politics and times are played out. Although Adams and Mydans participated through their photographic projects in U.S. nationalist discourse, their pictorial narrative evokes unwanted memories in our understanding of U.S. wartime politics. Thus, a re-reading of the pictorial history of the internment serves as a converging point of nationalist discourse of control and localized stories of ambivalence located between the historical continuity pursued by a nation-state and the individual times of differences and excess.

Introduction

While the Japanese American wartime experience has been recognized as one single historical event that has engaged perhaps the most critical attention in the past three decades of Asian American Studies, intriguing is that little attention has been paid to what this event means to the imagination of the U.S. as a nation. More precisely, whereas the constituting force of the Japanese American displacement and incarceration during the war in the making of Asian American history — in particular Japanese American history — has been made obvious, this history of internment, when put back to the national scene is usually dismissed either as a wartime anomaly of U.S. history or as a test stone in the linear development of US-American multicultural democracy. In *An Absent Presence: Japanese Americans in Postwar American Culture, 1945-1960* Caroline Chung Simpson uses the phrase "absent presence" to describe the paradox existing in the representational history of Japanese American internment experiences (2). The phrase "absent presence" was coined originally by Marita Sturken in her article "Absent Image of Memory: Remembering and Reenacting the Japanese Internment" where she conceptualizes it as a strategy for Japanese Americans to produce counter memories despite the governmental control of the wartime historiography. Sturken explores Japanese American efforts to generate presence out of absence: despite the lack of image icons of the internment, one remembers by bringing back the seemingly trivial and fragmentary living traces of the internment by tackling the intervals of the official narrative, hence reenacting memories out of their absence. In turn, Simpson calls our attention to another twist implied by the idea of the concept, namely not that we have to bring what is absent into presence, but that what appears to be present could be tamed and robbed of affective power. Presence could as such perpetuate a more profound level of absence. It should be noted here that few photographs about the internment were circulated during the war. First, cameras were listed along with knives and guns as contraband, forbidden in internment. Although some Japanese American internees, most notably Toyo Miyatake, did manage to produce underground photographic images, these pictures were not published until after the war. Moreover, even the photographs commissioned by the federal government for official reports and propaganda were allowed little public presence. For example, in the cases of Dorothea Lange and Clem Albers — who worked with the War Relocation Authority (WRA) — from the 107 photographs by Albers few were published (Robinson 35) while Lange's 691 photographs for the WRA were banned from circulation during the war (Robinson 41; Gordon and Okihiro 5-6).

The event and history of the Japanese American internment is often articulated within a general but dominant discourse and its traumatic effect is thus pacified and buried and because of this situation is that I postulate that it is of importance not only to remember and to analyze what happened during the internment, but to consider the form and the socio-political repercussions of the event itself and its memory. Here, I undertake a re-reading of the pictorial representations of internment in the photography of Ansel Adams in his Manzanar photographic collection, *Born Free and Equal* (1944) and in Carl Mydans's photography for *Life* magazine's 1944 feature article on the Tule Lake Relocation Center. I study Adams's and Mydans's photographic works not only because both photographers were white civilians involved in the task of representing the internment but also because their works are among the few of their kind with some public circulation when the war was still on. While most studies on Japanese American internment understand this historical trauma as belonging exclusively to Japanese Americans (or Asian Americans as a pan-ethnic group), Adams's and Mydans's internment projects sheds light on white people's personal involvement and emotional investments in the Japanese American wartime experiences. Moreover, the images captured, as well as the narrative framework invented in their photographic essays spell out both the popular discursive strategy and the feelings of the U.S. public vis-à-vis the internment policy.

I bring to the fore in my discussion below the trope of time partly because Adams's and Mydans's photographic works are in one way or another engaged with the issue of temporalities and, more importantly, because both attempt history making as negotiation with their time. The central role time plays in the imagination of a nation is evident in contemporary theories on nation and modernity. For one thing, the myth of modern nation is built upon an imaginary simultaneity shared by nationals inhabiting different places and classes (see, e.g. Anderson) and for another, the construction of a national history demands the elimination of distracting memories and unwanted pasts. And to repress certain memories is to repress times, as memories usually provide the shortcuts to other temporalities as well as alternative arrangements of times. In effect, if memory could be taken as a useful "method" in history-writing, it is because memories evoke the drama of times (I take the concept of "memory as method" from T. Fujitani's, Geoffrey M. White's, and Lisa Yoneyama's introduction to *Perilous Memories: The Asia-Pacific War[s]*). This conception about the play of different times that disturb the temporal homogeneity of the imagined nation could become even more visible and concrete when the acts of immigration bring about not only the encountering of people from different time zones on the globe but also the cultural exchanges and conflicts that generate, to borrow from Homi Bhabha, the "ghostly," the "double and split" time that a national history usually tries to but can hardly surmount (295).

When Bhabha theorizes the complex time of a nation in "DissemiNation: Time, Narrative and the Margins of the Modern Nation," he has in his mind the Freudian theory of the unconscious and the uncanny. I argue that the emergence of the uncanny temporalities from the US-American national unconscious, usually assuming the form of cultural and racial doubles, is staged in the popular documentary photography of the Japanese American internment. What appears as the "absent presence" of Japanese American wartime images may, under close inspection, turn out to bearing witness to the "ghostly presence" of the unwanted memories and alternative times that are integral to the US-American national symbolic.

Ansel Adams's *Born Free and Equal*

Among the white photographers involved in photographing the

internment, Adams remains one of the most controversial. His career rose when he put on his first solo museum exhibition at the Smithsonian Institution in 1931, in 1933 he opened his own art and photography gallery in San Francisco, in 1936 he had a solo show at the Stieglitz gallery *An American Place* in New York, in 1939 he became an editor of *U.S. Camera* (the most popular photography magazine at the time), and in 1941 worked with the U.S. Department of the Interior to make photographs of National Parks, Indian reservations, and other locations for public decorations (see, e.g., please Alinder). Adams entered Manzanar in the Fall of 1943 to undertake a photographic project at his own expenses. He explained his reason of declining sponsorship in the foreword to the 1944 version of *Born Free and Equal*: "I have intentionally avoided the sponsorship of governmental or civil organizations, not because I have doubts of their sincerity and effectiveness, but because I wish to make this work a strictly personal concept and expression" (13). His insistence on individual creative freedom is nonetheless undermined by the fact that he was allowed to photograph Manzanar because of his personal acquaintance with Ralph Merritt, the Manzanar camp director, who gave Adams the permission to photograph under the condition that he followed closely the three official restrictions in his work: "no barbed wire, no armed guard, and no guard towers" (Merritt qtd. in Creef 18). The ambivalence of Adams's work is also testified by the divergent receptions of his work. Adams was the only photographer of the internment whose photographs made to an exhibition at the basement gallery of the Museum of Modern Art in New York in 1944, when the war still raged on; he was also able to publish a photographic collection, *Born Free and Equal* owing to his affiliation with *U.S. Camera.* The exhibition, however, encountered harsh criticism and copies were even "burned by self-proclaimed patriots" (Robinson 27). In her article detailing the publication history of *Born Free and Equal*, Sue Kunitomi Embery mentions the unsubstantiated rumor about the censorship on Adams's photographic collection: "a rumor circulated. The book hadn't sold at all. They were pulled from the shelves by the federal agency that had approved the book for publication in the first place" (24). Yet, while his work was criticized by many from the mainstream society as "disloyal to the war effort" (Benti 123), a report indicates that the Office of War Information asked Adams for permission to use his photos to show "American kindness ... urgently requested from the Pacific outposts to combat Japanese propaganda which claims our behavior is monstrous" (Adams qtd. in Gordon 34).

A similar ambivalence is evident in Japanese Americans'

reception of Adams's work. Embery I refer to above, a former Manzanar internee and Emerita of the Manzanar National Historical Site Advisory Commission, was excited upon seeing the publication of a photographic book on the internment in 1944 and quickly bought "a couple of copies": "It was so exciting. Our story was finally being told, by a celebrated photographer no less" (24). This celebration of Adams's contribution to bringing Japanese American internment history to the public attention, however, has for long been counteracted by many critics' realization of Adams's at most compromised efforts in representing the internment: his compliance to the "no barbed wire, no armed guard, and no guard towers" regulations, as well as his euphemistic representations of the internment as "humane, orderly, and even beneficial" to Japanese Americans' ultimate assimilation into the US mainstream society (see Davidov 233). Certainly, much debate has derived from the self-contradictory nature of Adams's photographic essay. On the one hand, Adams was "sympathetic" to "the Japanese American people" (Miyatake 20). On the other hand, however, whatever protests might have been implied in his work, they are largely muffled and deferred by his recurrent reference to the "good administration of the Center by the WRA," and as well to "the basic character of the people" (Adams 57). Judith Fryer Davidov criticizes Adams for capturing in stills only "the accommodationist Nisei" (233) and Elena Tajima Creef argues that Adams tried to de-Orientalize Japanese Americans and fashioned them into "unambiguous all-American citizen subjects" and "docile American bodies" (19, 22). Moreover, reiterating that relocation was "only a rocky wartime detour on the road of American citizenship" (Adams 37), Adams downplayed the element of the racial oppression inherent in the internment policy. Other critics accuse Adams of bringing his personal worship of natural landscape into his Manzanar photographs: instead of presenting the barrenness and impoverishment of the desert land Japanese Americans were relocated to, he romanticized the relationship between the land and the internees (on this, see, for example, John Streamas's comparison of Toyo Suyemoto's poetic rendition of the landscape of relocation camps and Adams's photographic representations. Streamas argues that Adams projected "his own awe and wonder [toward natural landscape] onto the inmates of Manzanar" [51]). And Linda Gordon links the Manzanar project to Adams's own frustrated patriotism during the war: "he was disappointed not to be able to enlist; he would have done so, he wrote [in his autobiography], but was not offered a job appropriate to his skills, and could not 'carry a gun to the Japs because they tell us we are over thirty-eight'" (34). Cast in this light, Adams's Manzanar project has something to do with his personal unfulfilled desire. An oblique analogy between the photographer and the photographed subjects could be attempted: did Adams not find in his Manzanar project his own "detour" to US-American identity, while claiming that the internment was "a detour" for Japanese Americans to attain their American citizenship?

Probing into the divergent critical opinions about Adams's internment photographs, I do not intend here in the least to determine, or fix, the meaning of Adams's photographic images. Rather, Adams's works are indeterminate in meaning precisely in that they were produced out of crisscrossing narrative requirements and temporal interpellations. They were products of the U.S. situation caught in a moment of historical ambiguity and national ambivalence: the nation's international image as an upholder of democratic liberalism did not coincide with the racist anxiety permeating its domestic spheres; its proclamation on civil rights was in conflict with its wartime internment policy; its insistence on national unity was challenged by the existence of differences along the lines of race, ethnicity, class, geographical location, etc.; and its pursuit of nationalist synchronicity was complicated by the multiplicity of immigrant times, ethnic histories, and everyday individual temporalities. To add to these ideological and temporal divergences was also Adams's own sense of being left behind in time in U.S. wartime patriotism, that is, the fact he was too old to enlist in the army when the war broke. Clearly, he had to do something for the war in compensation for his inability to join in the national armed force. Wynne Benti reports in his "publisher's note" to the 2002 republishing of *Born Free and Equal* that at "the onset of the war, Adams was told by the [*U.S. Camera*] magazine's publisher, Tom Maloney, that nature photographs were inappropriate during wartime" (124). Thus, a landscape photographer, Adams changed his photographic subject and focused primarily on portraits in his Manzanar photographic project largely because he had to catch up with the U.S. national time.

Partly as a reaction to the anxiety brought about by the wartime disjointed temporalities, Adams made an obvious effort to screen his Manzanar images away from specific historical contexts and times. For one thing, a quick glance through his close-up portraits such as "Catherine Natsuko Yamaguchi, nurse," "Sam Bozono, policeman," "Private Margaret Fukuoka, W.A.C."; etc. (see Figures 1, 2, 3), one would notice that Adams presented intentionally the internees not in terms of their immigrant backgrounds and ethnic identities but as productive individuals and loyal citizens known through their professions. Capturing most of these figures in uniform, Adams allowed the clothes to signify more than the racial bodies. Besides, Adams's preference of shooting individual close-ups against the sky or unspecified white backgrounds rather than taking group pictures with clear indication of material contexts of the camp barracks testifies to his attempt to strip the photographic images of immigrant times and the realities of the internment. This point is reinforced by Adams's statement about the goal of his photographic project: "This book in no way attempts a sociological analysis of the people and their problem. It is addressed to the average American citizen, and is conceived on a human, emotional basis, accenting the realities of the individual and his environment rather than considering the loyal Japanese Americans as an abstract, amorphous, minority group" (Adams 13). Upholding universal humanism over racial differences, Adams managed to take each Japanese American subject as an average US-American citizen, an individual free from his/her ethnic past and racial memories, hence assimilated to an imagined national identity.

Adams's attempt to negotiate disparate times is also visible in his invocation of the permanence of landscape to displace conflicting temporal experiences characteristic of wartime U.S. Expressing his interest in recording "the influence of the tremendous landscape in Inyo on the life and spirit of thousands of people living by force of circumstance in the Relocation Center of Manzanar," Adams indicated in his essay that "the huge vistas and the stern realities of sun and wind and space symbolize the immensity and opportunity of America — perhaps a vital reassurance following the experiences of enforced exodus" (13). In the section entitled "The Land," he further dwelled on the position of Sierra Nevada as transcending any form of arbitrary division of land and people enacted by humans: "maps and surveys establish arbitrary boundaries — but the spirit of this valley is not encompassed by such definite restrictions" (31).

In addition to appealing to nature's transcending power that fosters the oneness and continuity of the nation, Adams also resorted to the technological capacity of camera to snap temporal flows into carefully framed and hence more manageable instants. This emphasis on the instant is obvious, for example, in his narrative description of one photograph on "Manzanar Free Press" (Figure 4): "Early on a bright, cold, autumn morning, I remember Roy Takeno, Yuichi Hirata, his business manager (also relocated), and a staff member, standing in the sun before the Office of Reports and reading a Los Angeles paper just in by stage from the Southland. The moment was impressive; the clean, light, crisp air, the eternal mountain, and the transitory shacks, people of human creative quality avid for news and opinion of the great world in which they rightfully belong" (Adams 64). In this passage Adams not only reiterated the "eternal mountain" vs. "transitory shacks" theme but further brought into relief an "impressive" moment of seeming national simultaneity, the moment a few internees read a Los Angeles newspaper together under the office sign of *Manzanar Free Press*, a sign rich in symbolic meaning. Yet, a closer reading of the narrative description would compel one to notice that Adams had jumped too quickly to the conclusion about national simultaneity implied in this photographic image. That the newspaper had to come "by stage from the Southland" points to the fact that newspapers are not as accessible to the internees as one would like to expect following Adams's line of thinking. While Adams tried to present Manzanar as an integrated part of the U.S. national community in his distilled photographic moment, one cannot help but seeing the displacement of Japanese Americans, their exile into a place and existence disparate from what was expected to be a unified national space.

Despite Adams's attempt to replace time with neat instants of framed photographic images, obvious is that he had no complete control over his images and narratives; neither had him control over the way how his pictures and narratives would be perceived. He wanted to capture moments in the guise of normality, but the viewers would keep seeing the intervals, the slips, and gaps in-between the moments, the hybrid times constituting wartime U.S. In addition to the example above, Gerald Robinson points out that "a high camera angle" among Adams's work "betrays the existence of elevated guard towers that were not permitted to be photographed," "most of the middle range images" show "the shabby background of tar-paper covered barracks," and although the interiors may appear as normal and even cozy at first sight, careful viewers notice the "dangling light fixtures, crude walls, and home-made furniture, as well as the overwhelming feeling of temporariness" (30). Moreover, whereas Adams attempted to portray Manzanar, in his own words, as one of the miniature of "an average American metropolis," the fact that one has to pass through "solider-guarded gates" in order to enter Manzanar (37) reveals the relocation camp as a differentiated space segregated from normal domesticity. Further, an intriguing temporal structure plays out in the photographic image with which Adams attempted to show that

"Manzanar is only a detour on the road to American citizenship" (Figure 5). By presenting young internees in school uniforms holding books and walking in small groups away from the camp barracks into the foreground of the picture, Adams in a way stages through his photograph a tripartite past-present-future scenario: the relocation history embodied by the barracks is pushed to the background of the photograph and hence reduced — symbolically — into part of the national past; the walking internees then feature the present in a teleological movement towards the future of US-American citizenship, which, although remaining an abstract idea and invisible in the picture, is supposed to lay beyond the photographical frame. Yet, as one would notice, it is only within the photographic frame that these young internees appeared to walk away from the barracks. This specific photo actually captured an instant when the internees were moving inside the spaciousness of the relocation camp. They were walking between, rather than beyond, barracks. Besides, the urban manner of the internees — their citified outfits and hairstyle — rendered them as incongruent subjects in the expanses of the desert. Connoting a sense of dislocation of the subjects, the picture presents an image of spatial and temporal ambiguity. While Adams might have intended to weave the inconsistence and the ambiguity into a progressive national temporal narrative, the picture in one way or another commemorates, ironically, a detour in time and space: it records in image a space and time that remains difficult to be incorporated into the U.S. national symbolic.

Carl Mydans's *Life* report on Tule Lake

In 1944, *Life Magazine*, one of the most popular magazines noted for photojournalism in the United States during the period, published a feature article on the Tule Lake Relocation Center. Claimed by its editors to be "the first of its kind" (25), a publication like this was anticipated to set the tone of the US-American imaginary of internment. The problematics of the narration revealed by it were tellingly symptomatic of the general US-American take of this specific event. At first sight, the *Life* report adopts the framework of nationalist discourse. Choosing to document the infamous Tule Lake Relocation Center, the most notorious of internment camps as it housed those reportedly most resistant to the nation's internment policy, the *Life* editors predicated the introductory section of the article on the division of loyalty/disloyalty. The first headline of this eleven-full page pictorial report reads: "At this Segregation Center Are 18,000 Japanese Considered Disloyal to U.S." (25), bearing interesting echo to the subtitle of Adams's book, *Born Free and Equal: The Story of Loyal Japanese Americans*. While Adams tried to capture in stills the Japanese American internees as submissive and assimilated individuals, the *Life* article depicted mostly the disloyal "trouble-makers" as the "segregees" of the nation (25, 34). To be noticed is that both publications followed a war-time logic that insisted on a clear-cut binary division between "loyal (Japanese) Americans" and "disloyal Japanese," to prevent any blurring of those associated with Japan and those paying allegiance to the U.S. Although approaching the internment from seemingly opposite directions, the two publications in a way shared a very similar politico-historical agenda: as Adams justified the internment as it offered a way, albeit a "detour," for the loyal to achieve their US-American citizenship, the *Life* report also found the internment justifiable by pointing to certain Japanese subjects as "disloyal." Both brought the issue of the internment into the presence of the U.S. public, but only for smoothing over what appeared to be a wartime anomaly.

However, just as my above analysis of Adams's work exposes the ambivalence his project and the ambiguity of individual photographic images, a close investigation of the photographs by the magazine's staff photographer Carl Mydans and the captions attached to them reveals that the *Life* report could not be as stable and discursively constraining as it appears at first sight. In *Absent Presence*, Simpson also points to the ambiguities and contradictory meanings of the report (Simpson is to date the only one have provided a lengthy discussion of the *Life* article). Reading the report as marking an "inaugural" moment of the "nation's engagement with the question of Japanese American identity" that was to come in the immediate postwar years, Simpson points to the article's "harbinger" position in advancing the "disturbing effects" of the nation's attempted discursive incorporation of the internment (9). On the one hand, the *Life* article focused on the "pressure boys," the Japanese Americans refusing to swear allegiance to the U.S. government during the war as posing a menace to the nation and thus the justification for the internment. On the other hand, the article also tried to illustrate the "functional, normal aspects of the camp life," in a way to subsume the story of the U.S. domestic racism within the democratic and humanitarian image of the nation in the postwar international context (9). Although Simpson does not emphasize the issue of temporality specifically, implied in her discussion is that the *Life* report was produced at the juncture of times: U.S. domestic racism in wartime and the postwar time of U.S. international humanitarianism. Curiously enough, whereas Adams tended to depersonalize Japanese internees by transforming them into national subjects void of immigrant histories and a racial identity, a tendency of Mydans's photographs is to introduce detailed personal information in long explanatory captions. Frequently, it is through the long captions that we read personal stories that disrupt the discursive framework that the report as a whole seems to assume. For example, despite the demand to portray "disloyal Japanese," the family photo of the Manjis is ambiguous in terms of this dichotomy of loyalty/disloyalty (see Figure 6). Instead of presenting images of threatening Japanese, the photograph presents an image of a harmonious family, except for the fact that the nine members of the family are crowded into a small corner of their barrack in the internment camp; the four Nisei daughters are working and laughing at what appears to be a dining table; the three boys sit on the floor, reading quietly; the Issei mother and father sit at the corner, one reading a quarto newspaper or magazine and the other absorbed in thought. The caption to the picture begins by reiterating the loyalty/disloyalty theme of the report: "The Manji family, in their Tule Lake apartment, are all classed as disloyal" (28). It nonetheless does not proceed to narrate any concrete "crimes" committed by the Manjis; instead, the caption digresses into introducing each family member: the Issei father and mother came from Japan to the U.S., where the father became a "rice farmer." Also, the caption mentions that "the children are all U.S. citizens," in spite of the fact that this piece of information is incongruent with the theme of disloyalty. And as if intending to make the indictment of the Manjis as "disloyal" even more self-contradictory, the caption reveals that two more Manji children, who are not physically present in the photo — yet whose images are shown in the photographs on the bookshelf, are "in the U.S. Army" (28). After looking at the picture and reading the caption, one may wonder why on earth the Manjis were "considered disloyal" except — perhaps — that the parents were originally from Japan. All the bits and pieces of seemingly trivial and harmless information provided by the caption expose dramatically the racist implication of the internment policy.

The second difference between Mydans and Adams lies in their different ways of presenting time in their photographic images. As mentioned earlier, Adams usually rid his images of specific racial context and community background. Usually shot against an empty space (or a piece of sky, an unidentified landscape, etc.), the subjects are taken out of time. Or, if there is a temporal dimension implied in Adams's work, it must be a time pointing toward a teleological future of attaining U.S. citizenship — an imaginary time embedded in the scenario of the "American dream." In contrast to Adams's intention to present his subject out of temporal complexities, the captions attached to Mydans's photographs bring in personal pasts and immigrant times. For example, the caption to the Manji family photo specifies that the Issei father "came to the US from Yamaguchi, Japan, in 1904"; he "became a rice farmer in Nelson, Calif., where he and his family were living when war came" and his wife "arrived here in 1918" (28). Details like these place our understanding of the immigrant family into past time. They provide the historical depth to show that the Manjis, instead of being racial others or alien enemies coming from nowhere, were just human beings going through immigrant processes and, like most US-Americans, chose to build a family of their own in the U.S. The fact that the family "were living" in Nelson, Calif. "when war came" further aligns them with US-American residents of other ethnic origins.

Nationalist discourse is usually predicated upon the emptiness of time. Like racism, the mutually exclusive opposition between Japan and the U.S., between one's association with Japan and one's allegiance to the U.S., is a-historical. By providing details of the Manjis's routes and times of immigration, the captions, albeit unintentionally, compel readers to move beyond a static nationalist present to become aware of the temporal flows, the change of time, and the movement of history. Besides, the captions' frequent references to the internees' life and professions before the war evoke a phantom-like "double" time that emerges from, and at the same time haunts, the narrative present of the report. Information such as that the Manji father used to be a farmer, that May Iwohara was a college graduate managing a flower shop, or that Byon Akisuki came from Los Angeles and was "an engineer" before the war, all reminds us of the past, a time alternative to wartime. This evocation of another time renders the U.S. government's wartime policy ambiguous. The inadequacy and heavy-handedness, if not self-contradiction, of the internment policy is best illustrated in the following passage from the report: "These interned Japanese are not criminals. In peace-time they would be living normal civilian lives. But this is war and they are loyal to Japan, i.e., disloyal to the U.S. They must, of necessity, be put in a place where they cannot hurt the U.S." (34). The use of "and," "i.e.," and "of necessity" in the passage are but convenient linguistic covers of the gaps in the argument. Is being "loyal to Japan" the same thing as being "disloyal to the U.S."? And if they were "normal civilians," why was it "of necessity" for them to be segregated? Ultimately, is the argumentative movement from "there is war" to "they are loyal to Japan" through an awkward "and" not an avoidance of a difficult logic of causality? How could one jump from the fact that "there is war" so easily and quickly to the conclusion that "they are loyal to Japan"?

The wartime logic as such is disturbed by the "peace-time" order, reminding the reader that the wartime logic does not apply to or speak for all. The caption of another portrait introduces "Yohitaka Nakai": "26, has bought $8000 in war bonds. When Nakai was picked up for relocation, his farm crop went bad. Angry, he refused to take allegiance oath. Now he wants to" (30). This exposition of Nakai's life story, although short, is unusually enlightening. It narrates that before the relocation, Nakai purchased war bonds, in other words investing in the U.S. Army. More importantly, the story reveals that he refused to take allegiance oath not in the least because he was loyal to Japan (or disloyal to the U.S.) but simply because he was angry, for his "farm crop went bad" when he was "picked for relocation." Captions like this expose the absurdity of the dichotomy of loyalty/disloyalty.

The last photograph included in the *Life* article I discuss here is a full-page representation of a "pressure boy" (Figure 7). The photo shows a young man sitting in his small cubicle holding a guitar. In a way, it seems appropriate for Mydans to use such a snapshot to illustrate the theme of the "disloyal Japanese." However, except for the young man's sullen facial expression that may indicate to an extent a sense of rebellion, hence reinforcing the Japanese internees' image as threatening aliens, the disloyalty of the young "pressure boy" — the implication of his rejection of U.S. values — is cast into question when we look closely into the photo and, in particular, the caption: what it feels to be a prisoner is shown in the expression of this young Japanese boy in the stockade. He was singing "Home on the Range" when Mydans entered the barracks and Mydans writes that "He sang it like an American. There was no Japanese accent. He looked at me the same way I guess I looked at a Japanese official when he came to check on me at Camp Santo Tomas in Manila. At the back of my mind was the thought: 'Come on, get it over and get out. Leave me alone.' This boy felt the same way. He was just waiting, killing time" (31).

Several points deserve our attention to this passage. First, being a "no-no boy," who is considered a traitor to the U.S., the young man nonetheless sang, "like an American," "Home on the Range," a song known as the unofficial anthem of the US-American West, usually performed in programs of patriotic music. What is supposed to be an incarcerated body of a resisting alien here sings without accent a song symbolizing US-American individualism and patriotism. In her reading of this photo, Simpson also argues that this young man "straddles the presumed divide in the camps between the rejection of and identification with the familiar Western concepts of rugged individualism and unfettered freedom so ironically hailed in his sullen-faced singing of 'Home on the Range'" (38). And this disruption of the line between Japanese aliens and loyal US-Americans actually pushed Mydans into a moment of ambiguity when he entered the young man's small cubicle. Mydans found in the image of the Japanese young man a mirror of his: he saw in the eyes of the "pressure boy" a look of his own when he was imprisoned in Manila in a prisoner of war camp (as *Life* magazine's war photographer, Mydans was dispatched to cover the war in Asia, where he was interned with about 3,500 US-American and Allied nationals by the Japanese forces in Manila [see Luther]). Feeling what the boy felt as a prisoner, Mydans established with the Japanese American "pressure boy" a cross-racial emotional link, which is pinpointed by their shared experiences of "waiting, killing time."

Mydans's identification with the boy could be subject to various interpretations. Simpson, for example, notes in this cross-racial identification not simply Mydans's sympathy toward Japanese American internees but as part of the report's project to incorporate the internment into U.S. postwar humanitarian discourse against the cruelty of war: "a parallel between US and Japanese experience … subtly denies the unique experience of Japanese Americans" (40). The poetic ending note of the caption, the idea of "killing time," as such does not only refer to the pressure boy's waiting, his need to "kill time" (by playing the guitar) because he was deprived of his occupations in regular life, but also refer to a universal "wartime," to which the pressure boy was by no means the only victim. In this way Mydans annexes the traumatic force of the internment in U.S. politics by weaving the event into the postwar appeal for global peace. Yet, the caption could also evoke other layers of meaning. While looking at the image and reading the caption, I am drawn into the various possible implications of the idea of "killing time." In addition to its reference to wartime, does "killing time" not also evoke the fact that there was indeed "too much time" in the relocation camp, "time" that had to be constrained, i.e., "killed"? Does the idea of "killing time in the camp" not ironically point to the mission of the official documentation of the camps? Is it not important for a national discourse to get rid of the temporal "excesses" as implied by the existence of the camp, the racial memories and the unwanted temporalities embodied by the internment and the internees? Or, more precisely, would it not be one of the goals of internment to "kill time" — to suspend the immigrant histories and memories — of Japanese Americans for they exceed the U.S. national time of singularity? Confronting his ghostly double in the body of a Japanese American boy, Mydans was pulled into the whirlwind of time at least at one moment of his photographic project: the young man's past, his own past, the cruelty of wartime, the time wasted in prison, the time repressed by the official history, the immigrant time of excess, the constraining time of a national discourse.

To conclude, I attempt in this article to read documentary photography on Japanese American internment not as much for recovering what truly happened in the internment or for redressing the racism people of Japanese descent suffered during the World War II; rather, I read the photographs and their captions in order to restore the internment's integral position in U.S. national historiography. The history of the internment as such is of significance not only to Japanese Americans but to US-Americans in general in that it enacts temporal dislocation, the ambiguity and self-contradictions characteristic of U.S. wartime politics. Adams's and Mydans's work help reveal how documentary photography on the internment could serve as a mediating ground between the public appropriation of the internment, the white photographers' personal investments in this event, and the internees' experiences of displacement, dislocation, and deprivation. Taking photography as a converging point between nationalist discourse of control and localized stories of ambivalence, between the historical continuity pursued by a nation-state, and the individual times of differences and excess, I propose the possibility of writing the history of Japanese American internment beyond its "minor" containment — its "absent presence" — by enacting the flow of ethnic memories and US-American national consciousness.

Works Cited

Adams, Ansel. *Born Free and Equal: The Story of Loyal Japanese Americans Manzanar Relocation Center, Inyo County, California*. Ed. Wynne Benti. Bishop: Spotted Dog P, 2002.

Alinder, Mary Street. *Ansel Adams: A Biography*. New York: Henry Hold and Company, 1996.

Anderson, Benedict. *Imagined Communities: Reflection on the Origin and Spread of Nationalism*. London: Verso, 1991

Benti, Wynne. "Publisher's Note." *Born Free and Equal: The Story of Loyal Japanese Americans Manzanar Relocation Center, Inyo County, California*. By Ansel Adams. Ed. Wynne Benti. Bishop: Spotted Dog P, 2002. 122-24.

Bhabha, Homi K. "DissemiNation: Time, Narrative, and the Margins of the Modern Nation." *Nation and Narration*. Ed. Homi K. Bhabha. New York: Routledge, 1990. 291-322.

Creef, Elena Tajima. *Imaging Japanese American: The Visual Construction of Citizenship, Nation and the Body*. New York: New York UP, 2004.

Davidov Fryer, Judith. "'The Color of My Skin, the Shape of My Eyes': Photographs of the Japanese American Internment by Dorothea Lange, Ansel Adams, and Toyo Miyatake." *The Yale Journal of Criticism* 9.2 (1996): 223-44.

Embrey, Sue Kunitomi. "Born Free and Equal." *Born Free and Equal: The Story of Loyal Japanese Americans Manzanar Relocation Center, Inyo County, California*. By Ansel Adams. Ed. Wynne Benti. Bishop: Spotted Dog P, 2002. 24-26.

Fujitani, T., Geoffrey M. White, and Lisa Yoneyama, eds. *Perilous Memories: The Asia-Pacific War(s)*. Durham: Duke UP, 2001.

Gordon, Linda. "Dorothea Lange Photographs the Japanese American Internment." *Impounded: Dorothea Lange and the Censored Images of Japanese American Internment*. Ed. Linda Gordon and Gary Y. Okihiro. New York: Norton, 2006. 5-45.

Luther, Claudia. "Carl Mydans, 97; Noted *Life* Magazine War Photographer." *Los Angeles Times* (18 August 2004): <http://articles.latimes.com/2004/aug/18/local/me-mydans18>.

Miyatake, Archie. "Manzanar Remembered." *Born Free and Equal: The Story of Loyal Japanese Americans Manzanar Relocation Center, Inyo County, California*. By Ansel Adams. Ed. Wynne Benti. Bishop: Spotted Dog P, 2002. 15-23.

Robinson, Gerald H. *Elusive Truth: Four Photographers at Manzanar*. Nevada City, California: Carl Mautz, 2007.

Simpson, Caroline Chung. *An Absent Presence: Japanese Americans in Postwar American Culture, 1945-1960*. Durham: Duke UP, 2001.

Streamas, John. "Toyo Suyemoto, Ansel Adams, and the Landscape of Justice." *Recovered Legacies: Authority and Identity in Early Asian American Literature*. Ed. Keith Lawrence and Floyd Cheung. Philadelphia: Temple UP, 2005. 141-157.

Sturken, Marita. "Absent Images of Memory: Remembering and Reenacting the Japanese Internment." *Perilous Memories: The Asia-Pacific War(s)*. Ed. T. Fujitani, Geoffrey M. White, and Lisa Yoneyama. Durham: Duke UP, 2001. 33-49.
"Tule Lake." Photographs by Carl Mydans. *Life Magazine* 20 (March 1944): 25-35.

Author's profile: Hsiu-chuan Lee teaches English at National Taiwan Normal University. Her interests in research include Asian American literature, women's literature, psychoanalysis, and cinema studies. She is the author of *Re-Siting Routes: Japanese American Travels in the Case of Cynthia Kadohata and David Mura* (2003), translator of Toni Morrison's *Sula* to Chinese (2008), and she has published articles in *EurAmerica, Concentric: Literary and Cultural Studies, Review of English and American Literature, Zhongwai wenxue* (Chung Wai Literary Quarterly), and other scholarly journals.

Appendix

Figure 1: Catherine Natsuko Yamaguchi, nurse. Photographs by Ansel Adams. Library of Congress, Prints & Photographs Division (reproduction number LC-DIG-ppprs-00046)

Figure 2: Sam Bozono, policeman. Photographs by Ansel Adams. Library of Congress, Prints & Photographs Division (reproduction number LC-DIG-ppprs-00402)

Figure 3: Private Margaret Fukuoka, W.A.C. Photographs by Ansel Adams. Library of Congress, Prints & Photographs Division (reproduction number LC-DIG-ppprs-00441)

Figure 4: Roy Takeno, editor, and group reading paper in front of office. Photographs by Ansel Adams. Library of Congress, Prints & Photographs Division (reproduction number LC-DIG-ppprs-00363)

Figure 5: School Children. Photographs by Ansel Adams. Library of Congress, Prints & Photographs Division (reproduction number LC-DIG-ppprs-00153)

Figure 6: Family in their apartment at Japanese internment camp, Tule Lake, CA. Photograph by Carl Mydans. Courtesy Time & Life Pictures/Getty Images (image number 92934113)

Figure 7: Young Japanese Nisei playing guitar in the stockade at
Tule Lake Segregation Center. Photograph by Carl Mydans.
Courtesy Time & Life Pictures/Getty Images (image number
50693609)

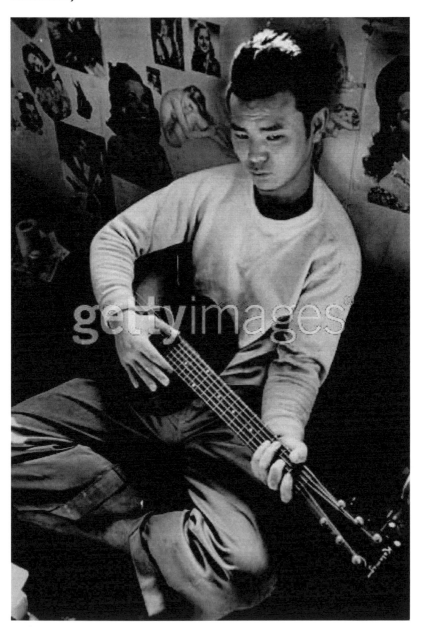

Interculturalism and New Russians in Berlin
Giacomo Bottá

Abstract: In his article "Interculturalism and New Russians in Berlin" Giacomo Bottà discusses aspects of the community of Russian artists in contemporary (post-1989) Berlin. The Berlin-based *Russendisko* night has been held in Tel Aviv, Milan, or Frankfurt, where enthusiastic people danced to songs of obscure Russian bands. In 2008, a new CD compilation, *Ukraine do Amerika*, was published and in 2009 *Meine russische Nachbarn*, the seventeenth book by Russian-born and Berlin-based author Wladimir Kaminer appeared in book stores. Russian culture is experiencing global success curiously tied to Berlin. How could the German capital have channelled this interest? Is there a particular historical, social, geographical, or cultural factor which has been decisive in this phenomenon? Why are these artists in Berlin? How important has Berlin been in the production of Russian artists? These are the basic questions Bottà explores in his study in an exploration of Berlin as an intercultural city and the locus of a Russian artistic community as intercultural practice.

Multiculturalism and interculturalism are concepts in order to relate to changes in society by migration and by the "coexistence of differences" in many European cities. Globalization and the continuous movement of people, goods, and information throughout the globe are slowly eroding clear national identities. As Jude Bloomfieldand Franco Bianchini and Phil Wood and Charles Landry point out, interculturalism could be seen as an important element of mutual recognition, openness, and dialogue within the urban environment. Culture is here addressed through the idea of "change," it is not something fixed, static, immutable; it is something which continuously adapts, evolves, mutates in time and space. From the individual point of view, cultures are something which we adopt, recreate, and modify every day by interacting with the city as spatial and social entity and negotiating our place in it. Wood and Landry emphasize the role played by intercultural innovators, normally people of second generation or mixed origin — in particular artists — in boosting the dialogue among cultures at the urban level. A second element of Wood's and Landry's analysis is the role played by civic recognition in interculturalism. Identifying yourself with your city or to a district and feeling committed to them by some sort of in-place activity creates the basic instruments for integration. A third important element is provided by Ash Amin where he points at the idea of "micro-cultures of place" and the chances in intercultural dialogue given by habitual places of encounters and by seeing these places as resources.

The modern city has always been the place where cultures, as ways of life, meet, and coexist. In the city "the other" is encountered and the subject is continuously torn between homologisation and distinctiveness (see Simmel). Every year the magnetic power of the city attracts new people looking for better living conditions, a new beginning or the freedom to pursue their own happiness. Different understandings of space, time, and life gather and coexist in the same city, often in conflict or in total ignorance of one another. Nevertheless, sometimes a particular urban context happens to be vital to the birth of an intercultural practice, of a border that cannot be ascribed to one culture but that becomes a cognitive link between identities, cultures or worlds. Geographically, Berlin lies in the middle of Brandenburg, a sandy region of lakes, fields, and small villages, far from the core of Western Europe; the Polish border is only 120 kms away. Even culturally, the German capital has been defined as a city on the border between "East and West," a definition that seems catching, at first sight.

The main feature of Berlin's locus on the border between East and West, apart from its tragic political reality as the dividing point of the Iron Curtain in the Cold War era, lies in its evanescence: you might find yourself searching for it in vain, just like tourists looking for the Berlin Wall. Berlin is neither a city of the East, of the West, nor a city between East and West. It is a city that can only be defined interculturally, in the sense that East and West, as vague cultural connotations, had the chance to interact and define a homogeneous urban context, where actors are to be found both in the ruling powers and in grassroots subcultural activities of various origins. The German capital is not on a border; it is a border itself; a place where cultures meet and interact (on the notion of Central and East European borders and the cultures of the region as a locus of "in-between peripherality," see, e.g., Tötösy de Zepetnek; see also Lisiak). Its identity cannot be determined by any single definition: Berlin has always absorbed and "digested" architectonical, social, and cultural influences that should be perceived as contents within the city-container, but that cannot be used to explain it as "on the border": the project of an intercultural city remains, especially in the case of Berlin, self-significant. The intercultural connotation of Berlin is also endorsed by its multilingualism: apart from German, the languages spoken in the four allied sectors after World War II (English, French, and Russian) left their influence and toponyms. After 1989 Russian, as we will see, has regained prominence, along Turkish, which has been widely spoken since the 1960s, especially in "Little Istanbul" (i.e., Kreuzberg, a distinctively ethnic quarter). Nowadays English is widely used as a language of business and tourism. In everyday use or in literary expression, all considered languages mirror cultural differences, existing in different urban perceptions. The spatial definition of Berlin made, for example, by

German, Turkish, or Russian speakers reveals singular cultural determinations of space and original cognitive mappings, which should always be kept in mind, when speaking about the city " in general." Starting with the 1990s, for the first time in Europe, cities had to face new urban phenomena such as gentrification, massive immigration, poverty, and segregation; in particular, new lines of division set by social boundaries appeared in Berlin, outnumbering the former ideological division. At the same time, the aim to compete in the world scenario, with the other "world cities" collapsed partly under the weight of a bottomless financial bankruptcy; on a global level, many big cities have lost their economic and political supremacy, previously connected to their "centrality" in production, communication, and power (see Savage and Warde). Culture has been used as a means to regain this superiority: art, performance, and entertainment, originating in popular subcultural settings, have been moved to serve the marketing interests of the city. Free cultural production, institutionalised through the organisation of city festivals or otherwise subsidized, has turned into "city culture"; part of what Sharon Zukin calls "symbolic economy" (3). This new cultural policy turned the newly reunified Berlin into a film and video location, a gigantic dance-floor (with the Love Parade and the Christopher Street Day), and a tourist stage for the *Erlebnisgesellschaft* (event society). In the 1990s, Berlin baptized a new civil society whose lifestyle was shaped as a mixture of the roaring twenties cultural fascination (*die goldenen Zwanziger Jahre*) and the most contemporary of global corporate concerns. The recent past was quickly obliterated, at least from promotional material. At the same time, the city was chosen again as German capital (in 1991), greeted by the birth of a new political class: the *Berliner Republik*, which was biographically separated from Germany's nazi past and initiated the normalisation of the country within the European Union.

Having been passive and unheard spectators of all this, many grassroots artists and intellectuals, felt the need to preserve or renew pre-existent local practices in the city, the features of which were traditionally participation, autonomy, and a deep disbelief in any form of hierarchy, capitalistic exploitation, and profit. In fact, Kreuzberg in West and Prenzlauer Berg in East Berlin represented islands of alternative urban lifestyles and cultural experiences that could not just be put away by the reunification and sacrificed in the name of a city-marketing plan that was eager to forget the past and substitute it with an idealized and flat "pop history" (Jameson 25).

Artistic and intellectual work, outside official circles, has emphasized the importance of urban liveability and local practices, and has opposed the market-ruled policies of city governance. The big projects that made Berlin "the biggest construction site in Europe" ("die grösste Baustelle Europas")), such as the Potsdamer Platz or the Friedrichstrasse left out real citizens' needs and the problems that they had to face every day. An interesting metaphor describing the reunified Berlin is that of a medieval palimpsest (see Huyssen). According to Andreas Huyssen, the city was rubbed and rewritten several times during the twentieth century, and just like in an old manuscript, valuable texts in ancient tongues are still partially visible under the freshly written words, pointing at various historical markers, both towards the past and the future of the city. The textual metaphorisation of Berlin has always been fascinating for its semiotic connotations but it seems questionable, when analysing also visual (pictorial, photographic, filmic) representations of the German capital and its socio-spatial image. For example, the Reichstag, one of the most contested symbols of the new Berlin was originally built between 1884 and 1894 as the parliament of the German empire and then of the Weimar republic. It was burnt down in 1933 and destroyed during World War II, becoming a symbol of nazi defeat, for example through the famous (staged) photo, portraying a Soviet soldier with the red flag on its roof. After Berlin's division among the allied forces, it ended up in the British sector and was partly restored in 1961. After the 1991 *Wiedervereinigung* (reunification), the building was chosen as the place for the parliament (Bundestag) of the German federation of states and a major restoration began, following a project by Norman Foster, who decided to top the roof with a new futuristic dome. The nicknamed "space egg," made of glass and steel, the dome contains two ramps leading the visitors to a 360-degree panorama of the city. The dome has been interpreted as an expression of the transparency of the new unified democracy (see Köpenick). Inside, in the renovated entrance, some Cyrillic graffiti, left by the red army soldiers, is marked with light. The stratification of radically different political and historical meanings is recalled continuously by visible and invisible signs, by public or personal memories bound to the place, to its history, and to its medial representations.

In 1995, just before the restoration of the Reichstag began, the artist pair Christo and Jeanne-Claude "wrapped" the Reichstag with thickly woven polypropylene fabric with an aluminium surface, lending it an unreal, fairy tale dimension and underlining its spatial importance within Berlin's landscape (Christo and Jeanne-Claude

<http://www.christojeanneclaude.net/wr.html>). Christo and Jeanne-Claude's wrapping transformed the building into a "shimmering and abstract form" without any clear message, and more than five million people strolled and relaxed around the temporary work of art, enjoying its vacuity (Ladd 88-90). All semiotic meanings related to the building's future and past disappeared: for two weeks it included everyone looking at it. The palimpsest had turned temporarily into blank paper and everyone became able to read it. Nevertheless, and more profoundly, Berlin's image interfered in the artistic and cultural life of the city. Every book about Berlin had the moral task confronting "its ghosts" (Ladd 1). Writing about Berlin became an overwhelming challenge: too big was the confrontation with its history and its myth, and the expectations of the reading public and of the critics had been exaggerated. On the other hand, the socio-cultural scenes and subcultures of the 1990s, left out of the big speeches and of the expectations related to "high culture," acquired new autonomous features through mutual intermingling / exchanging / mixing and interaction. The chance to overwhelm the weight of history was bound to the recognition that Berlin does not belong just to History or to Myth. Berlin is also a place where millions of people live every day and where every day new ways to read the city are created and new meanings are attributed to places. The Russian-speaking minority in post-1989 Berlin has been one of the most active and original in reshaping the everyday city as a cultural environment and constitutes an interesting case study related to the intercultural city thesis. In fact, practices that renewed the urban cultural environment, mirroring social life, have been fuelled extensively by Russian-speaking immigrants and by their work. Berlin has always been the first step into the West for Russian-speaking emigrants, used both as a point of arrival or transit. In the twentieth century, five waves of migrations to the West can be identified, the first and the fifth of which interest the German capital in particular. The first wave, which had a peak of about 350.000 people in the 1920s, was a consequence of the Bolshevik Revolution. It is the most celebrated, owing to the extensive presence of intellectuals and to its taking place in an era when Berlin acquired the qualities of a world city in size, infrastructure, and cultural life. It is often forgotten that Berlin in the *goldenen Jahren*, was extremely diverse not only in sexual orientation but also culturally in diverse contexts: Nabokov, Majakowski, Gorki, and Kandinsky were among the many Russian artists without those contribution German art movements, for example, Expressionism or Dada, would never have begun.

Nevertheless, although influences spread among fellow poets, painters, and revolutionaries, the social independence of nationalities remained. Cafes such as the Prager Diele or institutions such as the *Haus der Kunst* (*Dom Iskusstv*) and the writers' club (*Klub Pisatelej*) were Russian-speaking outposts. The quarter of Charlottenburg (in the Western part of the city) became a centre for the Russian-speaking community and was familiarly called Petersburg by the immigrants — or Charlottengrad by the Berliners (see Shrivastava 35). This wave of immigration can be characterized by the preservation of the national cultural identity, which was evident, for example, in the refusal to learn and use German and in the consolidation of a Russian-speaking infrastructure in communications and media. Striking is the fact that more than seventy publishers and printing houses, putting out approximately 200 newspapers and magazines were active in the German capital until 1941 (Kasack; Andreesen <http://www.ifla.org/IV/ifla64/096116e.htm>) and the fascination of this era is tangible in several of Nabokov's novels.

The second wave of immigration was a result of World War II; many war prisoners remained in West Germany after 1945, fearing repercussions if they return to the Soviet Union. At the same time, a sector of Berlin was controlled directly by the Soviet Union, involving the moving in of troops, functionaries, and various officials. The third wave was an outcome of repression in the USSR with a high tide in the 1970s: dissident writers and intellectuals escaped or were sent abroad under international pressure. The fourth wave of immigration to Germany involved people of Jewish background who were allowed to leave USSR in the 1980s: some of the Russianspeaking emigres with a Jewish background, while most settled in Israel, also settled in West Germany or used Berlin — owing to its proximity to St. Petersburg (Leningrad) and Moscow as a transit point to Israel or the US/Canada. The fifth wave, the one that is central to this paper, is related to the fall of the Berlin Wall and to the end of the Cold War and of the Socialist Block. Inthis last wave, three interrelated typologies of Russian-speaking immigrants to Berlin can be identified. The *Deutsch-Russen*, Russian-speaking citizens with German ancestors, misplaced during or soon after World War II constitute the first group; then there were people of Jewish religion (*Kontingentflüchtlinge*) who were often also of German origin; finally there were people who, independent of any ethnic or religious identity, moved for economical reasons and saw Berlin as the nearest place to find better living conditions. It is interesting to note how the first two categories relate to historical events that took place fifty years before, as if the Cold War had frozen time. From the legislative point of view, they were a direct consequence of the new immigrant legislation (*Asylrecht*) approved by the German parliament in 1993. Germany's Basic Law (*Grundgesetz*) guarantees people of German ancestry the right to enter the country and to obtain citizenship (i.e., the *ius sanguini*) if they suffered persecution after World War II because of their heritage, even if they do not speak the language and have no direct ties to the country. In 1990, almost 400,000 ethnic Germans arrived. Since 1993, a maximum 220,000 persons per year can be granted recognition as ethnic Germans, although not all of them will move immediately to Germany. Statistics aside, in Berlin the official number of Russian-speaking immigrants should take into account the existence of illegal immigrants. Their presence could mean something between 50.000 to 200.000 people facing, at the same time, the problem of who to identify as "Russian" (all Russian speakers? Only the people from the Russian Federation?). Relevant for my study is the fact that, whether or not of German origin, some intellectuals and writers started working extensively in German and felt immediately at home in the new, precarious, and exciting reunified Berlin, changing radically the whole image of Russian-speaking immigration in the city. As far as writing is concerned, German intercultural literature is not a new phenomenon: already in the 1960s, guest workers from Italy and Turkey started adopting the guest language to document, in poetry and prose about identity and ethnicity issues, but with a strong political and realist attitude, sometimes filled with hostility (see Chiellino 60-61; see also Nell). In fact, Carmin Chiellino identifies the fifth-wave of Russian-speaking immigrants as the *Neunte Stimme*, (ninth voice; Chiellino 56) of German-language intercultural literature.

Contemporary Russian-speaking authors use German naturally, not as a weapon to fight back discrimination, but as a positive means to assert their own identity among the German and non-German speaking population of Berlin. The membership of the wider subcultural Berlin scene (Prenzlauer Berg) is of course a decisive factor in this attitude. In fact, the scene attracts outsiders and minorities from various cultural and national environments. Their attitude liberated the German language from its negative historical connotations very much present in Russia. There is an assembly of factors which could only be found in the German capital at the beginning of the 1990s central to the redevelopment of Berlin as an original cultural space and that explain the extensive use of the German language. Firstly, the housing situation in the district Prenzlauer Berg must be considered. This working-class district is located in the central East side of the city; its buildings, called *Mietskaserne* in German, were built no later than the 1920s and needed renovation, especially after World War II. Instead of carrying out renovations, the East German government, since the 1960s, preferred to build new block of apartments (*Neubauten*), embodying the socialist ideal with all kinds of facilities, in quarters further east such as Marzahn and Hellersdorf. The offer of brand new apartments somewhere else led Prenzlauer Berg to decay for a long time. At the end of the 1970s, a small group of outsiders, punks, and dissidents started repopulating the area, owing to the abundance of empty buildings with apartments (see Felsmann and Gröschner). Despite this, after the fall of the Berlin Wall in 1989, one-sixth of the district's dwellings were vacant, 43% of the apartments lacked a private bathroom, 22% had an outdoor toilet and 83 % were inadequately heated (see Levine 95). These factors, plus the Bohemian reputation, prompted many "pioneers" to move to Prenzlauer Berg, both from West Germany and from East Europe. The run-down quarter was an ideal place for gentrification, i.e., the social and physical process of inner city regeneration (Friedrichs). Many original residents had decided to leave their apartments and move to West Germany; West German members of the "creative class" occupied these apartments and started rearranging the public and private space they now claimed their own at their will. Soon the transformation of the working-class quarter into a gentrified one began to be apparent. Nowadays, in areas such as Kollwitz Platz and in some parts of the Schönhauser Allee, the gentrification process seems to have been accomplished. Also from the infrastructural point of view the quarter represented, together with some parts of the more central *Mitte*, an ideal setting for social and cultural experimentation because of the presence of modern buildings, warehouses, available basements, and other service- or industry-related buildings that were turned, more or less illegally, into clubs, bars, galleries, or restaurants. Thus, the parallel of gentrification and the birth of a subcultural scene is obvious.

The urban environment described above was decisive for Wladimir Kaminer's popularity, which relies on the unique interaction between his Russian origin and identity and their embeddedness in practices typical of Berlin. Kaminer, a trained sound-engineer and theatre student, was born in Moscow in 1967. He came to East Berlin in 1990, as the avant-garde of the fifth wave of immigration obtaining a visa as a Russian of Jewish origin. After a series of various jobs and shortterm occupations, he decided to become a writer and performer. Today, he can be considered one of the most influential writers of post-1989 Berlin. His multifaceted career was started by meeting Bert Pappenfuß, an East German dissident poet, active in the pre-1989 Prenzlauer Berg scene. In the bar Kaffe Burger, whose furniture remains untouched by history, Kaminer founded NPK: Neue Proletarische Kunst (New Proletarian Art) and later joined the *Reformbühne Heim und Welt*. Both are groups of spoken word artists. In Kaffe Burger and in other small bars and clubs of Prenzlauer Berg, he started reading his short stories, surreal and humorous texts, full of autobiographical anecdotes related to his identity, the difficulties of living in Berlin and the city's Russian underworld. The spoken word scene was a phenomenon limited to the East and to Prenzlauer Berg in particular, where veterans from the former East Germany (GDR) oppositional movements got in contact with Western artists and writers and with foreigners. Kaminer's short stories aroused interest: they were published, among others, by *TAZ* (*Die Tageszeitung*), a left-wing newspaper. The Russian author was also working for *Multi-Kulti*, a radio station broadcasting in various languages. At the same time, he organized a regular party in Tacheles (a run-down department store from the 1920s in the eastern quarter *Mitte* of the city, which squatters occupied in the early 1990s and turned into a culture centre) where, as a DJ, he played only obscure Russian rock and pop music from the 1960s and 1970s. This selection suited the Western audience that attended the parties, read the *TAZ*, and listened to *Multi-Kulti*, always in search of something distinctive. Kaminer became a sort of catalyst for the "invisible" minority of East European immigrants in Berlin and at the same time revived the myth of the first wave immigration, when the Russian intellectuals set trends. His popularity grew in 2000 with the Goldmann publishing house publication of *Russendisko*, which contained most of his short stories. The book, with an explicit red star on the cover, was greeted with great success in Germany and, thanks to various translations, abroad. Along with the book, also his work as spoken word performer, journalist, DJ, talent scout, and event promoter acquired more and more national and international visibility. Every book published by Kaminer was followed by a reading tour associated to a DJ night, transforming the promotional job into a multimedia event (see Schulze). Kaminer's entrepreneurial ability is striking: *Russendisko* became a "trademark," in the form of a CD, a weekly DJ night, a book, a website <http://www.russendisko.de>, and an "event," maintaining a subcultural and Bohemian credibility that many other artists would have then lost. His attitude, as a performer, is in fact strikingly low-profile and relaxed, celebrating humorously his own amateurism and marking continuously his condition as immigrant and outsider — a well-established way of self-irony practiced by many Central and East European writers and artists. "Don't take it too seriously" is a sort of motto of the whole Prenzlauer Berg scene, where the intermingling of subcultural elements, marketing strategies, and anti-professionalism are the norm, Kaminer used this attitude and brought it to success. Kaminer's sensation brought Russian culture, music, and aesthetics into fashion, the ethnic minority, which was previously linked, especially in the yellow press, only to mafia or criminality, was suddenly surrounded by a previously unknown hype: Russian artists were invited or moved to Berlin, Russian bars opened and Russian music events began populating the programs of various clubs. A brief internet look-up suggests the existence of websites and articles, both in Russian and German, promoting the Berlin "Russian scene" and all its activities (concerts, exhibitions, readings, disco nights, etc.). A visit to Kaffee Burger (the established location for the party after its beginning in Tacheles) on a Saturday could easily testify the enormous popularity of the "Russendisko night" for non-Russians. This fascination has been explained by *Ostalgie* (a fusion of the worlds Ost i.e., East and *Nostalgie*, i.e., nostalgia), which idealised the GDR and East Bloc aesthetics and which found expression in the partly melancholic mood of films such as the vastly popular *Good Bye! Lenin* (2003) or in the ironic re-release of East German products and furniture. An insight into Kaminer's work shows its actual distance from this phenomenon, which is bound to a post-reunification desire for *Heimat*, solidarity, and tradition. *Ostalgie* is not sufficient to explain Kaminer's efforts or the "Russian mania" as a whole, as its above-mentioned intercultural dimension is far from the idealisation of a German monocultural past.

   Russendisko's short stories are not centred on the past; they describe Berlin's reality and chronicle the author's assimilation into Berlin's contemporary social and urban fabric. Mental maps are the routes in our minds, which organize our moving, orienting and living in spaces and that influence our recollection and meaning (on this, see, e.g., Downs and Stea; Lynch). In *Russendisko*, Kaminer sets the majority of his short stories at the beginning of the 1990s, as the fifth wave of immigration was beginning to hit East Berlin (when Honecker granted GDR citizenship to Russians of Jewish background) or even in during the years when Kaminer was planning in Moscow to emigrate. Analysing time and space references, we can identify a slow shift in perception through the book: in the oldest descriptions, there are no real mental maps and no references to prototypical elements of the German capital: the city is still an imaginary goal, filtered through Russian narratives and images (TV reports, friends, books, etc.). The stories set in the east of the city, at the very beginning of the 1990s belong to a second level of perception. "Centrality" is represented by Marzahn (an eastern district in the outskirts of the city where the refugees' apartments were located) and the Lichtenberg Railway Station (where the trains from Moscow and St. Petersburg arrive). They both represent the first consequential places encountered by a Russian immigrant. Socially, in these first stories there are few references to Germans; the protagonists are Russian compatriots of, real or presumed, Jewish Russians, Roma, Africans, and Vietnamese, which constituted the ethnic minorities already present in the GDR before 1989. A key short story in the book is "Die erste eigene Wohnung" ("My First Apartment"), where Kaminer describes the gentrification of Prenzlauer Berg, according to his own experience as a pioneer. The first phase of this process is depicted vividly. Prenzlauer Berg is identified as a secret hint and starts attracting pioneers from the West: "Punks, foreigners, members of the church of the holy mother, strange guys, and life artists of every kind" ("Punks, Ausländer und Anhänger der Kirche der Heilingen Mutter, schräge Typen und Lebenskünstler aller Art" [28]; unless indicated otherwise, all translations are mine) who replace the original dwellers. The author and two friends fed up with life in the refugee dormitory, join this Western wave (from the east!) and take up squatting. Only later does the city become able to identify and regulate the housing through ordinary rent contracts. This will eventually lead to a normalisation and to the consequent third and fourth stages of gentrification. Three streets are named in the story: Stargarder, Greifenhagener, and Lychener (the last being the one chosen by the author for his 25-square-metre apartment), which nowadays are very "central" areas of the gentrified Prenzlauer Berg. Moving into a private home is also linked to a change in the social environment: the majority of stories reel around his Russian family and friends, West Europeans, and bizarre characters from the intercultural Prenzlauer Berg community. The ethnic references are limited to Vietnamese and Turks and are mainly connected to their commercial and restaurant activities flourishing in the district. This slow shift in the author's perception of the city and of its inhabitants continues in the second book, *Schönhauser Allee* (2001). The title refers to the long street (2775 meters) running north to south, one of the main axes of Prenzlauer Berg. It is unusually taken over almost completely by the U2 metro line, which is elevated far over the street level in the middle. Its metro stations are traditional meeting points, especially the ones called Eberswalder Stasse and Schönhauser Allee, where beggars, street vendors, and musicians are present. The street has always had a literary and filmic fascination, which found expression during GDR times in films such as *Berlin. Ecke Schönhauser* (1957), about youth gangs. Many of its bars and shops are often portrayed in photographs, to evoke the "alternative Berlin" or as a symbol for the gentrified East. Today it constitutes a microcosm of Berlin and an urban village with connotations that could be defined interculturally and not only ethnically. Unlike Kreuzberg, where the Turkish majority has set a certain national flair on many streets, the Schönhauser Allee constitutes an inter-relational cultural space. This is also historically visible, for example, in its Jewish cemetery, the second oldest in Berlin, where epitaphs are bilingual German and Hebrew displaying an ongoing assimilation. The street is adorned by an incredible number of bars, cafés, and ethnic restaurants, small shops with curious names, a mall called Arcaden (opened in 1999), a cinema complex, Colosseum (founded in 1924), and a big cultural centre, the Kulturbrauerei. The street is also full of residential apartments. All buildings along the street have their own courtyard, with apartments also located at the wings and back of the buildings; this means that behind every entrance exists a hidden and crowded "square." The street constitutes a huge meeting point, where every day many people walk, travel, eat, work, shop, and mingle. Owing to the gentrification of the area, its population is rather mixed: the gentrifiers live beside the original Prenzlerberger and the ethnic minorities, which are mainly involved in commerce also share the same locations.

As we know from *Russendisko*, Kaminer's real postal/residential address is on Schönhauser Allee. For him, it represents a home, a starting point to explore the city, and at the same time a mythical place to be abstracted or emphasized. His wandering along the shops, in the Arcaden mall or by the Burger King, during the day or at night, shows a deep confidence in the street, especially through the use, of his supposed, everyday mental maps, his locations of existence. The ease with which he recognizes places, routes, and manners typical of Prenzlauer Berg, could be one explanation of his popularity, as they establish a familiarity with the readers. His ironical questioning of trademarks, chain shops, and fast food outlets, and his keen descriptions of people's manners could also lead one to think of him as a post-modern *flâneur*. Post-modern *flânerie* because of its minimalism and because "it could not care less about possible conflicts between authenticity and simulation" (Goebel 1279). Kaminer operates a sort of "urban archaeology" in the shops and trash bins of the busy street by enumerating products on display in a Vietnamese corner-shop, books found in a dustbin or in cheap bookstores. This shows the speed and craziness, achieved by consumption. His criticism, although politically loaded, is never prevailing, and it is offered in a humorous way, pointing at the comic more than at the dramatic aspects of contemporary capitalism. Nevertheless, also in this collection, the idea of interculturalism remains essential; for example in "Singles and Family Economy" ("Jungeesellen und Familienwirthschaft") he describes the building, where he lives with his wife and children. Russian, "modern Islamic," Vietnamese families, and German singles live side-by-side, sharing space, sniffing exotic food from behind the neighbouring door, listening to unknown languages and noises and every day observing "the other," the strange, and the uncommon. This is the real multiculturalism in place here where different cultures have their own place to express themselves (the apartment), but at the same time, inevitably, they interact in real life through noises, smells, and words, in sharing the same building and street. Socially, it is interesting to note that, besides foreign families, the German *autochthons* are often single, involved in artistic or cultural work, and perform urbanity through a distinctiveness, which at times turns into caricature or cliché (for example in the "black only" outfit of the "lässige Junggesellin" on the first floor). This shows implicitly the limits of gentrification, here without an intercultural counterpart. Again, following the rapid succession of short stories, the author wanders along his cognitive maps of the city, which remain deeply rooted in the East. West Berlin is for Kaminer, as for many other contemporary authors, an unexplored and most likely uninteresting site. At the same time, there are no references to the "contested places" of Berlin, to tourist attractions, or to prototypical elements of the city. Stylistically, many of the short stories maintain a common bizarre structure, where an episode of the past, in Moscow, is linked abruptly to something contemporary in Berlin, with sentences such as "here too, on our Schönhauser Allee" ("auch bei uns in der Schönhauser Allee" [22]): the phrase shows complicity with the reader. The Schönhauser Allee acquires in Kaminer's text the features of an urban intercultural village, where social and ethnic diversities coexist and interact. At the same time, the realistic dimension of the street is strengthened by abstractions: the fictional episodes where famous persons are met by the author in the street (for example Bill Clinton, Charles Bukowski, Albert Einstein) assert a mythical and dreamy dimension, which modify the dynamics of its perception and its canonisation. Kaminer refers repeatedly to the importance of the street, as a subject for urban research. As Marshall Berman noted, the street is the place where the subject comes in contact with social forces, the showcase of modernity, the place where social classes interact, where strangers bump into each other and where riots and political rallies are performed. In Paris, the Boulevard was the symbol of modernity and modernisation, just like the Newsky Prospect in St. Petersburg, and in Berlin it is the Schönhauser Allee that exemplifies the intercultural character of the German capital, its being built upon history but also its being deeply entrenched in the everyday encounter of diverse but interacting ways of life.

Next, I introduce another Russian immigrant to Berlin, Natalia Hantke: born 1967 in Kazakhstan, Hantke studied social sciences in St. Petersburg, before moving to Berlin in December 1991. She belongs to the spoken word group *Erfolgsschrifsteller* im *Schacht*. The group of seven authors, previously known as *Blaue Drache*, established itself as one of the most active within the Prenzlauer Berg literary "off" scene, participating actively in reading nights and poetry slams and hosting a literary night every Monday at the Bergwerk, in the district *Mitte*. The spoken word movement in Germany originated from social beat and from slam poetry activities, which flourished in East Berlin after 1989 (on this, see, e.g., Neumeister and Hartges). These literary practices were first conceived in the USA in the 1960s: they adopt performance and entertainment to bring literature back to nightclubs and bars and to a wider and more mixed audience than the written book. Gathering in groups mocks the "rock-band" attitude and at the same time helps the performers to gain confidence. Besides learning German, in a way that could allow her to "play" with language, Hantke had a double task: to establish herself as the "Russian girl" within a scene almost completely German and male. In fact, Hantke's texts, never collected in a book, are connected to the questioning of her own identity, of her home country's and family's history, and constitute a fascinating counterpart to her "Western" colleagues. For example, "Germany Searches for Its Gagarin Statues" ("Deutschland sucht seine Gagarin-Büsten") is a humorous reportage which mixes a variety of time/space associations: the inauguration of "Flight to the Sky" ("Flug zum Himmel"), an exhibition by the painter Andrej

Rudjev at the Prenzlauer Berg planetarium, a childhood cosmonauts stamp collection, a letter from a Siberian Russo-German woman to the newspaper *Evrasia Direkt* concerning the Soviet cosmonaut Jurij Gagarin, with the editor's answer. "Space" is the connecting element of the text, which jumps from Prenzlauer Berg to Siberia, from Berlin to the sky and back, through unexpected and sudden associations. The link to the work of Kaminer is clear, as she points out in an interview: "I believe without Kaminer I couldn't do what I'm doing" ("ich glaube, ohne Kaminer konnte ich nicht tun, was ich tue" Hantke qtd. in Ahne 20). In fact, in the above-mentioned text, she adopts Kaminer's strategy of linking the past to Russia and the Soviet Union and to the present, the "new life" in Germany. Her texts also appeared in the newspaper *TAZ;* among them a reportage about the nazi scene in the outskirts of Berlin and some humorous stories about intercultural communication. Her studies in social pedagogy, in St. Petersburg and then at Berlin's Freie Universität have surely been extremely relevant to her literary work. At the same time, following Kaminer's example again, she started her own DJ night called *Disconova*.

My next example, the painter Vladimir Skokov, born in 1966 in Prijekule, Latvia and studied art in Toljatti (Russia) (<http://www. skokov.de>): I consider his work the visual equivalent of Kaminer's and Hantke's work. Skokov moved to Berlin in 1997 and apparently left the city a few years later to move to Moscow. From 2002 he lived between the two capitals and he resides currently in Frankfurt. The intercultural dimension of Skokov's work consists of the mix of historically loaded elements of the Russian tradition with pop art and with themes which are clearly bound to the specifics of living in Berlin. Briefly put, he uses techniques of the Orthodox icon painters to portray the contemporary urban environment. Skokov started painting icons in 1991 after working as a graphic and shop window designer (in 1988 his shop window design of the Melodia music shop earned him a prize from the Leningrad City Council); he paints mainly on simple wooden surfaces such as wardrobe boards and doors and in small formats. For my purposes here, I discuss briefly two of his paintings, *Der Warteraum II* (1999) and *Game Boy Spieler* (1998), as these represent the Berlin series of the artist. *Der Warteraum II* (acrylic on wood, gold leaf, 77x85 cm) depicts the queue in the employment office, as if it were a Biblical apocalypse. The plastic features of an icon are maintained, both in the human figures and in the setting. Following the traditional rules, even if the scene is happening in an interior, the people are placed outside; the entrance and exit of the office are seen in the background. All faces are staring to the top, where, substituting the eye of God and surrounded by logos of the *Arbeitsamt* (employment office), is the display with the number of the next person in the queue (the number refers to the actual number of unemployed in that period). The humor of the painter is clear: high culture, established by historical and religious values and surrounded by a sacral aura is deconstructed by the use of contemporary urban "icons," logos, and everyday situations. Nonetheless, the subject dealt with in the icon is typical of the German capital: the employment office is filled to capacity; since reunification Berlin is straddled with an enormous unemployment rate (as is all of the former East Germany). At the same time, there is also an ironic meaning, specific to Russian immigrants: many of them have the chance to work only through special programs of the employment office (Kaminer himself at the beginning of the 1990s had to visit the office several times, to obtain jobs as an immigrant from the former Soviet Union). Game Boy Spieler (acrylic on wood, gold leaf, 21.5x29.5 cm) is a more conventional icon, representing a full frontal figure, in the way Jesus and saints are normally portrayed. In the hands of the boy is a videogame console, in his shirt pocket a large container of fast-food beverage, both symbols of contemporary, globalized urban lifestyle. The background shows the electronic circuits of the videogame. Again the intermingling of high and low culture is clear, similar to the one between Russian heritage and elements belonging to the Western urban world, recognizable also in Berlin. Other Skokov icons present prominent German or Russian politicians or even reprisals of famous pop art masterpieces (Andy Warhol's Campbell soup can), always keen on stylistic faithfulness to religious art on one hand and on the humorous, nearly comical effect on the other, in portraying contemporary urbanity.

The *Verheimatung* (established as in a home) of Russian artists in Berlin has led to the creation of an original intercultural production and at the same time has contributed enormously to the canonisation of the "image" of the city and of some of its areas around the world. Kaminer and Hantke are recognized today as initiators of the Prenzlauer Berg intellectual scene and their visibility in national newspapers and other media has contributed to the normalisation of much of the eastern immigration and to the spread of an intercultural understanding of Berlin. The results of the present study suggest at least three levels of intercultural practice in Berlin: 1) a sociospatial practice of interculturality: the Prenzlauer Berg district, and more generally the whole of Berlin, gave the discussed artists the chance to find their "own apartment" to pursue

a career and to create places and infrastructures to perform and to "invent" intercultural work. The inherited richness of the cultural cityscape offered itself up for exploration, interaction and comparison to the home country. The particular social and spatial dimensions of Berlin are the *sine qua non* conditions for the artists' production. On the other hand, these artists gave a personal commitment to Prenzlauer Berg, both as gentrifiers and as promoters of the district's social life, which, in turn, became basic to its survival. Kaminer in particular brought the district to national and international attention; 2) there is a biographical level of interculturality in place: the artists discussed immigrated to Berlin for different reasons, but with an open mind and the capacity to interact with the place and its people. Migration to Berlin increased and guided their professional expectations and their artistic careers; and 3) the content of intercultural production, namely the texts and paintings show an intense and determined use of interculturalism: the Russian components, supported by stylistic and thematic references, are always mixed with Berlin's urbanity. German as a language or, in the case of Skokov, German icons and logos are used as a means of artistic expression, but at the same time also as instruments to affirm his existence as a minority member of German society. Thematically, the references to visas, employment offices, and citizenship applications relate to real and personal situations. Of importance is also that the portrayal of de facto Russian and/or foreign artists in the texts of Kaminer and Hantke promote other intercultural work. Christo and Jeanne-Claude's wrapping "liberated" temporarily the Reichstag of the burden of history and made it a piece of art, belonging to everyone, to its haters and admirers, thus to a wide audience. In the same way the work of many intercultural or bicultural artists of today's Berlin, when confronted with an urban framework, tend to create new and positive ways to "read" the city as a social and spatial entity.
Note: The above article is a revised version of Bottá, Giacomo. "Interculturalism and New Russians in Berlin." *CLCWeb: Comparative Literature and Culture* 8.2 (2006): <http://docs.lib.purdue.edu/clcweb/vol8/iss2/5/>. Copyright release by Purdue University Press.

Works Cited

Ahne, Petra. "Russland in Berlin." *Berliner Zeitung* (9 October 2003): 20.
Amin, Ash. *Ethnicity and the Multicultural City: Living with Diversity.* Report for the ESRC CITIES Programme and the Department of Transport, Local Government and the Regions (2002): <www.aulaintercultural. org/IMG/pdf/ash_amin.pdf>.
Andreesen, Walter. "New Russian-Language Newspapers in Berlin." Paper

Presentation. 6th *Conference of IFLA*: *International Federation of Library Associations and Institutions* (1998): <http://www.ifla.org /IV/ifla64/096-116e.htm>.

Berman, Marshall. *All That is Solid Melts Into Air*. New York: Simon and Schuster, 1982.

Bloomfield, Jude, and Franco Bianchini. *Planning for the Intercultural City*. London: Comedia, 2004.

Chiellino, Carmine. *Interkulturelle Literatur in Deutschland. Ein Handbuch*. Stuttgart: Metzler, 2000.

Christo, and Jeanne-Claude. *Wrapped Reichstag. Berlin 1971-95* (2006): <http://www.christojeanneclaude.net/wr.html>.

Downs, Roger, and Stea, David. *Maps in Minds*. New York: Harper & Row, 1997.

Felsmann, Barbara, and Gröschner, Annett. *Durchgangzimmer Prenzlauer Berg. Eine Berliner Künstlersozialgeschichte in Selbstauskünften*. Berlin: Lukas, 1999.

Friedrichs, Jürgen. "*Gentrification*." *Großstadt. Soziologische* Stichworte. Ed. Hartmud Häußermann. Opladen: Leske & Budrich, 2000. 57-67.

Goebel, Rolf J. "Berlin's Architectural Citations: Reconstruction, Simulation, and the Problem of Historical Authenticity." *PMLA: Publications of the Modern Language Association of America* 118 (2003): 1268-89.

Hantke, Natalia. "Stichwort Nazi." *Die Tageszeitung* (24 July 2004): <http://www.taz.de/pt/2004/07/24/a0288.1/text.ges,1>.

Huyssen, Andreas. *Present Pasts*: *Urban Palimpsests and the Politics of Memory*. Stanford: Stanford UP, 2003.

Jameson, Fredric. *Postmodernism or the Cultural Logic of Late Capitalism*. London: Verso, 1991.

Jandt, Fred E. *Intercultural Communication: A Global Reader*. Thousand Oaks: Sage, 2004.

Kaminer, Wladimir. *Russendisko*. München: Goldmann, 2000.

Kaminer, Wladimir. *Schönhauser* Allee. München: Goldmann, 2001.

Kasack Wolfang. *Die russische Schriftsteller-Emigration im 20. Jahrhundert*. München: Otto Sagner, 1996.

Köpnick, Lutz. "Redeeming History? Foster's Dome and the Political Aesthetic of the Berlin Republic." *German Studies Review* 24 (2001): 303-23.

Ladd, Brian. *The Ghosts of Berlin*. Chicago: The U of Chicago P, 1997.

Levine, Myron. "Government Policy, the Local State and Gentrification: The Case of Prenzlauer Berg (Berlin), Germany." *Journal of Urban Affairs* 26.1 (2004): 89-108.

Lisiak, Agata Anna. *Urban Cultures in (Post)Colonial Central Europe*. West Lafayette: Purdue UP, 2010.

Lynch, Kevin. *The Image of the City*. Cambridge: MIT Press, 1960.

Nell, Werner. *Reflexionen und Konstruktionen des Fremden in der europäischen Literatur*. St. Augustin: Gardez!, 2001.

Neumeister, Andreas, and Marcel Hartges. *Poetry! Slam! Texte der Pop-Fraktion*. Reinbek bei Hamburg: Rohwolt, 1996.

Sartori, Giovanni. *Pluralismo, Multiculturalismo e estranei*. Milano: Rizzoli, 2000.

Savage, Mike, and Alan Warde. *Urban Sociology, Capitalism and Modernity*. London: Macmillan, 1993.

Schulze, Gerhard. *Die Erlebnisgesellschaft. Kultursoziologie der Gegenwart*. Frankfurt: Campus, 1992.

Shrivastava, Anjana. "Neue Russen im neuen Berlin." *Die bewegte Stadt*. Ed. Thomas Krüger. Berlin: FAB, 2000. 34-42.

Simmel, Georg "The Metropolis and Mental Life." 1903. *The Sociology of Georg Simmel*. New York: Free P, 1950. 409-24.

Teraoka, Arlene. "Multiculturalism and the Study of German Literature." *A User's Guide to German Cultural Studies*. Ed. Scott Denham, Irene Kacandes, and Jonathan Petropoulos. Ann Arbor: U of Michigan P, 1997. 63-78.

Tötösy de Zepetnek, Steven. "Configurations of Postcoloniality and National Identity: Inbetween Peripherality and Narratives of Change." *The Comparatist: Journal of the Southern Comparative Literature Association* 23 (1999): 89-110.

Wood, Phil, and Charles Landry. *The Intercultural City: Planning for Diversity Advantage*. London: Earthscan, 2007.

Zukin, Sharon. *The Cultures of Cities*. Oxford: Blackwell, 1995.

Author's profile: Giacomo Bottà teaches urban studies at the University of Helsinki. Bottà is particularly interested in the representations of popular culture in European cities in general, and Helsinki, Berlin, and Manchester in particular. His recent publications include the article "The City that was Creative and did not Know Manchester and Popular Music 1976-97," *European Journal of Cultural Studies* (2009).

From Diaspora to Nomadic Identity in the Work of Lispector and Felinto
Paula Jordão

Abstract: In her article "From Diaspora to Nomadic Identity in the Work of Lispector and Felinto" Paula Jordão analyzes Clarice Lispector's *A Hora da Estrela* (1977; *The Hour of the Star*, Trans. Giovanni Pontiero, 1992) and Marilene Felinto's *As Mulheres de Tijucopapo* (1982; *The Women of Tijucopapo*, trans. Irene Matthews, 1994). Despite being stylistically different, Lispector's *A Hora da Estrela* and Felinto's As *Mulheres de Tijucopapo* depict protagonists who share the same social and ethnic background and diasporic identity as women from the Northeast of Brazil. A closer look at the narrative trajectory of these two main characters shows us that they complement each other in the questioning and reformulation of their female identity. Although in a completely different way, they both defy a stereotyped female identity built upon patriarchal standards and put forth a nomadic identity in which memory, trauma, and gender play a central role. As "conscious pariahs," they are maybe the promise of the "New Brazilian Woman."

What can two such different novels as Clarice Lispector's *A Hora da Estrela* (1977; *The Hour of the Star*, trans. Giovanni Pontiero, 1992) and Marilene Felinto's *As Mulheres de Tijucopapo* (1982; *The Women of Tijucopapo*, trans. Irene Matthews, 1994) possibly share, one might ask. Dissimilar in their approach to female identity and subjectivity, the two novels do not seem to have much in common, except that their protagonists share the same ethnic background: the Brazilian *Nordeste.* In the case of Lispector's novel, the "anti-heroine" does not go beyond an image of anti-femininity according, at least, to patriarchal standards: Macabéa is ugly, dirty, and dim-witted. By contrast, Rísia, the amazon of *As Mulheres de Tijucopapo*, has all that Macabéa lacks: a will to rebel against those standards, which she evinces during her journey back to the mythic community of Tijucopapo. However, despite their differences, the two novels share what Helena Parente Cunha sees as an explosion of female speech (16), a common trait of Brazilian literature in the 1970s and 1980s. Further, they seem to establish a kind of dialogue in their reformulation and reconstruction of female identity as well as in the way they relate to the collectivity to which they belong. Macabéa and Rísia share a similar destiny as poor *nordestinas* who try to survive in the big city and complement each other in their questioning of a stereotyped female identity according to patriarchal standards. They also put forth a new, nomadic identity in which memory, trauma and gender play a central role.

As novels that describe the psychological, social, emotional, and relational development of their protagonists, *A Hora da Estrela and*

As Mulheres de Tijucopapo contain characteristics that confirm but also contradict the ones usually attributed to the genre of the *Bildungsroman*. This apparent paradox is present in Clarice Lispector's novel, since we witness both the creation and the parodic destruction/deconstruction of the main character Macabéa by the narrator Rodrigo S.M. Macabéa, who left the Northeast for the big city, is characterized as a typical anti-heroine, not only because of her physical and intellectual shortcomings but also due to her social class and ethnic identity. If her initial position as poor *nordestina* in a predominantly white and bourgeois society is already challenging, her situation becomes even harder when her individual limitations become apparent. She is physically unattractive, has a weak health, is very poor, is intellectually underdeveloped and lacks the most basic notions of hygiene. Her emotional relationships with other characters are equally off-putting. Gloria, the co-worker she relates to and who could mean a slim chance of a friendship, ends up as her rival in love matters, once she "steals" Macabéa's boyfriend. Olímpico, who for a short period functions as her (again very slim) promise of romance, turns into a clear disappointment when he exchanges her for Glória. Macabéa's limited life and inability to realize who she is becomes repeatedly and painfully clear in the words of the narrator, who describes her as "inept for living" (24), and as someone remaining outside the world. Her "absence" from the world and emptiness of existence change only briefly at the end of the story, when the *clairvoyante* makes it clear to her who she really is (not), she is run over by a car. Her ignorance, lack of understanding of her own situation and incapacity of changing her destiny would therefore hardly make her an example of a protagonist from a *Bildungsroman*.

Rísia's story begins with her departure from São Paulo in order to return to her mother's birthplace Tijucopapo. Besides having a symbolic meaning since it implies her return to her northeastern roots (partly symbolized by the strong and courageous women of Tijucopapo), Rísia's journey is also her answer to the diverse and multiple traumatic events she experienced in her childhood and youth. Her physical abuse by her father, her very complex and contradictory love-hate relationship with her mother, her awareness of her position as Other in a society that disparages her identity as poor *nordestina*, and finally her pain as a result of having been (figuratively or literally) deserted by her loved ones (Nema and Jonas) are a few of those traumas. During her therapeutic journey through which she constantly recalls her traumatic and painful past, Rísia affirms her determination to fight for a socially, ethnically and sexually less prejudiced reality and future. On her way to achieve it, she is willing to join a revolution that will eventually make it possible. Her exile and her symbolic ninemonth-journey finishes with what seems to be the end of her own private and individual revolution, and her son's and her own (re)birth. She eventually reaches her new reality: one without traumas and where the Other has finally his or her respectable and respected place in a multicultural and multiethnic society.

In her study *O Bildungsroman Feminino. Quatro Exemplos Brasileiros* on novels written by Brazilian women writers in the 1930s to the 1950s, Cristina Ferreira-Pinto points out a few characteristics of what she sees as being typical of the Brazilian female *Bildunsgroman*. Ferreira-Pinto begins by mentioning a few aspects that are also characteristic of the novels of apprenticeship written by men. Among others, she mentions the conflict between the character and his or her background (usually limited and backward), the character's isolation, conflicts with her/his parents, a journey to the big city or to another environment, emotional problems, a process of self-education, and an open end. Besides these aspects, the novels of apprenticeship written by women reveal a clear concern regarding the search for a female identity. Whereas in the case of male writers, the male character is generally in conflict with his father, the heroine's conflict involves her mother, who is usually absent, either physically or emotionally. Furthermore, while the hero searches to fulfill his calling and strives to develop his particular worldview, women look for an identity and wish to develop their own selves in their own terms. Finally, another fundamental difference has to do with the end of the narrative. If, in the case of the male character, he is lead to integrate in his social group, a quite different thing happens to the female character who ends with another journey, either physical or metaphorical (see Ferreira-Pinto, *O Bildungsroman Feminino* 147-49). The characteristics exposed above are significant to the analysis of *A Hora* and *As Mulheres*, in that they show how both novels constitute an alternative to the male novels of apprenticeship, and, consequently, contribute to the reformulation and construction of an alternative female identity.

Following the framework developed by Ferreira-Pinto, we can see that Macabéa and Rísia too are involved in a situation of conflict with the world they live in, which is partly caused by their ethnic and social origins. As often happens to so many *nordestinos*, they are confronted with a socially, geographically, and morally hostile environment that, predominantly white and bourgeois, does not accept their otherness. As diaspora subjects, they too are forced to flee the poverty associated to that environment, as well as the (in)direct threat of violence that is associated with it. Or, to apply Paul Gilroy's definition of identities of diaspora, they flee "the threat of violence rather than [decide upon] freely chosen experiences of displacement" (318). Consequently, they leave in search of another place and of an opportunity for a new life and eventually a new identity, even if that new place is not quite the answer to their initial difficulties. In spite of sharing the same background, the two protagonists not only proceed in different directions in their trajectory, but also develop in very different ways. While the big city seems to be the final destination for Macabéa, Rísia chooses to travel back to the symbolic and mythical Tijucopapo. Furthermore, while the city represents to Macabéa isolation and, eventually, her literal and figurative end, it means to Rísia the beginning of a new life and above all, an alliance with others in her struggle for a world with more justice. Their diversity notwithstanding, both protagonists search for and finally reach a reformulation of their identity. Rísia's departure from São Paulo and symbolic return to the northeastern Tijucopapo seems to be her answer to Macabéa's unsuccessful efforts to start a new and more prosperous life in the big city after leaving Alagoas. Rísia thus answers Macabéa's powerlessness and silence with her own cry of revolt and with her struggle for ethnic, social, and moral justice.

Macabéa's attitude of silence is also an attitude of exile. To Cláudia Nina, *A Hora* shows the intimate relation between a narrative of silence and of exile. In Lispector's novel, we witness a dominant atmosphere of silence that is the expression of loneliness, immobilization, and expatriation. According to Nina, in the narratives of silence (which is the case of *A Hora*) characters "are strangers not only in the world, in the landscape with which they do not interact, but also inside themselves for they feel unable to risk a self-knowledge journey. In a depersonalized society in which they are barely known, they feel anguish and nausea but they are so indifferent and passive that they ignore the word 'revolt'" (Nina 22-39). Furthermore, Macabéa's silence is significant not only as a sign of her nonquest for her identity, but also as an effect of the overbearing attitude of the male narrator. As he begins his narrative in *media res* ("I am about to begin in the middle by telling you that — that she was inept. Inept for living" [24; here and in subsequent quotations the English versions of the novels are used]), Rodrigo S.M.'s domineering stance goes so far as to imprison the female protagonist in "an impersonal limbo, untouched by what is worst or best" (23). Later in the text, he refuses her any possibility of escaping such imprisonment in her search for an (affirmative) identity. Macabéa's "impersonal limbo" becomes, however, a two-edged sword for it deconstructs Rodrigo's identity as a creative entity. If, on the one hand, we are able to detect in his words a possessive attitude towards his own creation, as the quotation above demonstrates, on the other hand he is the one subverting that same domineering stance by using a self-reflexive parodic discourse. Lets us recall Rodrigo's own words: "I must add one important detail to help the reader understand the narrative: it is accompanied from start to finish by the faintest yet nagging twinge of toothache, caused by an exposed nerve" (23). This self-reflexivity and self-subversion goes even further when he confesses his complicity (and why not also his solidarity) with Macabéa. As a social and individual failure, her weakness and annihilation become his own: "The typist doesn't want to get off my back" (21); "I see the girl from the Northeast looking in the mirror and — the ruffle of a drum — in the mirror there appears my own face, weary and unshaven. We have reversed roles so completely" (22); "Macabéa has murdered me" (85).

According to Cynthia Sloan, we can interpret the narrator's self-subversion as a sign of the "game" Lispector plays with the reader, by which she undermines the masculine libidinal economy that is clearly present in the narrative (91). Macabéa regains in this way a kind of power over Rodrigo that will eventually cause his narrative death as her creative father, and, even more significantly, the destruction of his normative and symbolical law. Contrary to what happens to Lispector's protagonist, Rísia's story is not one of ignorance of her identity, nor it is one of enunciative silence. Hers is rather an auto-diegetic text in which she affirms her revolt in a strong, and almost excessive and obsessive way: "My mouth is filled with dirt, it tastes of red, I spit grit, I grind my teeth. I was five years old and I was eating dirt and shitting roundworms like crazy, my eyes bulging out like a dolphin's; that didn't stop me from stampeding out the next day, however, and sliding from the top to the bottom of the mound of dirt, wrapping myself in dirt, and rolling in it, and eating and spitting and shitting and bawling into the four winds to go tell them: 'You go to hell and take my worms with you, papa and mama, and take your quarrelling and your quarrelling about me and your quarrels that make me cry so hard'" (12). To Macabéa's situation as an orphan and to her general passivity Rísia opposes not only her conflict with her parents, especially with her mother and aunt, but also her active efforts to change her situation, translated in constant movement. As Marilena Chaui reminds us in her preface to the novel, Rísia is a woman who is always on the verge of leaving for somewhere, either by taking boats made of paper, or airplanes, or flat bed trucks (9). Rísia's incessant departures are also the metaphorical translation of her identity's constant transformation. For Rísia, to exist means to leave for other places, to have other experiences, and to be connected to others, either in the present or by making a (frequently painful) journey to past events and past relationships. Her trajectory is one of change, and of confrontation with her fragmented self. The narration of this relational process can therefore only be a repeated and a repeating one, since it translates the constant (circular) movement of approach and separation from others and from herself. Felinto's protagonist thus corresponds to what Rosi Braidotti defines as a nomadic subject: "she/he connects, circulates, moves on; s/he does not form identifications but keeps on coming back at regular intervals" (35). This nomadic subject identity can be characterized as: "a play of multiple, fractured aspects of the self; it is relational, in that it requires a bond to the "other"; it is retrospective, in that it is fixed through memories and recollections, in a genealogical process" (Braidotti 166). Rísia's quest for her identity should therefore not be understood in terms of phases or stages of growth and development, as it is usually the case in novels of apprenticeship. Rather, Felinto's protagonist seems to establish her own rules of nonapprenticeship by the constant renewal of her identity, a process in which memory plays a central role.

As I mention above, the protagonists of the two novels represent complementary approaches to female identity. Rísia experiences what Macabéa was not able to do entirely: a new life as *nordestina* in the big city. This new life includes the social, ethnic and even religious discrimination that comes with her social background, as well as emotional disappointments, and, finally, her return to her origins in an effort to cope with and to recover from her traumatic experiences. According to Ferreira-Pinto, Rísia's journey comprises three facets: a geographical one (her return from São Paulo to the *Nordeste*), a psychological one (by which she reinvents herself in her violent litany to her mother), and a mythical one (involving mythical characters of Brazilian culture, such as Lampião and the Amazons of Tijucopapo) (*Gender, Discourse, and Desire* 70-71). Although Ferreira-Pinto touches upon some of the main aspects of Felinto's novel, she does not mention a topic that is key to the understanding of the formulation of identity in *As Mulheres*, namely the role of memory in the protagonist's recovery from her traumas.

The neglect of her mother, the physical and psychological abuse by her father and his sexual involvement with her aunt, the departure of both her friend Nema and, later on, of her lover Jonas constitute the main reasons for Rísia's feeling of abandonment and betrayal. Her repeated and unarticulated references to those events reveal not only the depth of her trauma, but also show the relevance of memory as a means of coping with pain and of recovering from it. As Marita Sturken states in her two essays on recovered memory and victims of trauma, "remembrance is an activity that will help one recover ... fragmentation is a primary quality of traumatic experiences ... Recovered memories are not produced in isolation. Rather, they emerge in dialogue with a therapist, or in the context of a therapy group, where testimony falls not on silence but on affirmation ... Testimony involves a constitutive relationship between a speaker and a listener ... The listener is the means through which the traumatic memory can be spoken, known, and made real" ("The Remembering of Forgetting" 104; "Narratives of Recovery" 235-37). Sturken's words might apply to Rísia's situation, whose fragmented, repeated and associative narration reveals her efforts to confront, cope with and eventually exorcize her past (and present) ghosts. Her narrative contrasts visibly with Macabéa's silence that, imposed by the narrator's overbearing ventriloquism, confirms her impossibility to give voice to and therefore to recover from her traumatic existence. In Rísia's case, we witness not only the confirmation but also the reiteration of the possibilities inherent in narration. Besides being the recollection of past scenes and episodes of her life, her narrative also includes a symbolic letter. In this text she unveils conflicts that have hurt her, and, above all, the emotional distance she establishes between her and others, which is particularly clear in her usage of English words: "I want this particular letter to go in English because English is the most alive language in the world ... English is made of foreign stuff that fascinates me and separates me from all that closeness of sending a letter from me in the language of my own people, in my own language. I don't want them to know about me like that, so closely. I want them to not understand me" (53). Among all the addressees she mentions in her letter, her mother occupies undoubtedly a central place. This is due to the emotional distance between them, which played a crucial role in her identity formation.

When seen from a psychoanalytic point of view, the neglect of the mother originates a fracture in the development of the child's most essential emotional center. According to psychoanalysts Jessica Benjamin, Nancy Chodorow, and Dorothy Dinnerstein, the mother is: "simultaneously the first love, the first witness and the first source of frustration of the child" (qtd. in Williams, "Which Came First?" 139). The protagonist of *As Mulheres sees* herself bereft of such emotional basis. Confronted with the trauma that results from such abandonment, Rísia becomes involved in an identification process with her mother by which she tries to minimize and even resolve that traumatic loss. As Diana Fuss affirms in her study *Identification Papers*: "All identification begins in an experience of traumatic loss and in the subject's tentative attempts to manage this loss" (38). In her attempt to manage or diminish this loss, Rísia addresses her mother in a way that evokes the different stages generally delineated in a psychoanalytic analysis: ambivalence, violence, repetition, and remembrance. In her frequently violent discourse, she seems to oscillate between love and total detachment symbolized by the words in English she often uses, in a paradoxical effort to finally reach harmony in the relation with her mother (and with herself), as her final words in the novel reveal: "So, that's it, mama. I want my life to have a finale like a big screen movie in another language, in the English language. I want to have a happy ending" (120).

The image of Rísia's mother is not only associated with emotional abandonment, but also with a refusal of her ethnic origins. As a daughter of a black mother and of a Native Brazilian father, Rísia's mother was given away for adoption as a young child and has consequently lost any attachment to her emotional and ethnic background. She unconsciously tries to pass her detachment to her daughter, a fact that is symbolized by the brilliantine she rubs on Rísia's hair in order to conceal her ethnic origins: "It was at Poti, and my mother was the adopted daughter of sister Lourdes, auntie's mother. My mother had lost all contact with the truth of herself. Mama's last native link died out with the rays of the moon on the moonlit night when she was given way. Everything about mama is adopted and adoptive. My mother has no origins, in reality, my mother doesn't exist. I don't know if my mother ever was born ... Manjopi — my hair looked like a hangman's ropes kneaded with the brilliantine mama put on it and that the sun melted at midday ... A family with crinkly hair: you used to hate our hair, mama" (23, 59, 117). Finally, Rísia's emotional and physical detachment from her mother has another reason: her mother's weakness and passivity towards life in general and towards her husband's infidelity, in particular. In Rísia's eyes, her mother belongs to the group of

women whom she despises and condemns, either for their betrayal
(as it is the case with her father's mistresses), or for their hypocrisy
(as it is the case with the women of her religious community). These
are the women she regards as traitors of their own gender because
of their lack of dignity and self-esteem. This lack of dignity and
self-esteem become clear in the following quotation: "My street had
women in it who carried their Bible under their arm and wore long
skirts at the door of the church, and, at the door that gave to the
guava tree, went in for copulation after a beating" (70). It is then
not surprising that she turns to the mythical Amazons of Tijucopapo
in search of an example of strength or resistance, establishing
therefore what one could call a feminine genealogy with Latin-
American characteristics.

Rísia's criticism itself should, however, not be considered
uncritically. In fact, her incapacity and even refusal to regard her
mother as a victim or at least as a product of Brazilian patriarchal
culture, makes her a reproducer herself of the negative (misogynist)
aspects of that culture. In other words, although Felinto denounces
maternity and gender stereotypes as oppressed elements within
Brazilian society, she does not address the possible reasons for such
oppression. On the contrary, she does not allow Rísia's mother any
kind of autonomy either in her behavior or in her speech that would
enable her to escape her subaltern fate. Imprisoned in that
oppressed situation, Rísia's mother remains a character that has
neither a voice, nor the means to regain it. She becomes therefore a
double victim of silence: in the plot and in her text, a kind of
silenced Jocasta, to use Marianne Hirsch's expression in her
introduction to her *The Mother/Daughter Plot: Narrative,
Psychoanalysis, Feminism* on the image of the mother in feminist
studies in the 1980s: "What earns the Spinx, the non-maternal
woman, privilege over Jocasta, the mother? Why do even feminist
analyses fail to grant Jocasta as mother a voice and a plot?" (3).

In spite of Rísia's ambiguity towards her mother, she puts forth
a kind of identity that is characterized by independence, autonomy
and rebellion against the values represented by the (female)
characters she relates to, and therefore attempts to subvert a
stereotypical conceptualization of gender. In this subversion, we
can find to a certain extent the continuation of the issues already
raised in *A Hora*. In fact, even if in a timid way, Macabéa too seems
to question some of the patriarchal values prevalent in Brazilian
society, such as female fertility and the submission of women to
men. Contrary to Glória who, possessing large hips, "was made for
bearing children" (59), "Macabéa, by comparison, had all the signs

of her own unmistakable doom ... [Macabéa] had ovaries as shrivelled as overcooked mushrooms" (59, 58). Described initially as if she had a physical deficiency, Lispector's protagonist eventually challenges the ideal of fertility cherished in and by a patriarchal society, when it becomes clear that her (lack of) fertility does not prevent her from feeling and behaving like a woman. In fact, expressed frequently in the text, her sensuality and desire show Macabéa as capable of loving someone, and not as someone who is deprived from any hope of romantic fulfilment, as Williams says in her study "Macabéa in Wonderland" (26). Macabéa does not become a stereotype of asexuality or frigidity, either. The sensual strength and intensity of her longing make her a challenge to the moral standards that are accepted by bourgeois culture, which dismisses female desire as hysterical, and therefore as abnormal: "She [Macabéa] understood what desire meant -- although she didn't know that she understood. That was how it was: she was starving but not for food, it was a numb sort of pain that rose from her lower abdomen, making the nipples of her breast quiver and her empty arms starved of any embrace came out in goose bumps. She became overwrought and it was painful to live. At such moments, she would shake with nerves and her workmate Glória would rush to get her a glass of water with sugar" (44). In her relationship with Olímpico, Macabéa also shows a behaviour that does not conform to the passivity and subordination often attributed to women in heterosexual relations in a patriarchal society. To Olímpico's petulance and megalomania, she opposes her own wise ignorance, which often unveils his superficiality and sexist mentality.

As mentioned above, Rísia's overt criticism of the promiscuous and hypocritical behavior of the women of her religious community also unveils her subversion of stereotyped gender values. This subversion acquires a more radical facet when she expresses her openness and acceptance of a moral and sexual behaviour that challenges the moral rules of a heterosexual and patriarchal order. This is for instance clear in her reaction to the disappearance of her lover Jonas. In a provocative and even almost self-destructive way, Rísia's violent disruptive discourse and unrestrained (sexually and morally) behavior seem to refuse any kind of rules or moral boundaries. Love alternates with hatred, and her sexual experiences are unrestrained: "And that, as far as fairies and pansies and my own morality are concerned, I almost had an affair with a woman" (72); "I'm a whore, take me anywhere you want to (84); "Because that was the only way I could surrender myself to the complete and total indifference that comes from giving my own body, without pride, without dignity, without love, without pain" (85).

In *As Mulheres* we witness a frequent intertextuality between the novel and the Bible that provides another example of transgression of moral and religious principles. The first instance of this intertextuality is embodied in Jonas, Rísia's lover. As a homonym of the prophet in the Old Testament who fled God's imposed responsibilities and duties, the name Jonas reasserts the character's symbolic association with (human) selfishness and treason. On the other hand, however, since it concerns a mere (failed) romantic relationship, it belittles its religious connotation, and makes it (too) secular. Rísia's frequent references to Psalm 91 are other examples of a disruptive Biblical intertextuality. Originally a text of spiritual comfort, forgiveness, and hope, it loses its original symbolism, because it also represents Rísia's power over others, her will to take revenge on others for having despised, hurt, and left her, and her despair and self-destructive feelings:

[I] wanted to be like the Bible, the greatest book, the 91st Psalm, God's commands. I wanted to be God so I could kill all the people I wanted to, and make the world in my own way ... Until I was a certain age I knew the 91st Psalm by heart. If I still knew it, I probably wouldn't hesitate to recite it in the middle of these nights ahowled by packs of starving wolves, sung by swollen frogs, by little crickets, by snakes lying in ambush, in the middle of these menacing nights where I lie down to sleep and glimpse stars through the openings in the shacks I'm stopping at, almost dead from the death of him who died and left me exposed to all dangers. If only I could pray. I am too scientific to believe in what I pray for. If only I could believe. If only I could telephone. If only I could hear, coming from the heavens, the voices of a choir of angels: the 91st Psalm. (70-81)

Rísia's "naked" and daring perspective of her relationship with Lampião, one of the mythical characters of Brazilian culture and history, provides a last example of her rebellion against the dominant morality she is immersed in: "But today my body needs a man ... I wanted to be seduced ... I wanted a man with all the acts of the previous men, and with new acts. I wanted the perfection of an act. The man and I moved together in every act. We still didn't sleep. And when I tried to enwrap the man's member with my hands and he got aroused, and when I wanted to appease it in my mouth and he wet himself like a child wets itself, I cried. I cried with my mouth full of liquid salted with tears, I fondled the man's member that I had sucked and slept like someone who has just emerged from the waves of the sea" (95-96). Described in non-conventional and daring terms for its sexual transparency and eroticism, her relationship can be seen as the beginning of a new era as far as gender and sexuality are concerned (see Ferreira-Pinto, *Gender, Discourse, and Desire* 68). In this new order, women and men would be in a position of equality and women would be able to reaffirm their independent, free, and autonomous subjectivity in a thoroughly enjoyed sexual relationship.

The new order Rísia wants to bring forth is not limited to her individual identity, but is also closely related to the community to which she belongs. This collective side of her identity becomes particularly relevant when we consider her ethnic origins and, consequently, the diasporic fate she shares with so many other *nordestinos*. Tijucopapo is to Rísia a promised land. Both a crystallized mythical image in her memory and the symbol of a paradisiacal future, Tijucopapo shares some of the characteristics Pierre Nora attributed to his *lieux de mémoire*. According to Nora, the *lieux de mémoire* comprehend the three senses of the word: the material, the symbolic, and the functional one. The first one addresses tangible and changeable realities. The second one is the product of imagination and it sustains the crystallization and the transmission of mementos. The third one concerns rituals (see on Nora in Ricoeur 528). As a reminder of the heroines who fought the Dutch invaders in Pernambuco in the seventeenth century, Tijucopapo is not just an element of Rísia's symbolic reality but is also part of Brazilian reality and (mythical) history. Moreover, by passing on her recollection of that (mythical) place to other generations, Rísia fulfills the task attributed to the *lieux de mémoire* — the enrichment of its meaning to a community, and in this particular case, to (a part of) the Brazilian Northeastern community. Finally, by reviving events that are part of a forgotten history in which women played an essential role, Rísia broaches another aspect of Tijucopapo as a *lieu de mémoire*, namely the making of another history or of a renewed history that belongs to the legacy of gender of the Brazilian *Nordeste*.

Rísia's renewal of history is also present in the way she addresses historical dates and periods. By relating them to events which other characters are part of, those dates and periods acquire a more personal dimension that contributes to the personalization of History. That is the case of 1935, her mother's date of birth and the date of the first failed coup of the communist party against the Vargas government. Because of the meaning of political and historical failure attached to that year, her mother's birth becomes overshadowed by a general feeling of impossibility and impotency. Something similar happens with 1964, the beginning of the dictatorship led by Castelo Branco and the year of her newborn brother's death, owing to a lack of medical assistance. Metonymically speaking, it is as if Rísia's grief and despair became a reflection of the country's own suffering, both protagonist and country sharing the consequences of poverty and misery. Finally, the concomitance of her friend Nema's departure with the leaden years of the dictatorship during the Médici government originates again the symbolic interrelation of Rísia's individual tragedy and the country's predicament. By mentioning these dates, Felinto thus contributes to a recovery of collective and historical memories that are essential to a Brazilian cultural and historical legacy, and therefore to Brazilian identity, never dismissing the individual aspect of those memories in this process.

Rísia's involvement in such a recovery does not mean, however, that she accepts to play the role of unifier of the nation, or of a so-called "building-block," to use Paul Gilroy's concept. In fact, in her refusal to compromise with any kind of rules or principles of the patriarchal, white and bourgeois order, she evinces a diasporic identity, which can be described as: "an alternative to the accepted gender hierarchy and 'family as building-block' basis of the nation-state, offering instead anti-national and anti-essentialist accounts of identity formation based on contingency, indeterminacy and conflict, and offering possibilities for different forms of political action" (Gilroy 339). Her answer is to fight for a revolution (regardless of how mythical it may be): "The landscape I brought painted on the white sheet of paper turned into a revolution. I came to make the revolution which knocks down not my Guaraná on the counter, but those who are guilty of all the lovelessness I suffered and of all the poverty I endured" (119).

A Hora da Estrela and *As Mulheres de Tijucopapo* portray female identity as an identity of exile and of Diaspora. Both novels are a good example of the deconstruction in literature of cultural myths of femininity, beauty, or youth in their questioning of issues of identity, sexuality, and desire (Ferreira-Pinto, *Gender, Discourse, and Desire* 2). Further, in their subversive (re)formulation of female identity, *A Hora* and *As Mulheres* also instantiate what Lúcia Helena Vianna characterizes as typical of the literary work written after the 1960s: a renewal of the *Bildungsroman* insofar as this genre deals with the construction of subjectivity. In their trajectory of reconstruction and questioning of identity, the protagonists complement each other in their particular quest. Rísia seems to take Macabéa's end as point of departure, or at least appears to wish to accomplish what Lispector's protagonist was not able or allowed to do. She recuperates the voice Lispector's protagonist does not seem to have entirely, and takes part in a revolution Macabéa did not hear of. As they are both part of a Northeastern Diaspora, they seem to correspond to the notion of "the conscious pariah" defined by David Brookshaw as "self-excluding ... which denotes someone whose status as an outsider enables him/her to depict society more freely" (12). As "conscious pariahs," they are maybe the promise of the "New Brazilian Woman," to use Ferreira-Pinto's expression (*Gender, Discourse, and Desire* 7).

Note: The above article is a revised version of Jorãdo, Paula. "From Diaspora to Nomadic Identity in the Work of Lispector and Felinto." *CLCWeb: Comparative Literature and Culture* 11.3 (2009): <http://docs.lib.purdue.edu/clcweb/vol11/iss3/8>. Copyright release by Purdue University Press.

Works Cited

Braidotti, Rosi. *Nomadic Subjects*: *Embodiment and Sexual Difference in Contemporary Feminist Theory*. New York: Columbia UP, 1994.
Brookshaw, David. "Migration and Memory — From forgetting to Storytelling: José Eduardo Agualusa's *O Vendedor de Passados* and Moacyr Scliar's *A Majestade do Xingu*." *Postcolonial Theory and Lusophone Literatures*. Ed. Paulo de Medeiros. Utrecht: U of Utrech Portuguese Studies Center, 2007. 9-20.
Chaui, Marilena. "Prefácio." *As Mulheres de Tijucopapo*. By Marilene Felinto. Ed. Marilena Chauí. Rio de Janeiro: Editora 34, 1992. 7-10
Cunha, Helena Parente. "Desafiando o desafio." *Desafiando o cânone*. Ed. Helena Parente Cunha. Rio de Janeiro: Tempo Brasileiro, 1999. 15-20.
Felinto, Marilene. *As Mulheres de Tijucopapo*. Rio de Janeiro: Editora 34, 1982.
Felinto, Marilene. *The Women of Tijucopapo*. Trans. Irene Matthews. Lincoln: U of Nebraska P, 1994.
Ferreira-Pinto, Cristina. *O Bildungsroman feminino. Quatro exemplos brasileiros*. São Paulo: Editora Perspectiva, 1990.
Ferreira-Pinto, Cristina. *Gender, Discourse, and Desire in Twentieth- Century Brazilian Women's Literature*. West Lafayette: Purdue UP, 2004.
Fuss, Diana. *Identification Papers*. London: Routledge. 1995.
Gilroy, Paul. "Diasporas and the Detours of Identity." *Identity and Difference*. Ed. Kathryn Woodward. Thousand Oaks: Sage, 1997. 301-43.
Hirsch, Marianne. "Introduction." *The Mother/Daughter Plot: Narrative, Psychoanalysis, Feminism*. By Marianne Hirsch. Bloomington: Indiana UP, 1989. 1-27.
Lispector, Clarice. *A Hora da Estrela*. Rio de Janeiro: Editora Rocco, 1998.
Lispector, Clarice. *The Hour of the Star*. Trans. Giovanni Pontiero. Manchester: Carcanet P, 1992.
Nina, Cláudia. *Exilic/Nomadic Itineraries in Clarice Lispector's Works*. Utrecht: Utrecht UP, 2001.
Ricoeur, Paul. *La Mémoire, l'histoire, l'oubli*. Paris: Seuil, 2000.
Sloan, Cynthia A. "The Social and Textual Implications of the Creation of a

Male Narrating Subject in Clarice Lispector's *A Hora da Estrela.*" *Luso-Brazilian Review* 38.1 (2001): 89-102.

Sturken, Marita. "The Remembering of Forgetting. Recovered Memory and the Question of Experience." *Social Text* 16 (1998): 103-25.

Sturken, Marita. "Narratives of Recovery: Repressed Memory as Cultural Memory." *Acts of Memory: Cultural Recall in the Present*. Ed. Mieke Bal, Jonathan Crewe, and Leo Spitzer. Hanover: UP of New England, 1999. 231-48.

Vianna, Lúcia Helena. *Escenas de amor y muerte en la ficcion brasilena. El juego dramatico de la relacion hombre-mujer en la literatura*. La Habana: Casa de las Américas, 1996.

Williams, Claire. "Which Came First? The Question of Maternity in Clarice Lispector's 'O Ovo e a Galinha'." *Women, Literature and Culture in the Portuguese-Speaking World*. Ed. Cláudia Pazos Alonso. Lewiston: Edwin Mellen, 1996. 135-53.

Williams, Claire. "Macabéa in Wonderland: Linguistic Adventures in Clarice Lispector's *A Hora da Estrela*." *Elipsis* 3 (2005): 21-38.

Author's profile: Paula Jordão teaches Brazilian and Portuguese literatures at the University of Utrecht. Her interests in scholarship include Brazilian and Portuguese contemporary literature and Brazilian contemporary cinema. Jordão's recent publications include "Inleiding," *The Value of Literature in the Seventies: The Case of Italy and Portugal* (Ed. Monica Jansen and Paula Jordão, 2007), "Da Memória e da contra memória em *O vento assobiando nas gruas*," *Para um leitor ignorado. Ensaios sobe a ficção de Lídia Jorge* (Ed. Ana Paula Ferreira, 2009), and "O cruzamento do desejo e da memória em 'O Belo Adormecido' e 'Assobio na Noite' de Lídia Jorge," *Bulletin of Hispanic Studies* (2009).

Part Three
Thematic Bibliography

Selected Bibliography of Work on Identity, Migration, and Displacement
   Li-wei Cheng, Steven Tötösy de Zepetnek, and I-Chun Wang

This bibliography is also available online at <http://docs.lib.purdue.edu/ clcweblibrary/migrationbibliography>. For further bibliographies relevant to migration studies see Steven Tötösy de Zepetnek, "Selected Bibliography of Works about Postcolonial Writing," *CLCWeb: Comparative Literature and Culture* (*Library*): <http://docs.lib.purdue.edu/clcweblibrary/postcolonial bibliography> and Steven Tötösy de Zepetnek and Carlo Salzani, "Bibliography for Work in Travel Studies," *CLCWeb: Comparative Literature and Culture* (*Library*): <http://docs.lib.purdue.edu/clcweblibrary/travelstudies bibliography>.

Aissaoui, Rabah. *Immigration and National Identity: North African Political Movements in Colonial and Postcolonial France*. New York: Palgrave Macmillan, 2009.
Aitchison, Cara, Peter Hopkins, and Mei-po Kwan, eds. *Geographies of Muslim Identities: Diaspora, Gender and Belonging*. Burlington: Ashgate, 2007.
Akpinar, Aylin. *Male's Honour and Female's Shame: Gender and Ethnic Identity Constructions among Turkish Divorcées in the Migration Context*. Uppsala: A. Akpinar, 1998.
Anderson, Bridget L. *Migration, Accommodation and Language Change: Language at the Intersection of Regional and Ethnic Identity*. New York: Palgrave Macmillan, 2008.
Anderson, Wanni W., and Robert G. Lee, eds. *Displacements and Diasporas: Asians in the Americas*. New Brunswick: Rutgers UP, 2005.
Ariel, Ari. *Trust Networks, Migration, and Ethno-National Identity: Jewish Migration from Yemen to Palestine in the Late Nineteenth and Twentieth Centuries*. PhD Diss. New York: Columbia UP, 2009.
Bainbridge, Susan. *Culture and Identity in Belgian Francophone Writing: Dialogue, Diversity and Displacement*. Bern: Peter Lang, 2009.
Bammer, Angelika. *Displacement: Cultural Identities in Question*. Bloomington: Indiana UP, 1994.
Barbiera, Irene. *Changing Lands in Changing Memories: Migration and Identity during the Lombard Invasions*. Firenze: All'Insegna del Aiglio, 2005.
Bates, Crispin, ed. *Community, Empire, and Migration: South Asians in Diaspora*. New York: Palgrave, 2001.
Bender, Barbara, and Margot Winer, eds. *Contested Landscapes: Movement, Exile and Place*. New York: Berg, 2001.
Benmayor, Rina, and Andor Skotnes, eds. *Migration and Identity*. New Brunswick: Transaction, 2005.
Bottà, Giacomo. "Interculturalism and New Russians in Berlin." *Perspectives on Identity, Migration, and Displacement*. Ed. Steven Tötösy de Zepetnek, I-Chun Wang, and Hsiao-Yu Sun. Kaoshiung: National Sun Yat-sen U, Humanities and Social Sciences Series, 2010. 163-181.
Braidotti, Rosi. *Nomadic Subjects: Embodiment and Sexual Difference in Contemporary Feminist Theory*. New York: Columbia UP, 1994.

Bravo-Moreno, Ana. *Migration, Gender and National Identity: Spanish Migrant Women in London*. Bern: Peter Lang, 2006.

Brettell, Caroline. *Anthropology and Migration: Essays on Transnationalism, Ethnicity, and Identity*. Walnut Creek: Altamira, 2003.

Brookshaw, David. "Migration and Memory — From forgetting to Storytelling: José Eduardo Agualusa's *O Vendedor de Passados* and Moacyr Scliar's *A Majestade do Xingu*." *Postcolonial Theory and Lusophone Literatures*. Ed. Paulo de Medeiros. Utrecht: U of Utrech Portuguese Studies Center, 2007. 9-20.

Brown-Guillory, Elizabeth, ed. *Middle Passages and the Healing Place of History: Migration and Identity in Black Women's Literature*. Columbus: Ohio State UP, 2006.

Brown, Melissa, J. *Is Taiwan Chinese?: The Impact of Culture, Power, and Migration on Changing Identities*. Berkeley: U of California P, 2004.

Buckley, Cynthia J., Blair A. Ruble, and Erin Trouth Hofmann, eds. *Migration, Homeland, and Belonging in Eurasia*. Baltimore: Johns Hopkins UP, 2008.

Buckner, Phillip, and R. Douglas Francis, eds. *Canada and the British World: Culture, Migration, and Identity*. Vancouver: U of British Columbia P, 2006.

Bull, Philip, Frances Devlin-Glass, and Helen Doyle, eds. *Ireland and Australia, 1798-1998: Studies in Culture, Identity, and Migration*. Sydney: Crossing, 2000.

Canepa-Koch, Gisela. *Geopolitics and Geopoetics of Identity: Migration, Ethnicity and Place in the Peruvian Imaginary*. PhD Diss. Chicago: U of Chicago P, 2003.

Castillo, Susan. "The Ambivalent Americanness of J. Hector St. Jean de Crèvecoeur." *Perspectives on Identity, Migration, and Displacement*. Ed. Steven Tötösy de Zepetnek, I-Chun Wang, and Hsiao-Yu Sun. Kaoshiung: National Sun Yat-sen U, Humanities and Social Sciences Series, 2010. 48-57.

Cervantes-Rodríguez, Margarita, and Ramón Grosfoguel, and Eric Mielants, eds. *Caribbean Migration to Western Europe and the United States: Essays on Incorporation, Identity, and Citizenship*. Philadelphia: Temple UP, 2009.

Cesarani, David, Tony Kushner, and Milton Shain, eds. *Place and Displacement in Jewish History and Memory: Zakor V'makor*. London: Vallentine Mitchell, 2009.

Chamberlain, Mary. *Caribbean Migration: Globalised Identities*. London: Routledge, 1998.

Cheng, Chin-chuan. "Distance, Culture, and Migration in Ancient China." *Perspectives on Identity, Migration, and Displacement*. Ed. Steven Tötösy de Zepetnek, I-Chun Wang, and Hsiao-Yu Sun. Kaoshiung: National Sun Yat-sen U, Humanities and Social Sciences Series, 2010. 5-10.

Christou, Anastasia. *Narratives of Place, Culture and Identity: A Second Generation Greek-Americans' Return "Home."* Amsterdam: Amsterdam UP, 2006.

Civantos, Christina. *Between Argentines and Arabs: Argentine Orientalism, Arab Immigrants, and the Writing of Identity*. New York: State University of New York P, 2005.

Cohen, Robin, ed. *The Cambridge Survey of World Migration*. Ed. Robin Cohen. Cambridge: Cambridge UP, 1995.

Colic-Peisker, Val. *Migration, Class, and Transnational Identities: Croatians in Australia and America*. Urbana: U of Illinois P, 2008.

Cuba, Lee, and David M. Hummon. "A Place to Call Home: Identification with Dwelling, Community, and Region." *The Sociological Quarterly* 34.1 (1993): 111-31.

Dahab, F. Elizabeth. *Voices of Exile in Contemporary Canadian Francophone Literature*. Lanham: Rowman & Littlefield, 2009.

Davies, Carole Boyce. *Black Women, Writing, and Identity: Migrations of the Subject*. London: Routledge, 1994.

Dauvergne, Catherine. *Humanitarianism, Identity, and Nation: Migration Laws of Australia and Canada*. Vancouver: U of British Columbia P, 2005.

De Carvalho, Daniela. *Migrants and Identity in Japan and Brazil: The Nikkeijin*. New York: Routledge, 2003.

Delaney, Enda, and Donald M. MacRaild, eds. *Irish Migration, Networks and Ethnic Identities since 1750*. New York: Routledge, 2007.

Delanty, Gerard, Ruth Wodak, and Paul Jones, eds. *Identity, Belonging and Migration*. Liverpool: U of Liverpool P, 2008.

Diener, Alexander C. *One Homeland or Two? Territorialization of Identity and the Migration Decision of the Mongolian-Kazakh Diaspora*. PhD Diss. Madison: U of Wisconsin, 2003.

Dubey, Ajay, ed. *Indian Diaspora: Global Identity*. Delhi: Kalinga, 2003.

Edwards, Natalie, and Christopher Hogarth, eds. *Gender and Displacement: "Home" in Contemporary Francophone Womens Autobiography*. Cambridge: Cambridge UP, 2008.

Eigenbrod, Renate. *Travelling Knowledges: Positioning the Im/Migrant Reader of Aboriginal Literatures in Canada*. Winnipeg: U of Manitoba P, 2005.

Erickson, Gary, and Lois Anne Lorentzen. *Religion at the Corner of Bliss and Nirvana: Politics, Identity, and Faith in New Migrant Communities*. Durham: Duke UP, 2009.

Falola, Toyin, Niyi Afolabi, and Aderonke Adesola Adesanya, eds. *Migrations and Creative Expressions in Africa and the African Diaspora*. Durham: Carolina Academic P, 2008.

Fanning, Bryan, ed. *Immigration and Social Change in the Republic of Ireland*. Manchester: Manchester UP, 2007.

Fernández, Maria José. "Negotiating Identity: Migration, Colonization, and Cultural Marginalization in Lara Rios and Vicky Ramos' *Mo* and Carmen Lomas Garza's *In My Family/En mi familia*." *Children's Literature Association Quarterly* 28.2 (2003): 81-89.

Fitzgerald, Patrick, and Brian Lambkin, eds. *Migration in Irish History, 1607-2007*. New York: Palgrave Macmillan, 2008.

Galent, Marcin, Idesbald Goddeeris, and Dariusz Niedźwiedzki. *Migration and Europeanisation: Changing Identities and Values among Polish Pendulum Migrants and their Belgian Employers*. Kraków: Zakład Wydawniczy, 2009.

Gillan, Jennifer. "Focusing on the Wrong Front: Historical Displacement, the Maginot Line, and 'The Bluest Eye.'" *African American Review* 36.2 (2002): 283-98.

Gilroy, Paul. "It Ain't Where You're From, It's Where You're At: The Dialectics of Diasporic Identification." *Third Text* 13 (1990-91): 3-16.

Gilroy, Paul. "Diasporas and the Detours of Identity." *Identity and Difference*. Ed. Kathryn Woodward. Thousand Oaks: Sage, 1997. 301-43.

Goh, Robbie B.H., and Shawn Wong, eds. *Asian Diasporas: Cultures, Identities, Representations*. Hong Kong: Hong Kong UP, 2004.

Gordon, Edmund T., and Mark Anderson. "The African Diaspora: Toward an Ethnography of Diasporic Identification." *The Journal of American Folklore* 112.445 (1999): 282-96.

Gracia, Jorge J.E., Lynette M.F. Bosch, and Isabel Alvarez Borland, eds. *Identity, Memory, and Diaspora: Voices of Cuban-American Artists, Writers, and Philosophers*. Albany: State U of New York P, 2008.

Grasner, David. "Migration, Fragmentation, and Identity: Zora Neale Hurston's *Color Struck* and the Geography of the Harlem Renaissance." *Theatre Journal* 53.4 (2001): 533-50.

Gray, Breda. *Women and the Irish Diaspora*. New York: Routledge, 2004.

Gray, Breda. "Curious Hybridities: Transnational Negotiations Migrancy through Generation." *Irish Studies Review* 14.2 (2006): 207-23.

Guenther, Christina. "Exile and the Construction of Identity in Barbara Honigmann's Trilogy of Diaspora." *Comparative Literature Studies* 40.2 (2003): 215-31.

Guild, Elspeth. *The Legal Elements of European Identity: EU Citizenship and Migration Law*. Hague: Aspen, 2004.

Gupta, Akhil, and James Ferguson. "Beyond 'Culture': Space, Identity, and the Politics of Difference." *Cultural Anthropology* 7.1 (1992): 6-23.

Hammer, Juliane. *Palestinians Born in Exile: Diaspora and the Search for a Homeland*. Austin: U of Texas P, 2005.

Harrington, Sue. *Aspects of Gender Identity and Craft Production in the European Migration Period*. Oxford: John and Erica Hedges, 2008.

Hedberg, Charlotta. *The Finland-Swedish Wheel of Migration: Identity, Networks and Integration, 1976-2000*. Uppsala: Uppsala UP, 2004.

Herzberg, Yael. *Identity in an Era of Globalization and Transnational Migration Microform: The Discursive Construction of Identity of Israeli Immigrant Women*. PhD Diss. New Jersey: Rutgers UP, 2000.

Hoffmann, David L. *Peasant Metropolis: Migration to Moscow and the Politics of Social Identity, 1929-1941*. New York: Cornell UP, 1994.

Hsu, Madeline Yuan-yin. *Dreaming of Gold, Dreaming of Home: Transnationalism and Migration between the United States and South China, 1882-1943*. Stanford: Stanford UP, 2000.

Huebener, Paul. "'No Moon to Speak of': Identity and Place in Dionne Brand's *In Another Place, Not Here*. *Callallo* 30.2 (2007): 615-25.

Huyssen, Andreas. "Diaspora and Nation: Migration into Other Pasts." *New German Critique* 88 (2003): 147-64.

Hwang, Pao-i. "Ethnicity and Nationhood in Achebe's *Arrow of God*." *Perspectives on Identity, Migration, and Displacement*. Ed. Steven Tötösy de Zepetnek, I-Chun Wang, and Hsiao-Yu Sun. Kaoshiung: National Sun Yat-sen U, Humanities and Social Sciences Series, 2010. 58-73.

Ibrahim, Fouad N., and Helmut Ruppert, eds. *Rural-Urban Migration and Identity Change: Case Studies from the Sudan*. Bayreuth: Druckhaus Bayreuth, 1988.

Israel, Milton, and N.K. Wagle, eds. *Ethnicity, Identity, Migration: The South Asian Context*. Toronto: U of Toronto P, 1993.

Jansen, Tineke. *Defining New Domains: Identity Politics in International Female Migration: Indonesian-Chinese Women in the Netherlands*. Hague: Institute of Social Studies, 1992.

Jay, Jennifer W. "Sui and Tang Princess Brides and Life after Marriage at the Borderlands." *Perspectives on Identity, Migration, and Displacement*. Ed. Steven Tötösy de Zepetnek, I-Chun Wang, and Hsiao-Yu Sun. Kaoshiung: National Sun Yat-sen U, Humanities and Social Sciences Series, 2010. 11-24.

Jayasuriya, Shihan. *African Identity in Asia: Cultural Effects of Forced Migration*. Princeton: Markus Wiener, 2008.

Johansson, Anders W., and Maria Udén. "Information, Gender, and Innovation." *Perspectives on Identity, Migration, and Displacement*. Ed. Steven Tötösy de Zepetnek, I-Chun Wang, and Hsiao-Yu Sun. Kaoshiung: National Sun Yat-sen U, Humanities and Social Sciences Series, 2010. 74-85.

Jordão, Paula. "From Diaspora to Nomadic Identity in the Work of Lispector and Felinto." *Perspectives on Identity, Migration, and Displacement*. Ed. Steven Tötösy de Zepetnek, I-Chun Wang, and Hsiao-Yu Sun. Kaoshiung: National Sun Yat-sen U, Humanities and Social Sciences Series, 2010. 182-196.

Julios, Christina. *Contemporary British Identity: English Language, Migrants, and Public Discourse*. Burlington: Ashgate, 2008.

Jungbluth, Konstanze, and Christiane Meierkord, eds. *Identities in Migration Contexts*. Tübingen: Narr, 2007.

Kaes, Anton. "Leaving Home: Film, Migration, and the Urban Experience." *New German Critique* 74 (1998): 179-92.

Kandiyoti, Dalia. *Migrant Sites: America, Place, and Diaspora Literatures*. Lebanon: Dartmouth, 2009.

Kelly, Ursula A. *Migration and Education in a Multicultural World: Culture, Loss, and Identity*. New York: Palgrave Macmillan, 2009.

Kerkyasharian, Stepan. *Migration and Australia's National Identity*. Sydney: Ethnic Affairs Commission of New South Wales, 1991.

Kleiner-Liebau, Désirée. *Migration and the Construction of National Identity in Spain*. Frankfurt: Vervuert, 2009.

Kofler, Angelika. *Migration, Emotion, Identities: The Subjective Meaning of Difference*. Wien: Braumüller, 2002.

Koning, Juliette. *Generations of Change: Migration, Family Life, and Identity Formation in a Javanese Village during the New Order*. Bulaksumur: Gadjah Mada UP, 2004.

Korhonen, Teppo, ed. *Encountering Ethnicities: Ethnological Aspects on Ethnicity, Identity and Migration*. Helsinki: Suomalaisen Kirjallisuuden Seura, 1995.

Krasner, David. "Migration, Fragmentation, and Identity: Zora Neale Hurston's *Color Struck* and the Geography of the Harlem Renaissance." *Theatre Journal* 53.4 (2001): 533-50.

Ku, Agnes S. "Immigration Policies, Discourses, and the Politics of Local Belonging in Hong Kong (1950-1980)." *Modern China* 30.3 (2004): 326-60.

Kung, Shao-ming. "British Muslims and Limits of Multiculturalism in Kureishi's *The Black Album*." *Perspectives on Identity, Migration, and Displacement*. Ed. Steven Tötösy de Zepetnek, I-Chun Wang, and Hsiao-Yu Sun. Kaoshiung: National Sun Yat-sen U, Humanities and Social Sciences Series, 2010. 111-126.

Laroussi, Farid. "Literature in Migration." *The European Legacy* 7.6 (2002): 709-22.

Larson, Pier M. "Reconsidering Trauma, Identity, and the African Diaspora: Enslavement and Historical Memory in Nineteenth-century Highland Madagascar." *The William and Mary Quarterly* 56. 2 (1999): 335-62.

Lavie, Smadar, and Ted Swedenburg, eds. *Displacement, Diaspora, and Geographies of Identity*. Durham: Duke UP, 1996.

Lee, Hsiu-chuan. "Popular Documentary Photography on the Internment of Japanese Americans." *Perspectives on Identity, Migration, and Displacement*. Ed. Steven Tötösy de Zepetnek, I-Chun Wang, and Hsiao-Yu Sun. Kaoshiung: National Sun Yat-sen U, Humanities and Social Sciences Series, 2010. 139-162.

Lee, Jade Tsui-yu. "(Im)migration and Cultural Diasporization in Garcia's *Monkey Hunting*." *Perspectives on Identity, Migration, and Displacement*. Ed. Steven Tötösy de Zepetnek, I-Chun Wang, and Hsiao-Yu Sun. Kaoshiung: National Sun Yat-sen U, Humanities and Social Sciences Series, 2010. 127-138.

Lewis, Laura A. "Of Ships and Saints: History, Memory, and Place in the Making of Moreno Mexican Identity." *Cultural Anthropology* 16.1 (2001): 62-82.

Liebkind, Karmela, ed. *New Identities in Europe: Immigrant Ancestry and the Ethnic Identity of Youth*. Brookfield: Gower, 1989.

Lin, Tse-min, Chin-en Wu, and Feng-yu Lee. "'Neighborhood' Influence on the Formation of National Identity in Taiwan: Spatial Regression with Disjoint Neighborhoods." *Political Research Quarterly* 59.1 (2006): 35-46.

Lorente, Beatriz P., Nicola Piper, and Shen Hsiu-hua, eds. *Asian Migrations: Sojourning, Displacement, Homecoming and Other Travels*. Singapore: Asia Research Institute, 2006.

Lucassen, Jan, and Leo Lucassen, eds. *Migration, Migration History, History: Old Paradigms and New Perspectives*. Bern: Peter Lang, 2005.

Ma, Laurence J.C., and Carolyn Cartier, eds. *The Chinese Diaspora: Space, Place, Mobility, and Identity*. Lanham: Rowman and Littlefield, 2003.

Magat, Ilan N. "Israeli and Japanese Immigrants to Canada: Home, Belonging, and the Territorialization of Identity." *Ethos* 27.2 (1999): 119-44.

Mansouri, Fethi, ed. *Youth Identity and Migration: Culture, Values, and Social Connectedness*. Altona: Common Ground, 2009.

Marjanne, Goozé E. "The Interlocution of Geographical Displacement, Cultural Identity, and Cuisine in Works by Jeannette Lander." *Monatshefte für deutschsprachige Literatur und Kultur* 91.1 (1999): 101-20.

Massey, Douglas. *Worlds in Motion: Understanding International Migration at the End of the Millennium*. Oxford: Oxford UP, 1998.

McClennen, Sophia A. *The Dialictics of Exile: Nation, Time, Language, and Space in Hispanic Literatures*. West Lafayette: Purdue UP, 2004.

Mehta, Raj, and Russell W. Belk. "Artifacts, Identity, and Transition: Favorite Possessions of Indians and Indian Immigrants to the United States." *The Journal of Consumer Research* 17.4 (1991): 398-411.

Milz, Sabine. "The Hybridities of Philip and Özdamar." *Perspectives on Identity, Migration, and Displacement*. Ed. Steven Tötösy de Zepetnek, I-Chun Wang, and Hsiao-Yu Sun. Kaoshiung: National Sun Yat-sen U, Humanities and Social Sciences Series, 2010. 25-47.

Mishra, Omprakash, ed. *Forced Migration in the South Asian Region: Displacement, Human Rights, and Conflict Resolution*. Delhi: Manak, 2004.

Morgan, Stacy I. "Migration, Material Culture, and Identity in William Attaway's *Blood on the Forge* and Harriette Arnow's *The Dollmaker*." *College English* 63.6 (2001): 712-40.

Mortland, Carol A., ed. *Diasporic Identity*. Arlington: American Anthropological Association, 1998.

Mufwene, Salikoko S. "Creolization is a Social, not a Structural Process." *Degrees of Restructuring in Creole Languages*. Ed. Ingrid Neumann-Holzschuh. Amsterdam: John Benjamins, 2000. 65-84.

Murdoch, H. Adlai. "'All Skin' Teeth Is Not Grin: Performing Caribbean Diasporic Identity in a Postcolonial Metropolitan Frame." *Callaloo* 30.2 (2007): 575-93.

Murdoch, H. Adlai. "Re-Viewing Black Studies: Articulating Identity from Diaspora: A Response to Alexander Weheliye." *American Literary History* 20.1 (2008): 337-45.

Nash, Catherine. "Irish Placenames: Post-Colonial Locations." *Transactions of the Institute of British Geographers* 24.2 (1999): 457-80.

Neuzil, Anna A. *In the Aftermath of Migration: Renegotiating Ancient Identity in Southeastern Arizona*. Suite: U of Arizona P, 2008.

Newell, Stephanie, ed. *Images of African and Caribbean Women: Migration, Displacement and Diaspora*. Stirling: U of Stirling P, 1996.

Nicole, Roberts. "Haitian and Dominican E/migration and the (Re)construction of National Identity in the Poetry of the Third Generation." *Small Axe* 18.9 (2005): 86-103.

Okpewho, Isidore, Carole Boyce Davies, and Ali A. Mazrui, eds. *The African Diaspora: African Origins and New World Identities*. Bloomington: Indiana UP, 2001.

Peberdy, Sally. "Imagining Immigration: Inclusive Identities and Exclusive Policies in Post-1994 South Africa." *Africa Today* 48.3 (2001): 15-32.

Pérez, Gina M. *The Near Northwest Side Story: Migration, Displacement, and Puerto Rican Families*. Berkeley: U of California P, 2004.

Pilkington, Hilary. *Migration, Displacement and Identity in Post-Soviet Russia*. New York: Routledge, 1998.
Popoviciu, Liviu. "Migrating Masculinities: The Irish Diaspora in Britain." *Irish Studies Review* 14.2 (2006): 169-87.
Purcell, David E., ed. *Crossroads of the Southwest: Culture, Identity, and Migration in Arizona's Safford Basin*. Newcastle: Cambridge Scholars, 2008.
Rahman, Mahbubar, and Willem van Schendel. "'I Am not a Refugee': Rethinking Partition Migration." *Modern Asian Studies* 37.3 (2003): 551-84.
Ranchod, Kirty. *Citizenship and Identity, Brain Drain and Forced Migration: The Zimbabwe Case*. Johannesburg: U of Witwatersrand, Centre for Policy Studies, 2005.
Rapport, Nigel, and Andrew Dawson, eds. *Migrants of Identity: Perceptions of Home in a World of Movement*. New York: Berg, 1998.
Raussert, Wilfried, and John Miller Jones, eds. *Traveling Sounds: Music, Migration, and Identity in the U.S. and Beyond*. New Brunswick: Transaction, 2008.
Rice, Prudence M., and Don S. Rice, eds. *The Kowoj: Identity, Migration, and Geopolitics in Late Postclassic Petén, Guatemala*. Boulder: UP of Colorado, 2009.
Ridgway, Benjamin B. *Imagined Travel: Displacement, Landscape, and Literati Identity in the Song Lyrics of Su Shi*. PhD Diss. Michigan: U of Michigan P, 2005.
Rodríguez, María Cristina. *What Women Lose: Exile and the Construction of Imaginary Homelands in Novels by Caribbean Writers*. Bern: Peter Lang, 2005.
Rosario, Vanessa Perez, ed. *Hispanic Caribbean Literature of Migration: Narratives of Displacement*. New York: Palgrave Macmillan, 2010.
Saavedra, Maria Cristina. "Nation and Migration: Emigration and Exile in Two Cuban Films of the Special Period." *Atenea* 25.2 (2005): 109-24.
Sackmann, Rosemarie, Bernhard Peters, and Thomas Faist, eds. *Identity and Integration: Migrants in Western Europe*. Burlington: Ashgate, 2003.
Safa, Helen I., and Brian M. Du Toit, eds. *Migration and Development: Implications for Ethnic Identity and Political Conflict*. Hague: Mouton, 1975.
Schler, Lynn. "Ambiguous Spaces: The Struggle over African Identities and Urban Communities in Colonial Douala, 1914-45." *The Journal of African History* 44.1 (2003): 51-72.
Schneider, Arnd. *Futures Lost: Nostalgia and Identity among Italian Immigrants in Argentina*. Bern: Peter Lang, 2000.
Schubert, Laura Elizabeth. *Liberty, Equality, Anxiety: Identity and Displacement in Post-Revolutionary France, 1815-1840*. Cambridge: Harvard UP, 2005.
Schulze, Mathias, James M. Skidmore, David G. John, Grit Liebscher, and Sebastian Siebel-Achenbach, eds. *German Diasporic Experiences: Identity, Migration, and Loss*. Waterloo: Wilfrid Laurier UP, 2008.
Sernett, Milton. *Bound for the Promised Land: African American Religion and the Great Migration*. Durham: Duke UP, 1997.

Shao, Yu-chuan. "Cosmopolitanism in Zhu's *Ancient Capital* (*Gudu*)." *Perspectives on Identity, Migration, and Displacement*. Ed. Steven Tötösy de Zepetnek, I-Chun Wang, and Hsiao-Yu Sun. Kaoshiung: National Sun Yat-sen U, Humanities and Social Sciences Series, 2010. 99-110.

Shapiro, Michael J., and Hayward R. Alker, eds. *Challenging Boundaries: Global Flows, Territorial Identities*. Minneapolis: U of Minnesota P, 1996.

Shreiber, Maeera Y. "The End of Exile: Jewish Identity and Its Diasporic Poetics." *PMLA: Publications of the Modern Language Association of America* 113.2 (1998): 273-87.

Singh, Manju. *Assam, Politics of Migration & Quest for Identity*. Jaipur: Anita, 1990.

Spellman, W.M. *Uncertain Identity: International Migration since 1945*. London: Reaktion, 2008.

Spohn, Willfried, and Anna Triandafyllidou, eds. *Europeanisation, National Identities, and Migration: Changes in Boundary Constructions between Western and Eastern Europe*. New York: Routledge, 2003.

Suarez, Virgil, and Ryan G. Van Cleave, eds. *American Diaspora: Poetry of Displacement*. Iowa: U of Iowa P, 2010.

Subramanian, Ajantha. "Indians in North Carolina: Race, Class, and Culture in the Making of Immigrant Identity." *Comparative Studies of South Asia, Africa and the Middle East* 20.1 (2000): 105-14.

Tarr, Carrie. "Transnational Identities, Transnational Spaces: West Africans in Paris in Contemporary French Cinema." *Modern and Contemporary France* 15.1 (2007): 65-76.

Teitelbaum, Michael S., and Jay Winter. *A Question of Numbers: High Migration, Low Fertility, and the Politics of National Identity*. New York: Hill and Wang, 1998.

Thapan, Meenakshi. *Transnational Migration and the Politics of Identity*. New Delhi: Sage, 2005.

Totoricaguena, Gloria. *Basque Diaspora: Migration and Transnational Identity*. Reno: Center for Basque Studies, 2005.

Tötösy de Zepetnek, Steven. "Migration, Diaspora, and Ethnic Minority Writing." *Perspectives on Identity, Migration, and Displacement*. Ed. Steven Tötösy de Zepetnek, I-Chun Wang, and Hsiao-Yu Sun. Kaoshiung: National Sun Yat-sen U, Humanities and Social Sciences Series, 2010. 86-97.

Tsuda, Takeyuki. *Strangers in the Ethnic Homeland: The Migration, Ethnic Identity, and Psychosocial Adaptation of Japan's New Immigrant Minority*. PhD Diss. Berkeley: U of California P, 1996.

Tuimalealiifano, Morgan A. *Samoans in Fiji: Migration, Identity and Communication*. Suva: Institute of Pacific Studies, 1990.

Tunstall, Kate E. *Displacement, Asylum, Migration*. New York: Oxford UP, 2006.

Van Hear, Nicholas. *Migration, Displacement and Social Integration*. Genève: UNRISD, 1994.

Vertovec, Steven, and Robin Cohen, eds. *Migration, Diasporas, and Transnationalism*. Northampton: Edward Elgar, 1999.

Waever, Ole, and David Carlton. *Identity, Migration, and The New Security Agenda in Europe*. London: Pinter, 1993.

Wessels, David J. *Migration and Identity in a Uniting Europe*. Notre Dame: U of Notre Dame P, 1995.

Wild-Wood, Emma. *Migration and Christian Identity in Congo*. Boston: Brill, 2008.

Winland, Daphne. "The Politics of Desire and Disdain: Croatian Identity between 'Home' and 'Homeland'." *American Ethnologist* 29.3 (2002): 693-718.

Yolanda, M. Manora. "'What You Looking at Me For? I Didn't Come to Stay': Displacement, Disruption, and Black Female Subjectivity in Maya Angelou's *I Know Why the Caged Bird Sings*." *Women's Studies: An Interdisciplinary Journal* 34.5 (2005): 359-75.

Index